Mentoring student teachers

The growth of professional knowledge

John Furlong and
Trisha Maynard

London and New York

First published 1995
by Routledge
11 New Fetter Lane, London EC4P 4EE

Simultaneously published in the USA and Canada
by Routledge
29 West 35th Street, New York, NY 10001

Typeset in Palatino by LaserScript, Mitcham, Surrey
Printed and bound in Great Britain by
Mackays of Chatham PLC, Chatham, Kent

British Library Cataloguing in Publication Data
A catalogue record for this book is available from the British Library

Library of Congress Cataloging in Publication Data
A catalogue record for this book has been requested

ISBN 0–415–11393–8 (hbk)
ISBN 0–415–11394–6 (pbk)

Mentoring s' :t ` `chers

In the UK and elsewhere, the training of teachers is increasingly seen as a matter of partnership between schools and institutions of higher education. There is thus an urgent need within the profession to define more carefully what the role of teachers acting as mentors should be. Clearly some aspects of professional knowledge can only be acquired from practical experience in school, and this book draws on extensive research on students' school-based learning to isolate and analyse those aspects. Like any form of teaching, mentoring, the authors suggest, must be built on a clear understanding of the learning processes it is intended to support. In this book, they report on their research into the nature of students' school-based learning and what this means for the role of the mentor.

John Furlong is a Professor and **Trisha Maynard** is a Senior Research Associate and Lecturer in the Department of Education at University of Wales, Swansea.

Contents

Acknowledgements

The research project on which this book is based was one of five projects on 'mentoring' funded in 1992/3 by the Paul Hamlyn Foundation. We gratefully acknowledge their most generous support. We also wish to thank those teachers and students who so readily gave their time in our research; without their interest and their willingness to withstand our ever more probing questions, there would have been no project. For suggestions and for comments on earlier drafts of the book, we would particularly like to thank Frank Banks, Mary Darmanin, Gerald Grace, Susan Groundwater-Smith, Terry McLaughlin, Sheila Miles, Jean Rudduck, Sue Sanders, Eleanor Treen and Margaret Wilkin.

Introduction

During the last ten years, successive government interventions have transformed initial teacher education in Britain. As a consequence, it now has at least three very distinctive features. First, there is a great deal of emphasis on time spent in school – in the case of secondary postgraduate courses as much as 66 per cent of the overall course. Practical, school-based work therefore now assumes a central if not dominant role in professional preparation. A second feature is that training – whether it takes place in school or in a higher education institution – is understood as the achievement of a series of practical 'competences' that closely relate to the day-to-day work of newly qualified teachers. It is these government-defined competences that now form the basic curriculum of all initial teacher education courses. Finally, government-imposed changes now mean that it is schools, rather than higher education institutions, that are seen as having the key role in training and assessing students in the achievement of those competences. Teachers, acting as 'mentors', will in the future have a central role in the education of the next generation of teachers.

Competency-led, school-based teacher education is therefore here to stay in Britain. But simply because official policy has placed practical school-based experience at the heart of the training process, it does not mean that we yet fully understand what it is that students have to learn when they are in school. Nor are we necessarily clear what the role of the mentor, in supporting school-based learning, should be. At one level, the content of the teacher education curriculum is clear – students, mentors as well as those in higher education have to address the list of competences defined by the government. Students must, for example, be taught how to 'identify the current level of attainment of individual pupils' and be able to 'create and maintain a purposeful and orderly environment for the pupils'. But to list such competences, we would suggest, is deceptively simple. It is the basis of our argument throughout this book that as yet we have very little detailed understanding of how students develop their own practical professional knowledge in relation to such competences; how they combine their practical experience and other forms of learning in order to develop the skills, knowledge and understandings necessary to be competent practitioners. We believe that a fuller prescription of the role of the mentor will not be achieved until we have a more thorough understanding of the processes involved in learning to teach. Like any form of teaching, mentoring, we suggest, must be built on a clear understanding of the learning processes it is intended to support.

The aim of this book is therefore to contribute to the debate about how students do develop their own practical professional knowledge while they are in school and what the role of mentor should be in supporting that highly complex process. It takes for granted throughout that teacher education involves more than simply work in school. We start from the assumption that a coherent programme of professional preparation involves students drawing on a range of different forms of professional knowledge (Furlong *et al.* 1988), some of which are best acquired in school and some in Higher Education Institutions. Universities and colleges, we would suggest, continue to have a vital role to play in initial teacher education. Nevertheless, the focus of our attention in this particular book is on the nature of school-based learning.

The book is based on a research project on 'mentoring', one of five funded by the Paul Hamlyn Foundation in 1992/3. The particular focus of our project was to be on the *substance* of the mentor's work in supporting the student teacher. Several years previous experience in developing and running 'mentor training' courses had convinced us that although there was a growing body of knowledge and understanding about the 'process' of mentoring (how to observe students, how to give feedback), there was very little understanding about *what* it was that practising teachers could best contribute to the development of student teachers' professional knowledge.

Our particular way of researching the substance of mentoring has been to ask what is it that student teachers need to learn when they are in school. What is the nature of the professional knowledge that students can only learn from their practical experience in school, and in what ways does that professional knowledge complement and extend other sorts of learning that can go on elsewhere?

Our answers have led us to what we believe is a distinctive perspective on initial teacher education; one that focuses on how student teachers progressively develop greater and greater control over different aspects of their own teaching. We argue that while such learning can, by definition, only be achieved through direct practical experience, if students are to develop appropriate forms of practical professional knowledge they are unlikely to be able to do that unless they have carefully structured support in school. We argue that developing a clearer understanding of how students achieve control of their own teaching gives us a better view of the distinctive contributions that mentors as well as those in higher education can make in supporting students' professional development.

A BRIEF OUTLINE OF THE BOOK

We begin in Chapter 1 by exploring how it is that initial teacher education in the United Kingdom has come to focus so much on student teachers' school-based experiences; why it is that the development of practical teaching competence has assumed such centrality in our policy and practice; and why is it that teachers, acting as mentors, are now seen as key figures in the professional development of the next generation of teachers. In order to answer these questions we examine the changing political and professional context of teacher education in Britain, particularly focusing on different ideologies of education and their implication for the construction of 'the practical' in initial teacher education.

The next two chapters describe and evaluate different ways in which recent writing on teacher education has attempted to understand teachers' professional knowledge. Two models – the competency model and the reflective practitioner model – are presented and their implications for understanding the professional development of student teachers are explored. In each case we recognise the contribution that such models can make to our understanding of how students learn to teach. However, we argue that in neither case is their analysis based on detailed empirical study of the processes involved – as models they are ideologically rather than empirically derived. As a result, although useful, they remain 'partial' analyses, in both senses of the word.

The following four chapters report on our own research into the ways in which students learn to teach. We begin, in Chapter 4, by briefly describing the context and methodology of our research. We then present our findings in the form of three distinct studies. In Chapter 5, we focus on the developmental learning needs of student teachers as they change over time. Our research confirms the common-sense observation that students typically go through a number of distinct stages of development, each with its own focal concerns. We characterise these stages as 'Early idealism', 'Personal survival', 'Dealing with difficulties', 'Hitting a plateau' and 'Moving on'. In the early stages of their work in school, students are typically dominated by concerns with themselves as performers; it is only slowly, and with help from the outside, that they can come to 'de-centre' and learn to focus on the learning needs of their pupils. The developmental sequence therefore highlights what students most need or are most ready to learn at different stages of their training.

The next two chapters present the results of two further studies which explore what it is students need to learn from their school experience and the complexity of that learning. We use as examples two topics that typically assume importance at different stages of students' development. We begin in Chapter 6 by looking at classroom management and control – an issue that is often of pressing concern at the early stages of students' school experience. Here, we focus on the personal learning that must go on if students are to put into practice any of the more technical skills (voice control, body posture, movement) that typically form the content of professional training courses. It was coming to terms with themselves as an authority figure that the students in our study found their most pressing learning need in their early stages of teaching. This was the key to bringing this aspect of teaching under their own control, yet it was a learning experience that could only be addressed through direct school experience.

In the last empirical chapter, we examine a topic more relevant to later stages of training – how students achieve control of the process of pupil learning; how they develop what the teachers in our study called 'good ideas' for teaching. To achieve this control, students, we argue, must first develop what experienced teachers consider to be 'appropriate' understandings of how pupils learn. Only then can they draw effectively on the subject-matter knowledge they intend to teach in the construction of pedagogical strategies.

In Chapter 8 we begin by reviewing what we have learned from our study and propose our own model of students' school-based learning. In the last chapter, we briefly consider existing views on the role of the mentor and the models of student learning they imply before moving on to present our own model of mentoring.

Chapter 1

Practice makes perfect?
The development of school-based teacher education in Britain

The classroom, recognised as the critical productive site of all educational enterprise was – and remains – beyond the continuous control of church or state. Only the teachers were – and are – continuously there. For the interest of church and increasingly of state, an enduring problem, therefore, has been to ensure that the teachers operated as effective agents of a higher authority. This was the central purpose behind the state's entry into the sponsorship and certification of teacher training in 1846. From that moment, effective forms of training . . . were envisaged not simply as mechanisms to improve the quality of schools, but also to regulate and direct the daily activity of the teacher in the classroom.

(Gardner 1993: 23)

The Secretary of State publishes criteria by which he will judge whether courses offer suitable preparation for teachers, *in the context of the Government's policy objectives for schools.*

(DFE 1993a: para 8, emphasis added)

In the United Kingdom, a succession of government circulars (DES 1984, 1989; DFE 1992, 1993a) has ensured that in future, the vast majority of secondary and primary initial teacher education courses will be planned and delivered through partnerships between schools and higher education institutions. In addition, the 'curriculum' for these courses is now prescribed in a series of government-defined 'competences' on which students are intended to focus throughout the course of their training. In future, it will therefore be teachers, acting as 'mentors' to students, rather than those in higher education, who will have the key role in the professional preparation of the next generation of teachers. As a result of these changes there is an urgent need within the profession for a clearer understanding than we have had in the past of precisely what the role of the mentor should be.

As we indicated in the Introduction, the central argument underlying this book is that a fuller prescription of the role of the mentor will not be achieved until we have a more thorough understanding of the processes involved in learning to teach. Like any form of teaching, mentoring, we suggest, must be built on a clear understanding of the learning processes it is intended to support.

The primary purpose of this book is therefore to report our own research with PGCE (Post Graduate Certificate of Education) students at University College, Swansea, into how students do indeed learn to teach; how, through their school-based experience, they develop the practical professional knowledge necessary to become competent teachers. After reporting this research, we are then able to go on to propose what the role of the mentor should be in supporting that development. But in order to place our study in context, it is necessary to begin by asking how it is that policy on teacher education has come to take the form that it has. How is it that initial teacher education in Britain should be conceived primarily as the achievement of a series of practical competences and that practising teachers, working in schools, should be seen as prime contributors to professional development? Such a view of professional preparation is certainly very different from that promoted in other periods of our recent history and it is different from approaches adopted elsewhere in the world.

The purpose of this first chapter is therefore to place our current study in historical context by charting the political and professional development of policy and practice in initial teacher education. In that history we are particularly interested in the ways in which, at different times, the school-based aspects of teacher education have been understood as well as the relationship between school-based and other types of professional preparation.

THE FIRST APPRENTICE – THE PUPIL-TEACHER

The fortunes of initial teacher education in this country over the last century and a half have, necessarily, been bound up with the changing relationship between the state and the teaching profession as a whole. At times, governments of the day have been content to grant teachers a degree of relative autonomy in their work; at those times, teacher educators too have been granted some autonomy. At other times, governments have wanted to regulate the teaching profession more directly and teacher education has often been seen as a key strategy for achieving such regulation.

Direct regulation of the teacher through their professional formation was certainly an aim that was to the fore throughout the nineteenth century. Teacher education during that period was characterised by the twin aims of being pragmatic and moral. Its structure and content were closely regulated by government and specifically intended to make sure that elementary school teaching remained a craft rather than a profession. Each new generation of 'the teachers of the people' (Grace 1978) had to learn their craft in accordance with the government-imposed Revised Code.

The most important aspect of state-sponsored initial training was the pupil-teacher system. Set up in 1846 by Kay-Shuttleworth, the pupil-teacher system was initially designed as a 'supply mechanism', allowing working-class pupils who were 13 years of age to be apprenticed to the school managers for a period of five years prior to going on to college. As Gardner (1993) notes, the conventional view of professional preparation was reversed: practical training was to come first; personal education was to come second, if at all. The training, such as it was, was based on an apprenticeship model. Pupil-teachers would teach in the school during the day and were then supposed to receive instruction in school subjects from the master or mistress for a further 1½ hours (Aldrich 1990). However, as Gardner documents, in many cases this did not happen and most of the training was of the 'sink or swim' variety.

> In many cases, the trainees' education was neglected and he or she effectively became a full-time, if temporary, addition to the staff of a school. Pupil-teachers were often pitched in at the deep end, finding themselves at the age of 13 or 14 teachers of children who a year or two earlier, had been their playmates. It was a difficult baptism, but a surprising number of trainees . . . seem to have picked up the mechanical skills of classroom discipline and rote learning without much difficulty.
>
> (1993: 28)

Upon completion of their apprenticeship, candidates could compete for the Queen's scholarship which would enable them to go on to training college and so achieve a teacher's certificate. The majority, however, did not and remained uncertificated assistants paid at a lower rate than their colleagues.

Those students who did arrive at college were assumed to be competent classroom practitioners. As a consequence, college training was more concerned with their personal and moral education than improving competence in the classroom. Only six weeks of the two years were given to school practice, the rest of the time being devoted to academic subjects other than education. But the training that was provided was more than just academic – it was first and foremost 'moral'. As Hencke (1977) records, students were subjected to a long and arduous timetabled day and led a monastic existence and, as a result of this 'laborious and frugal life', they went 'forth into the world humble, industrious and instructed' (Kay-Shuttleworth, 1862, quoted in Aldrich 1990: 18). As we will see, this construction of training as a moral activity did not entirely pass away with the pupil teacher system – remnants continued into the training colleges of the 1950s.

FROM PUPIL-TEACHER TO STUDENT TEACHER

Throughout the nineteenth century, therefore, responsibility for the practical preparation of new teachers lay largely with the teaching profession itself. It was practising teachers who were granted primary responsibility for inducting the next generation into the craft of the classroom. But again, as Gardner (1993) documents, the pupil-teacher system started to wither on the vine once alternative routes into secondary education were opened up. Scholarships to grammar schools meant that it was no longer necessary for the more affluent working-class pupils to become apprentice teachers if they were to continue their education, and by the 1920s, the pupil-teacher scheme had largely fallen into disuse.

The end to the pupil-teacher scheme coincided with the emergence of a different relationship between the state and the teaching profession. In the early years of the century, Grace (1987) has suggested that relations between the state and the profession could be characterised as ones of 'cultural and professional condescension'. However, by the 1920s, with the threat of significant teacher and trade-union radicalism, the state adopted a more conciliatory attitude towards the profession. It was during this period that the Conservative President of the Board of Education, Eustace Percy, recognised that the best guard against the politicisation of education was to give teachers a reasonable sense of independence. It was the beginnings of what Grace has characterised as 'legitimised professionalism': reasonable pay, reasonable conditions, greater control over the curriculum, in return for a non-political professionalism. This period coincided with growing autonomy for teacher educators too.

The expansion of secondary education for prospective teachers had a profound effect on the role of the training colleges in two important ways. In the first place, colleges found that they had a changing clientele. They no longer had to provide secondary education for working-class students and this freed them to devote some of their curriculum time to the study of educational theory. This was particularly true of the more autonomous Day Training Colleges associated with the universities which began to appear after the 1890s. Second, colleges found themselves accepting students who were better educated than in the past but with no prior experience of teaching. Moreover, the growing number of middle-class recruits meant that an important proportion of the student population were quite unfamiliar with elementary schools. As the students were in college rather than in school, the task of preparing them in the practical business of elementary school teaching largely fell to college tutors. In the decades around the turn of the century, therefore, responsibility for the practical preparation of the next generation of teachers slowly moved out of the hands of the teaching profession and into the increasingly autonomous world of the college; teachers' formal responsibility for training all but disappeared for the next sixty years.

THE POST-WAR PERIOD

The growth of the relative autonomy of the teaching profession from state intervention, which had begun in the 1920s, reached its height in the post-war period. Between the 1940s and the early 1970s, teachers achieved significant control over the school curriculum. As Grace (1987) notes, they did not achieve the major economic rewards, nor the professional autonomy of other professions, but in that most central aspect of their professionalism, the school curriculum, they were granted substantial freedom by the state; it was a 'licensed autonomy' (Dale 1989). Indeed, their control over the curriculum became the most significant aspect of their claim to be a true profession. As we will see, that professional autonomy was mirrored by autonomy in the curriculum of teacher education too.

In his study of teacher education institutions in the same period, Bell (1981) charts the structural changes that affected institutions and the impact of those changes on the way in which teachers were actually trained. Three types of institution succeeded each other during the 1950s, 1960s and 1970s – the Teacher Training College was transformed into the College of Education which was itself later transformed into the Institute of Higher Education or Polytechnic. Bell suggests that the vision of teacher education offered in each type of institution was different, broadly following the progression of Weber's (1948) three ideal types of educational structure – from 'charismatic education', to education of the 'cultivated man', to 'specialised expert training'.

Teacher education in the Training College of the 1950s was, Bell suggests, a form of charismatic education. Colleges were typically small, single-sex and physically and intellectually isolated, 'all factors which enhanced its capacity for creating a moral community' (Bell 1981: 5). Colleges were run as a collegiate community and relationships between the staff and the students were close and personal. The curriculum was largely undifferentiated and although 'main subject studies' began in the 1950s, they did not achieve much significance until the 1960s. As a consequence, the most important person to each group of students was the education tutor, usually a woman (Taylor 1969), who had responsibility for education theory, curriculum work and for supervising teaching practice.

Tutors maintained close contact with local schools and, according to Taylor (1965), school teachers were their most significant reference group. Their main claim to expertise lay in their years of successful school teaching experience; their knowledge was based upon a stock of teaching skills that they had personally accumulated. There was, therefore, little distinction between 'theory' and 'practice'. Tutors' teaching in college was strongly classroom orientated and experiential; they then closely supervised 'their' students in school, occasionally taking demonstration lessons themselves.

Overall, therefore, it would seem that teacher education in the 1950s retained many continuities with the nineteenth century. Practical training was still achieved through a master (or, more frequently, mistress) apprenticeship relationship while the college saw its role as giving strong moral leadership on the nature of teaching. What was different from the nineteenth century was that instead of being apprenticed to a practising teacher, students were now apprenticed to a tutor acting as an 'expert teacher' who was responsible for overseeing their whole training as well as their personal development. As we will see below, the content of training had also changed dramatically. The new morality of the colleges was more concerned with the promotion of child-centred, 'progressive' education, rather than Victorian humility and self-discipline. However, if anything, the fact that college and school-based teacher education worked in tandem meant that the opportunities for promoting this modern morality were even stronger than that hoped for by Kay-Shuttleworth himself. Such is the nature of the total institution.

A fundamental change to teacher education came with the Robbins Report of 1963. That report recommended that teacher education should be massively expanded (a threefold increase in numbers between 1960 and 1972) and relocated within the higher education system. The policy arguments deployed in favour of these changes had little to do with teacher education as such – students who were training to be teachers, it was argued, had as much right to a liberal education as any other student. The result was the introduction of the BEd degree, and the redesignation of Training Colleges as Colleges of Education. In Bell's terms, this period signalled a transformation from 'charismatic' teacher education to education of the 'cultivated man' (or woman).

Both the organisation and curriculum of the new Colleges of Education were very different. The increased size, reduction in student and tutor residence and co-educational nature of the institutions meant that relationships were less personal. More significant from our point of view, the curriculum became more differentiated, academic and removed from the direct world of the school.

For example, existing approaches to educational theory were challenged by those in universities who were to validate the new degrees. As a consequence, new disciplinary specialists were recruited to replace generalist education tutors. These new lecturers

– in sociology, psychology, philosophy and history – saw themselves as 'equipping students for intelligent and informed discourse about educational issues, sharply distinguished from practical expertise' (Bell 1981: 13). And these moves were justified largely in terms of the liberal education of the students; studying the disciplines was conceived of as 'part of the education of the scholar, who happened to want to be a teacher' (Bell 1981: 13). A similarly rigorous academic approach was progressively introduced to main subject departments which aimed to become 'degree worthy' in their own right. Teacher education throughout the 1960s and early 1970s therefore increasingly became an academic affair, with a growing distance between the world of the college and the school. The Colleges of Education saw themselves as having more in common with the universities and newly created Polytechnics than with the old Training Colleges.

But how were students prepared for work in school? Formally they were prepared through professional methods courses which, Bell suggests, became the home of many of the older lecturers from the Training College days and which retained a strong professional ideology. However, in most institutions, these courses now had a much lower status than the new academic courses and were seldom included in the formal assessment procedures of the degree. Moreover, given the number of students recruited, and the fact that the colleges were unwilling to cede any responsibility for supervising teaching practice to schools, all lecturers, whether they were experienced teachers or not, had to take on teaching practice supervision. Some students therefore found themselves supervised in school by lecturers with a wealth of practical experience on which to draw, others did not. In reality, therefore, students found that they largely had to fend for themselves, finding help where they might. For many students, trial and error and *ad hoc* socialisation were the main features of their professional preparation. Perhaps unsurprisingly, given the vocational commitments of many of the students, the academic nature of the BEd increasingly came under criticism.

A key turning point in the move away from the academic approach to teacher education was the James Report of 1972. Its recommendation that teacher education should be 'unashamedly specialised and functional' (p. 23) was to set the tone of much subsequent debate, and indeed its influence can still be felt twenty years on. Bell argues that it was complaints by students and teachers about the excessively academic nature of courses which eventually led to the James Inquiry. Whether or not this was its origin, the report certainly reflected this view, demanding 'a more rationally explicit connection between academic knowledge and practical teaching skills' (Bell 1981: 17).

On the institutional front, the 1970s saw a period of rapid change with the contraction, amalgamation and closure of many colleges (Hencke 1977; Alexander *et al.* 1984). By the end of the decade, most Colleges of Education had gone and students on BEd degrees were studying in 'poly-technic' rather than 'mono-technic' institutions, often spending at least part of their time working alongside non-education students. The curriculum had changed too. The James Report had challenged the role of the educational disciplines of sociology, psychology, philosophy and history, except in so far as they could be seen as of practical use in contributing to the development of effective teaching. The result was a reinvigoration of professional studies which began to enter into a more systematic dialogue with these disciplines. The position of the semi-autonomous main subject departments was also questioned, which in turn led to a softening of the boundaries between main subject and methods work. The rationale for main subject study increasingly became instrumental; solid subject knowledge was now necessary as the background to teachers' professional performance – it was no longer a 'good thing' in itself. All in all, the aim of the new faculties of education located in Polytechnics and Institutes of Higher Education was to establish the truly 'professional degree' – it was, in Bell's terms, 'specialised expert education'.

Interestingly, despite this greater professional orientation, relationships with schools changed little. Experts in curriculum, classroom interaction, geographical and mathematical education now taught the students in college. But they were indeed 'experts'; sophisticated theoreticians in one specific aspect of professional practice. Course structures still left it to the students to integrate what they had learned from these different experts and then somehow 'apply' that knowledge in the classroom. Despite the move away from the academic to the professional degree, the BEd, and indeed the PGCE, still largely operated on a 'theory into practice' model. Schools were places where students tested out what they had learned in college, and classroom teachers, formally at least, remained marginalised.

IDEOLOGIES AND THE CONTENT OF TEACHER EDUCATION

Initial teacher education in Britain therefore went through a number of distinct stages of development in the post-war years, each of which implied a different view of the role of school-based experience in professional preparation. In the 1950s, students were 'apprenticed' to a highly experienced tutor acting as a 'master teacher' who personally supervised their work both in the Training College and in school. The world of college and school were one, each interpreted through the eyes of the omnipotent college tutor. During the 1960s, the move to a more academic orientation to initial teacher education meant that a divide opened up between the world of college and school. College work took on a life of its own; the world of the school, and indeed professional preparation, were marginalised from the dominant focus of courses. The 1970s saw the emergence of specialised expert training where students were prepared by experts in college. Despite the professional focus, the divide between college and school remained, for it was largely left to the students to 'integrate' what they had learned and 'apply' it in school.

It is important to recognise that, in the post-war years, these changes in the curriculum of initial teacher education were only indirectly introduced by the governments of the day. The Department of Education and Science (DES) certainly had a strong hand in the changing structure of provision, encouraging and overseeing expansion in the 1960s, and contraction and amalgamations in the 1970s. But as elsewhere in education, their control over the teacher education curriculum itself was indirect. Teacher educators enjoyed the same 'licensed autonomy' (Dale 1989) over their curriculum as did the teachers. The changes outlined above therefore came about slowly and in a piecemeal fashion. They arose largely as a professional response of teacher educators, and particularly the Council for National Academic Awards (CNAA), to the changing structural circumstances that they found themselves in (Wilkin 1991). Because of the 'relative autonomy' of the universities from Her Majesty's Inspectors (HMI) and many of the structural changes imposed on the colleges, there was, by the early 1980s, more variation in approach within that university sector than outside it (Patrick *et al.* 1982).

In understanding the next stage of development in initial teacher education policy in Britain, it is important to recognise that throughout the post-war period, none of the changes in the teacher education that we have outlined, challenged, or were intended to challenge, dominant values or 'ideologies' about school teaching itself. Debates about the *form* of training in the 1950s, 1960s and 1970s were sharply distinguished from debates about the *practice of teaching*.

In fact the dominant ideologies of teaching were remarkably consistent throughout the post-war period, even though different forms of training meant that students were introduced to them in varying ways. At least three different ideologies had a strong influence on the content of training during this period – 'progressivism', 'liberal education' and 'social reconstruction'. As we will see below (on p. 13), what is distinctive about teacher education policy after the mid-1980s is that debates about the form of training and approaches to teaching have become more and more intertwined. As government educational policy has increasingly come under the influence of a different group of ideologies associated with the New Right, the promotion of school-based teacher education has been seen as an important vehicle to promote their particular view of teaching and to suppress alternative views. As in the nineteenth century, the government is attempting to utilise teacher education as a means of regulating and directing 'the daily activity of the teacher in the classroom' (Gardner 1993: 23).

In order to understand the nature of current policy and why school-based training has been constructed in the way that it has, it is therefore necessary to pause for a moment to examine the ideologies that have traditionally influenced the content of initial teacher education. For it is these ideologies that the present government has sought to challenge through its promotion of a particular form of school-based teacher education. The concept of ideology is of course itself deeply contested and may have one of a number of different meanings. Here we intend to take a broad definition of the concept, seeing ideologies as historical and intellectual movements or traditions. As such they involve 'sets of beliefs, values and practical experiences as well as research findings about the character of human nature and society and the role that education should play in relation to these' (Furlong 1992: 165).

The first, and by far the most significant educational ideology of the post-war period, is *progressivism*. Over the years, progressivism has achieved virtual hegemony as a way of thought in the primary sector (Alexander 1984), though its influence is also readily apparent in many examples of curriculum development in the secondary sphere too. The founding fathers of progressivism (Rousseau, Pestalozzi and Froebel) all believed that education must begin with the child; all children, they asserted, are unique, and moreover, their nature is essentially different from that of adults. If it is to be effective, education must be adapted to the unfolding nature of children's interests and developmental needs. The progressivist's view of a professional teacher is therefore someone who has a deep understanding of the ways in which children develop and an ability to adapt their pedagogy and curriculum to the developmental needs of individual pupils.

A second ideology, one that gained in strength in the 1960s, is that of *liberal education*. Liberal education has much in common with progressivism for it too focuses on the development of the individual. However, liberal educationists argue that if it is to be worth its name, education must be more than simply following the 'needs of the child'; neither must it be determined solely by the 'needs of society'. Rather, the purpose of education should be the development of the learner as a rationally autonomous individual. As a consequence, Bailey (1984) for example, argues that education should be centrally concerned with learning which is both fundamental and general, for only in this way can autonomy be promoted and the child freed from the constraints of the 'present and particular'. The liberal educationist's view of the professional teacher is therefore someone who is themselves a rationally autonomous adult and who has the pedagogic and curriculum planning skills necessary to foster rational autonomy in pupils.

During the 1970s a further voice was increasingly added to the educational debate, that of *social reconstructionism*. What is distinctive about social reconstructionist thought is that its starting point is political. Its supporters are committed to achieving equality and justice in society at large and teachers are seen as key change agents in that process. This concern with equality has been expressed both in terms of support for particular educational policies (for example, special needs, equal opportunities, mixed ability grouping) and for particular curricular initiatives (such as anti-sexist and multi-cultural teaching). In pursuing these policies, those committed to social reconstructionist thought argue that teachers must come to see themselves as 'transformative intellectuals', transforming the consciousness of children and enabling them to develop critical thinking (Hillcole Group 1989).

Progressivism, liberal education and social reconstructionism are therefore broad intellectual traditions that have, in the postwar period, been influential in many aspects of British educational policy. They have, as many critics have observed (Lawlor 1990; O'Hear 1988), been particularly influential in the field of initial teacher education, though, as the dominant modes of teacher training changed, students were necessarily inducted into these ideologies in different ways.

In the 1950s, the need to promote progressive, child-centred teaching was overwhelmingly seen as a moral issue (Taylor 1965); personal socialisation through the moral community of the college was therefore a highly effective form of induction into this ideological position. However, the concern with progressivism did not diminish in the move to a more academic form of teacher education. In the 1960s, much of the focus of the disciplines of education which came to dominate courses was also to do with aspects of progressivism. Developmental psychology and sociology of education were particularly concerned with promoting a child-centred perspective. Philosophy of education, however, did much to promote another ideological voice, that of liberal education. In the 1970s, both of these ideological strands and that of social reconstructionism can be seen in the work of the curriculum developers and others. In their training to be specialised experts, students were urged to adopt forms of practice that incorporated all three of these different ideological positions.

These, then, have been the dominant ideologies that have, in complex and sometimes contradictory ways, come to inform much professional educational debate in post-war Britain. It is into these values that successive generations of student teachers have been inducted in the course of their professional preparation. However, it is precisely these values that have increasingly become the focus of challenge by the government. And one means of challenging their dominance has been to reassert the importance of practical work in school.

1984 – RE-ENTER THE STATE

The late 1970s saw the beginning of a fundamental break in the consensus that had grown up between the teaching profession and successive governments in the post-war period. In Grace's (1987) terms, 'legitimised professionalism' was replaced by the 'politics of confrontation'. A long-running dispute in the mid-1980s resulted in the removal of pay bargaining rights, the imposition of new contracts with defined hours of work and the introduction of appraisal. Most dramatically of all, with the establishment of the National Curriculum in 1988 came the challenge to what Grace had portrayed as the heart of teachers' professional autonomy – control over the curriculum.

It is against this background of the changing relations between the state and the teaching profession that we need to place the government's growing intervention in initial teacher education. On a wide range of issues the government has, since the late 1970s, sought to 'rein in' the autonomy of the teaching profession. State intervention in initial teacher education, as Wilkin (1992a) argues, is the last, and certainly the most ambitious, attempt to challenge the autonomy of the profession. Through their growing intervention in the detail of courses, the government are claiming a right to control more than the hours teachers work; they are claiming the right to control more than what teachers teach. Through their progressive intervention in this sphere, the government are claiming the right to have a say in the very construction of the professionalism of the next generation of teachers: to determine what they learn, to determine how they learn it and to determine the professional values to which they are exposed. As such, state intervention in initial teacher education represents an even greater challenge to professional autonomy than that foreseen by Grace in 1987; it goes to the very heart of professionalism itself.

But what has the character of that government intervention actually been in the last ten years? What sorts of policies have been pursued and why has so much focus been placed on the development of a particular sort of school-based teacher education? We will suggest that government intervention in this field needs to be understood in the context of contemporary Conservative educational policy. The government's felt need to intervene, and the character of the interventions it has made are, we suggest, informed by New Right political philosophy. It is our contention that it is this ideology that has encouraged the government to reform teacher education and specifically to reconstruct the role of the school within it.

As Whitty (1990) has acknowledged, it is now commonplace to identify two main strands of New Right thinking – neo-liberal and neo-conservative. According to Gamble (1983), what is distinctive about contemporary Conservative political philosophy is the successful bringing together of these two different strands of thought. Neo-liberal thinking is concerned with the promotion of free market economics. It places complete trust in the market as a mechanism for the production and distribution of goods and services, and successive Conservative governments have attempted to extend free market principles into whole new areas of social activity including the provision of welfare services. In the field of education, the establishment of open access to schools, league tables, local financial management and the introduction of new types of school (Grant Maintained Schools, City Technology Colleges) are obvious examples of attempts to introduce a competitive 'market'.

Neo-conservative ideas are rather different, for they emphasise traditional authority and national identity. They have particular force in the field of education. From the neo-conservative perspective, the central aim of education is the preservation of a refined cultural heritage. In the words of the Hillgate Group (1989), education 'depends on . . . the preservation of knowledge, skills, culture and moral values and their transmission to the young' (p. 1). Neo-conservative educational ideas necessarily stand in marked contrast to progressive, liberal or social reconstructionist philosophies outlined earlier. As a view of education, neo-conservatism found its first contemporary vocal expression in the Black Papers issued in 1969. One can also see the influence of this line of thinking in the establishment of the broad structure of the National Curriculum with its emphasis on traditional subjects as well as in more recent struggles about the nature of subjects such as English.

In the field of initial teacher education, the influence of both neo-liberalism and neo-conservativsm have been apparent in government policies of the last ten years. As we will argue below, the first direct intervention – Circular 3/84 – appears informed by neo-liberal forms of thought. More recent interventions have moved policy in a different direction, influenced as they are by neo-conservative ideas. New Right policy is, it seems, always based on a blend of doctrines. As a consequence those policies 'are sometimes complementary, but sometimes in tension' (Whitty

1990: 23). But whatever the tensions, adherents of both neo-conservatism and neo-liberalism agree that a central problem facing teacher education, as in other areas of state monopoly, is 'producer capture'.

Producer capture, as Ransom (1990) explains, occurs when a service comes to be organised more to suit the needs of producers than consumers. 'The professionals create a technical language which serves only to bamboozle ordinary people and they organise the system for their convenience rather than to respond to the demands of its consumers. The result is inertia and resistance to change' (1990: 8). This interpretation of the work of professionals is well illustrated by O'Hear (1988) in his critique of initial teacher education. According to O'Hear,

> a large vested interest has arisen in the form of a teacher-training establishment, which runs, directs and assesses the courses in teacher training. In assessing the value of this training, we shall thereby, indirectly consider whose interests it really serves.
>
> (1988: 6)

Policies which seek to reform, whether it be from a neo-liberal or neo-conservative perspective, therefore depend first and foremost on challenging the control of that teacher-training establishment. As we will argue below, opening up training to the world of the school and the adoption of a competency-based curriculum have been seen by successive Conservative governments as a key mechanism to put an end to this producer capture.

A NEO-LIBERAL INTERVENTION: CIRCULAR 3/84

Direct government intervention was first felt in 1984 with the issuing of DES Circular 3/84 (DES 1984); it represented a major turning point in initial teacher education in Britain. Through this circular, for the first time for nearly sixty years, the government attempted to define the content and structure of initial teacher education; the circular had statutory authority. Secretaries of State for Education had always had formal responsibility for granting new teachers Qualified Teacher Status (QTS) through powers conferred on them by the 1944 Education Act, but until 1984 they were happy to do so simply on the recommendation of initial training institutions. All students who had satisfactorily completed a course of training were automatically granted QTS by the DES. Circular 3/84 changed that practice fundamentally. From that date on, QTS was only to be awarded to graduates of courses that conformed to the criteria laid down in the circular. If training institutions did not conform to the new criteria, they could in effect, no longer train qualified teachers. In order to make sure that training institutions did indeed conform to the criteria, a new government-appointed body – the Council for the Accreditation of Teacher Education (CATE) – was established. In the years following the issuing of Circular 3/84, CATE formally inspected every initial teacher training establishment in England and Wales.

As in other areas of educational policy (Baron *et al.* 1981; Ball 1990; Ransom 1990), the initial legitimation for this government intervention was the inadequacy of existing standards. Throughout the 1980s, HMI and DES published an array of research findings, inspection reports and documents on initial teacher education (DES 1983, 1988; HMI 1983, 1987, 1988a, 1988b), many of them implicitly and explicitly critical of existing arrangements. In almost every case, the focus of those criticisms was on the development of students' practical teaching competence.

In the early 1980s, one report stands out as having particular political significance. It was the first national survey of newly qualified teachers in schools conducted by HMI (HMI 1982). What the survey reported was that while the majority of newly qualified teachers were well trained, appointed to appropriate posts and given appropriate support in their new schools, a significant minority were not. In the judgement of HMI, nearly one in four were in some respects poorly equipped with the skills needed for teaching. And this view was corroborated by the new teachers themselves. On a range of key practical teaching skills, between one-fifth and three-fifths of teachers rated themselves as having been inadequately prepared. In addition, they complained that in their courses too much emphasis had been placed on academic study in general and on education studies in particular and that there was too little emphasis on teaching method and teaching practice. The report gave rise to hostile headlines. Clearly, something had to be done.

In line with the tenets of neo-liberal thought, Circular 3/84, which followed the publication of the survey, aimed to improve the quality of initial teacher education by opening training up to the 'the realities of the market'. In this case 'the market' was conceived of as the 'customers' of training courses – primary and secondary schools. As a result of the circular, college and university lecturers responsible for 'pedagogy' in teacher education courses had to return periodically to schools to undertake 'recent and relevant' school experience; teachers had to be involved in the process of interviewing students; the time that students had to spend in schools during their training was defined for the first time; and CATE was established.

In reality, the substantive changes introduced by Circular 3/84 were not particularly radical, for they were not that different from policies already adopted in many institutions, particularly those validated by the CNAA. Whatever the government's intentions, it is clear that those who drafted the circular, and indeed CATE itself, saw themselves as promoting what they thought of as the 'best' professional practice of the day – 'specialist expert training'. When the circular insisted that lecturers should periodically return to school for 'recent and relevant' experience, or when it insisted that main subject studies should be related to the curriculum of the school, its intention was not to challenge the expertise of teacher educators *per se*. Rather, its aim was to insist that teacher educators followed the discipline of the market; that what they taught was appropriately related to the world of the school. In reality, the circular did little or nothing to enhance the responsibilities of schools in professional preparation. As long as teacher educators did what they were told and conformed to the circular's particular model of training, they were to be left in charge as the experts.

The view of training supported by the circular was therefore, in reality, not so different from that of the James Report of a dozen years earlier. It wanted specialised expert training, provided by the training institutions and 'tested out' in the realities of the school. As a consequence, the substance of the circular was only experienced as a significant challenge by those courses, particularly in the university sector (Patrick *et al.* 1982), that still adopted a more traditional, academic approach, to professional preparation. But although the circular was not radical in terms of the curriculum of initial teacher education, it was constitutionally revolutionary and sent shock waves through the teacher education system (Wilkin 1991; Booth *et al.* 1991). By re-establishing the right of governments to have a say in the detailed structure and organisation of initial teacher education, it opened the door for more fundamental reform in the years that followed.

THE NEO-CONSERVATIVE CHALLENGE

The second strand of New Right ideology is neo-conservatism. Since the late 1960s in Britain, a small group of pamphleteers, loosely aligned around neo-conservative philosophies, have mounted a sustained attack on many aspects of contemporary educational policy (Cox and Boyson 1975; O'Keefe 1990). As we have already seen, their views on education stand in marked contrast to progressive, liberal or social reconstructionist thought that has dominated much of post-war educational practice.

Although they have been an important voice throughout the present administration, the influence of neo-conservative groups has increased sharply since the late 1980s. They had a profound impact on the drafting of the 1988 Educational Reform Bill (Ball 1990), and since the passing of that Act have turned their attention to initial teacher education (Hillgate Group 1989; Lawlor 1990; O'Hear 1988). The link between their two interests is well expressed in the Introduction to the 1989 Hillgate Group's pamphlet:

> In December 1986 and September 1987 the Hillgate Group published two pamphlets arguing for radical reform of British education . . . a case which was partly recognised in the proposal for the Education Reform Act (1988). . . . Now that the Act is on the statute book, there is a need to ensure that there are enough good teachers to enable its aims to be realised.
>
> (1989)

Hence their concern with initial teacher education.

Their views on current provision are trenchant. Teacher education courses, they argue, are intellectually 'feeble and biased' and excessively concerned with topics such as race, sex, class and even 'anti-imperialist' education (Hillgate Group 1989). As O'Hear says,

> there is a disproportionate emphasis on questions of race and inequality, an emphasis which is surely unhealthy in its implicit assumption that education is to be seen in terms of its potential for social engineering, rather than as an initiation of pupils into proven and worthwhile forms of knowledge.
>
> (1988: 22)

Given that the primary task for teachers is indeed to induct the next generation of children into 'proven and worthwhile forms of knowledge', the primary task for initial teacher education is to develop professionals who are themselves experts in their own subject area. What is needed above all in a 'good' teacher is a 'sound knowledge and love of the subject one is teaching' (O'Hear 1988: 16). Such preparation should take precedence over training in pedagogy; indeed, according to Lawlor (1990), the chief weakness of current approaches to initial teacher education is that they are dominated by a concern with preparing students in *how* to teach rather than *what* to teach. Learning how to teach is not, it seems, necessary for the *delivery* of our National Curriculum. It is only of importance for those concerned with progressivism or other 'fads and fashions of the teacher training establishment' (O'Hear 1988: 6). At present it is through the study of pedagogy that students are introduced to such views. In consequence, neo-conservatives have increasingly come to the conclusion that without the radical reform or even abolition of initial teacher education, there will be no 'good' teachers and the principles embodied in the Educational Reform Act will not be achieved. Those principles will constantly be undermined by a teaching profession wedded to a different set of educational values.

For the neo-conservatives, therefore, college-based training shows all the signs of 'producer capture' (Berrill 1994). It is at best of secondary importance; at worst it is pernicious. Instead, they have argued for an atheoretical, school-based apprenticeship. For example, O'Hear argues that teaching is an essentially practical skill which cannot be learned from the kind of theoretical study of teaching which, he suggests, dominates current courses. In similar vein, the Hillgate Group argue that there is a long tradition going back to Aristotle that some skills, including many that are difficult, complex and of high moral and cultural value, are learned best by the emulation of experienced practitioners and by supervised practice under guidance. 'In the case of such skills, apprenticeship should take precedence over instruction and even when formal instruction is necessary it can never substitute for real practical training' (Hillgate Group 1989: 9).

The radical nature of the neo-conservative vision is best expressed by Lawlor, writing in 1990, urging the government on to yet further reform.

Much of the declared emphasis in the [teacher education] reforms of the 1980s was on the practical activity of teaching.
Students would be sent into the classroom to learn to teach as
an essential part of their training. The individual qualities of
the teacher would develop as he taught his subject. He would
develop the characteristics of the good teacher in the classroom, use his common sense and acquire confidence, rather than
be taught generalised theories irrelevant to good teaching. . . .
Paradoxically, school practice has turned out to be far from
practical. It is seen by the education departments as an opportunity to put theory into practice. Indeed, it is often a tenet of
the course, and a requirement for assessment that theory and
practice must be interlinked. This has two results. First, con-
trary to the intentions of the 1980s' reforms, general theory
continues to dominate at the expense of individual practice;
and students are not encouraged to approach classroom
teaching with an open mind, or to develop individually as
teachers. Instead they are expected to bring to the classroom,
and to apply to their teaching, the generalised educational
theories which they have been taught.

(1990: 21)

For Lawlor, and for her fellow pamphleteers, it is therefore practice that makes perfect in learning to teach. But that practical
experience is understood in a particular way; it is seen as an
atheoretical, common-sense activity. Indeed, theory of any kind
distorts what is seen as a *natural* process, for it prevents the
trainee approaching the task with an open mind. As we will see
below, it is these views that have progressively come to dominate
official policy in teacher education. By 1993, neo-conservative
views had all but replaced the 'expert training' model enshrined
in Circular 3/84.

RECENT GOVERNMENT REFORMS

Since 1984 there have been a number of important government
initiatives in initial teacher education. Most obvious have been
the issuing of three further circulars in 1989, 1992 and 1993. In
addition, however, there has been the introduction of a number
of 'new routes' into teaching. Although the numbers of trainees
entering teaching via these new routes has to date been small

(Barrett *et al.* 1992a; Barrett and Galvin 1993), politically each of them has been highly significant in indicating the direction of government thinking in this area.

During the late 1980s, government initiatives seemed to be based on a form of dualistic thinking; in Circular 24/89 (DES 1989) and the Articled and Licensed teacher schemes it is possible to identify elements associated with both the 'expert training' model (probably promoted by CATE and HMI) as well as neo-conservative views. For example, the circular seemed concerned to respond to many of the neo-conservative critiques of existing provision. It specified the minimum time students should spend in the study of their main subject; defined practical competences of teaching that newly qualified teachers should achieve; increased the amount of time students had to spend in school; and insisted on a far greater involvement of teachers in the training process. At the same time, however, it maintained a strong role for 'expert trainers'. It reasserted the importance of studying pedagogy, educational and professional studies, and insisted that school experience should be closely related to these more 'theoretical' dimensions of preparation.

A similar dualism is apparent in the two new routes into teaching launched at the same time. In the Articled Teacher Scheme (which ran from 1989 to 1994) it was the expert voice of the teacher educator that was to the fore. Despite the fact that articled teachers spent 80 per cent of the two years of training in school, schemes had been organised and coordinated through Higher Education Institutions. As a consequence, teachers and lecturers were required to work in close partnership in the development of highly sophisticated, professional training schemes in which 'theory' and 'practice' were carefully interrelated. The Licensed Teacher scheme which also began in 1989 is quite different. Here, trainees, who do not necessarily have to be graduates, are recruited to specific vacancies in schools. They are granted a 'licence' to teach and provided 'on the job' training appropriate to their particular needs. As Barrett and Galvin (1993) report, in some cases this training is highly professionalised, though in many other cases it is not.

More recent government interventions have seen neo-conservative thinking move into the ascendency. In 1993, two new routes into teaching were proposed that challenged, and were intended to challenge, the 'expert training' model. The first was the 'school-centred' teacher training initiative which allows schools to 'opt out' of higher education control and receive government funding to run their own training schemes. Schools are intended to work together, buying in higher education expertise if and when they see fit. In order to fund such consortia, new funding arrangements have had to be established. In England this has resulted in the transfer of all funding for teacher education out of the Higher Education Funding Council and the establishment of a new government-appointed Teacher Training Agency (TTA). In the future, it will be the TTA that decides how much funding goes to higher education and how much goes to schools.

The last-proposed, 'new route' was of a different sort, for it proposed the creation of a new one-year, non-graduate training scheme for early years teachers. These courses, which were to have been explicitly directed at parents and others with experience of working with children, constituted the most fundamental challenge yet to the idea that teaching involves the development of an expert body of knowledge. The 'common sense' of parents was portrayed as equal to that of the expert teacher. However, after overwhelming opposition from teachers and others in 1993, the proposal was dropped by the government.

But these new routes are, and will probably remain, appropriate only for a minority. The vast majority of the 45,000 students in training in England and Wales in any one year will continue, for the present at least, to be enrolled on conventional undergraduate and graduate training programmes. For them, the influence of two new circulars, Circular 9/92 (DFE 1992) covering secondary courses and Circular 14/93 (DFE 1993a), covering primary courses, will be far more significant. Here again neo-conservative thinking now seems dominant. In both circulars the role of the school in training is enhanced even further; indeed, in many places, the circulars imply that schools are the 'lead institutions'. As the secondary Circular 9/92, states:

> The Government expects that partner schools and HEIs will exercise a joint responsibility for the planning and management of courses and the selection, training and assessment of students. The balance of responsibilities will vary. Schools will have a leading responsibility for training students to teach their specialist subjects, to assess pupils and to manage classes;

and for supervising students and assessing their competence in these respects. HEIs will be responsible for ensuring that courses meet the requirements for academic validation, presenting courses for accreditation, awarding qualifications to successful students and arranging student placements in more than one school.

(DFE 1992: para 14)

In the primary circular, 'training' is explicitly presented as involving only two elements: subject knowledge, which is largely, though not exclusively, the province of Higher Education Institutions, and practical teaching skills, which students learn in school. The standards that newly qualified teachers need to achieve in both of these areas are expressed in the form of a comprehensive list of competences which 'Higher education institutions, schools and students should focus on . . . throughout the whole period of initial training' (DFE 1993a: Annex A, para 2.1). Unsurprisingly, that list of competences makes little reference to issues of pedagogy or to many other issues such as child development or the social and cultural dimensions of learning that have traditionally made up the curriculum of initial teacher education.

Teacher education, according to these circulars, is, therefore, in the future intended to be narrowly focused, functional and technical. The loss of autonomy for teacher educators is now explicitly stated; according to Circular 14/93, courses must in the future be explicitly designed to serve 'the Government's policy objectives for schools' (DFE 1993a). For the present, those policy objectives are the achievement of the original aims of the National Curriculum which New Right critics see as being undermined by the teaching profession itself. By the suppression of 'lengthy, doctrinaire and demoralising' training courses (Lawlor 1990) and the creation of a 'neutral' system, in which teachers, rather than teacher educators, prepare students on a list of predefined competences, the hope is to raise a different generation of teachers, whose professional values are untainted by views of the teacher education establishment.

With these new circulars, British teacher education has therefore come full circle. Not, as some have argued (Wragg 1991), in the sense of a direct return to the pupil-teacher system of Victorian days. As Gardner (1993) notes, that system belonged to a particular time which has passed. The continuity is at the deeper level and lies in the aspiration of government to utilise initial teacher education as a means of regulating the daily activity of classroom teachers. Whether it will be more or less successful than the pupil-teacher scheme remains to be seen.

CONCLUSION

The purpose of this chapter has been to chart the changing ways in which practical school experience has been seen in initial teacher education over the years. Following the end of the teacher-pupil scheme, we have recorded the ebb and flow of the relationship between school and Higher Education Institution in the training process. Contemporary government policy has, as we have seen, progressively placed school-based experience at the heart of initial teacher education. In doing so, it has, if sometimes grudgingly, retained the support of much of the teacher education profession. Most teacher educators now recognise that practical school-based work must form a central part in professional preparation and that teachers have a vital contribution to make to the training process.

Far more controversial, however, is the government's vision of how students do in fact achieve the complex process of learning to teach. As we have seen, the view sponsored in the latest circulars is similar to that of the neo-conservatives. Their view is that, at the level of theory, we know nothing and there is nothing to know about teaching and learning; teaching is therefore best learned simply through experience itself. All that is needed is the definition of a number of broad competency statements, sufficient to focus the attention of student and 'mentor' alike. As we noted at the beginning of this chapter, we consider such a view simplistic and the purpose of our research has been to explore the complexities involved in school-based learning. Moreover, in asserting that there is nothing to know, neo-conservatives overlook an extensive literature that has indeed tried to conceptualise the process of learning to teach. In the next two chapters we move away from the political debate to engage with this professional literature on teacher education. We examine two of the major traditions of research and writing concerned with the process of learning to teach – the competency movement, and the reflective practitioner movement.

Chapter 2

Learning to teach – the competency-based model

Higher education institutions, schools and students should focus on the competences of teaching throughout the whole period of initial training. The progressive development of these competences should be monitored regularly during initial training. Their attainment at a level appropriate to newly qualified teachers should be the objective of every student taking a course of initial training.

(DFE 1992: Annex A, para 2.1)

In the last chapter we focused on the development of teacher education within Britain, looking in particular at the ways in which practical work in schools had been constructed at different stages. As we saw, the recent history of teacher education has been characterised by growing political intervention. In the last ten years, the professional voice has been given less and less opportunity to join the national debate on teacher education policy. Yet despite this exclusion, research and development in the area has never been more vigorous. In the next two chapters, we move away from the political arena to explore that professional literature, reviewing some of the most influential attempts to conceptualise the nature of teachers' professional knowledge and how it can be fostered. Two major schools of thought which analyse how students can and should 'learn to teach' are presented and critically reviewed from our own perspective. In this chapter we consider the competency models, while in Chapter 3 we examine the reflective practitioner movement.

The idea that initial teacher education should be conceived of as the achievement of a series of competences first received official support in the government's 1983 White Paper 'Teaching Quality'.

Since that time, the idea has been extended and developed through a range of policy documents until today, as the quotation above demonstrates, official policy sees initial teacher education entirely in these terms. Students, teachers and lecturers now have to concentrate on the competences of teaching 'throughout the whole period of initial training'.

Competency training is the latest flowering of a long-established tradition in teacher education which has attempted to develop a 'technical rationalist' approach to training (Carr and Kemmis 1986; Popkewitz 1987). Typically, such approaches attempt to combine utilitarianism (focusing learning on what is 'useful') with rationalist or even scientific principles. Such models of training are certainly not new; neither is an interest in them confined to policy makers. Bell and Lancaster's monitorial system, popular at the beginning of the nineteenth century, had something in common with the modern competency approach, for it too was based on the idea of defining the components of classroom organisation, discipline and teaching which could then be passed on to largely uneducated and unpaid monitors (Dent 1977). Later in the nineteenth century, similar rationalist principles underlay the building of model classrooms attached to colleges, where observers could watch from galleries (Wragg 1991).

In the more recent past, 'scientific' approaches to training achieved considerable popularity in the 1970s in Britain with the development of interaction analysis (Flanders, 1970; Wragg 1991), micro teaching (Allen and Ryan 1967; Stones 1976; Wragg 1984) and some interest in the American competency movement (Houston and Howsam 1972). What all three approaches had in common was the attempt to use the findings from research into effective teaching as a basis for training. The hope was that through the systematic use of observation schedules or videos, students could be trained in those skills of teaching that 'process product' research (Rosenshine and Furst 1971; Medley 1977) had supposedly demonstrated were associated with high pupil achievement. In the 1980s, disenchantment with the possibility of using such research to isolate what Flanders (1970) had called the 'laws of teaching' meant that these training models for a time fell out of favour too.

What is different about contemporary approaches to competency training is that, rather than being based on research into effective teaching, competences are, ideally at least, derived from an analysis of the job itself. As Jessup states,

The NVQ statements of competence are derived, not from an analysis of education and training programmes or the preconceptions of educators and trainers, but from a fresh analysis of present day employment requirements. Moreover, it is the employers and employees in the relevant industrial sector, occupation or profession, who have responsibility for saying what the requirements for qualifications, and thus training, are.

(1991: 16)

It is in accordance with this spirit of linking competences to the job of teaching that recent British government circulars on initial training (DFE 1992, 1993a) begin each list of competences with the phrase 'Newly qualified teachers should be able to: . . .'. In reality, of course, current government lists are not based on research; rather, they have emerged as the result of a political process both within the profession and, increasingly, outside it. They are therefore a 'partial' interpretation of teaching competences in both senses of the word.

In any discussion of contemporary competency-based teacher education it is important to recognise the enormous variation in interpretations of the approach. When writers as theoretically diverse as Jessup (1991) and Elliott (1990) can both claim to be writing about competences, it is essential to approach the area with caution. Within the professional literature it is possible to identify at least two different models of competence. The first, and more traditional, approach, defines competence as 'performance'. In this model, according to the CNAA committee on teacher education, competence is characterised as 'an ability to perform a task satisfactorily, the task being clearly defined as the criteria of success being set out along side this' (CNAA: 1992, para 3.3). More recently, in response to criticisms of such a behaviourist view, a broader definition of competence has been proposed – one which encompasses 'intellectual, cognitive and attitudinal dimensions as well as performance; in this model, neither competences nor the criteria of achievement are so readily susceptible to sharp and discrete identification' (CNAA 1992 para 3.3). To date, official government circulars have adopted a broadly based approach, perhaps deliberately allowing for a wide range of interpretations in the construction of particular teacher education programmes.

PERFORMANCE MODELS

Probably the clearest contemporary example of the 'perform-ance' approach to competency training is the National Vocational Qualifications (NVQ) model (NCVQ 1989; Jessup 1991). Within this model, all occupations are seen as classifiable within one of five different 'levels'. Teaching is seen as being at Level IV in that it involves 'competence in the performance of complex, technical, specialised and professional work activities, including those in-volving designing, planning and problem solving, with a significant degree of personal accountability' (Jessup 1991: 23). Teaching is yet to be fully incorporated into such a scheme, though advocates such as Hargreaves (1990) and Beardon et al. (1992) clearly see the model as having great potential for initial training.

If the model were to be applied, the role of the teacher, in its social, organisational as well as pedagogical dimensions, would be analysed in terms of a series of 'units', each of which would be broken down into its constituent 'elements'. Each element would then be defined in terms of its own 'performance criteria' which would set out, with a precision 'approaching that of a science' (Jessup 1991: 134), exactly what a candidate was expected to *do* to demonstrate competence in that element of the role. In addition, such criteria would include 'range statements' indicating the range of situations (age groups, ability levels and so on) in which the candidate at that level should be able to perform.

Jessup (1991) himself recognises that, in professions like teach-ing, it is not possible to define tasks purely in behaviourist terms. This is because teachers constantly have to face complex and novel situations. Competence at a professional level therefore includes the underpinning 'knowledge and understandings re-quired for performance in employment'. Nevertheless, knowledge and understanding are not things to be spelled out directly within the statements of competence. Rather, they are an 'assessment issue'. If a candidate can meet the performance criteria and can demonstrate to an assessor that they can act in a professional way in an appropriate range of situations, then they are assumed to have acquired the appropriate knowledge and understanding. However, in a profession like teaching, it may not be possible for assessors to observe candidates in all the novel situations they might meet. As a consequence it may be necessary for assessors to supplement their observations of candidates' performance by some 'secondary' means. This could include some formal examination of their knowledge.

The emphasis on the outcomes, rather than the content of training, leads Jessup to argue that candidates do not have to undergo any particular programme of learning to achieve an NVQ. Qualification is based solely on assessment of performance. Such a view is taken to its logical conclusion by Hargreaves (1990) and Beardon *et al.* (1992), who advocate that teacher education programmes should no longer be of fixed length but should end 'as soon as the trainee [has] met the standards of outcome required' (Beardon *et al.* 1992: 28).

The performance model of competency training presents a radical challenge to conventional conceptions of teacher education and is claimed to have a number of significant advantages (Whitty and Willmott 1991). By focusing on what newly qualified teachers should be able to do, it is claimed that the model: demystifies the process of teacher education; democratises access; provides a clearer role for schools and those in higher education in the training process; gives greater confidence to employers in what beginning teachers can (and cannot) do; and provides clearer goals for students. Whether or not those claims are realised of course depends on the validity of the approach in the first place. Can teaching be understood purely in terms of the performance of a number of discrete units and elements? Is it possible to infer appropriate knowledge and understanding purely from performance? Such a model of teaching is highly contentious and, unsurprisingly, has been subjected to vigorous challenge.

The most frequently repeated criticism of the performance model is that it is behaviourist and therefore reductionist in its view of teaching (Marshall 1991). The charge of behaviourism is linked to a number of perceived weaknesses. First, it is argued that despite Jessup's (1991) caveats, the performance model of competences separates skills from knowledge and understanding. Elliott (1990), for example, argues that it is inappropriate to conceptualise professional competence in terms of a string of behavioural competences whose performance is measurable. There is a difference, he asserts, between know-how, or 'habitual skill knowledge', which enables an individual unreflectively to perform certain necessary routines, and 'intelligent skill knowledge', which involves the exercise of capacities for discernment, discrimination and intelligent action. It is impossible to conceptualise professional competence without due regard for these complex capacities.

A further consequence of the behaviourism in the approach is the assumption that teaching can be understood and evaluated in terms of the performance of a number of discrete elements. Clearly teaching is not like this, for, as Walker emphasises, professional competence demands far more complex preparation than mastering an isolated collection of elements, even if those elements include 'knowledge' and 'understandings' as well as skills:

> Teaching is more than a technology; it is a moral practice whose successful performance depends on a 'structure of competence' (Klemp 1980) in which abilities are not isolated discrete elements but are linked together structurally. For example, cognitive abilities, interpersonal abilities and motivational abilities are unified in competent teachers' powers of practical understandings which underpin complex professional judgements.
>
> (1992: 93)

As McElvogue and Salters (1992) say, the performance model's emphasis on the separation of elements within teaching can be compared to explaining the successful working of a car engine by listing the engine components and observing their behaviour rather than taking into account the basic principles on which the internal combustion engine works!

A final consequence of behaviourism is that the model implies a decontextualised view of performance. But teaching performance is not only multi-faceted, it is also highly dependent on context. Again, as Walker (1992) notes, teaching is culture-dependent:

> The individual is never merely an individual and the job is never merely a job, [thus] performance is rarely changed by merely changing any single variable, such as bringing a professional's knowledge up to date. In teaching, the combination of the complexity of the work, individual variation among teachers and multiple cultural affiliations means that quality in performance usually requires the orchestration of variables. Creative orchestration of the many performance variables can enhance both individual and collective performance. The key is identifying the developmental balance appropriate to the culture.
>
> (1992: 7)

But the performance model of competencies has not merely been accused of being behaviourist; it is also seen as functionalist (Marshall 1991). The image of the teacher is one who is a neutral expert; an expert in the performance of teaching as it is currently constructed rather than someone who has been educated to understand how and why it has come to take the form that it has. Competency training, like other forms of 'technical rationalist' education, implies that there is a common framework for people with fixed goals. Teaching is not seen as being based on values or interpretations. In the words of Popkewitz (1987), such an approach 'flattens reality and obscures the struggles which fashion and shape our world' (p. 12). According to Popkewitz, as a consequence of such approaches to professional preparation, the 'neutral professional' is in reality being asked to deliver an education that is increasingly defined by a political process over which the individual teacher has little control. As Marcuse said, 'Technology [in this case the "technology" of training] is always an historical-social project; in it is projected what a society and its ruling interests intend to do with men and things' (Marcuse, quoted in Roderick 1986). It is perhaps for this reason that, as we saw in Chapter 1, the more teacher education has come to be politicised by the New Right, the more official government documents have adopted the apparently neutral language of competences. As the latest circular on primary teacher education demonstrates (DFE 1993a), behind that apparent neutrality lies a vision of teaching that is itself far from neutral.

A COGNITIVE MODEL

As a result of the weaknesses of the performance model, many of those working in the field of teacher education today face a tension. That tension, according to McElvogue and Salters (1992), is that they recognise the inadequacies of traditional approaches to professional preparation that stressed understanding the process of teaching over and above the practical experience in doing it, but they see competency training as an inadequate alternative because it produces people who are able to teach but who do not understand what they are doing.

In an attempt to deal with that tension and to respond to some of the other criticisms of the performance model, a number of contemporary analysts have tried to develop a rather different approach to competency training. As we will see, this alternative model places greater emphasis on the knowledge and understanding underpinning action: it is a cognitive rather than a performance model. Much of the developmental work for this model has gone on outside the field of teacher education in relation to the police (Elliott 1992) and social work (Winter 1990), but a recent working party report from the Department of Education in Northern Ireland (DENI 1993) has proposed adopting a similar model for the education of teachers.

The cognitive model of competency training is intended to differ from the performance model in a number of significant ways. First, it adopts a very different approach to knowledge and understanding in initial teacher education; both are seen as intrinsic and essential to meaningful action rather than as optional extras. Without knowledge we cannot interpret events, neither can we act in a meaningful way. As McElvogue and Salters (1992) argue, 'what we see and what we select for attention is directly influenced by our previous learning and it is the framework of knowledge which we have which influences how we filter information from the environment'. A teacher education programme that sees only 'performance' and does not prepare students in appropriate knowledge leaves them 'gaping' at experience rather than 'seeing' it. Teacher education programmes must therefore have a content.

But knowledge and understanding are not the only issues that must be addressed in professional preparation. If student teachers are to be prepared to respond flexibly to complex professional situations, then, as McElvogue and Salters (1992) point out, they also need to be able to exercise judgement. This reference to judgement reminds us that teaching is not merely a technical matter but is fundamentally concerned with values. This is an issue that receives scant attention in 'performance' models yet somehow teacher education programmes must address it.

Professionals also need to develop certain habits of mind, including the ability and commitment critically to examine their own practice. In other words, they need to learn to reflect. Following McIntyre (1991), McElvogue and Salters (1992) argue that this sort of reflection involves students doing more than merely thinking about what they are doing; rather, they must

assimilate theoretical knowledge into a framework of professional thinking and then consider the relevance of this to teaching
by examining their own practice.

Competence, from this perspective, therefore involves judgement, commitment, habits of mind as well as knowledge, understanding and skills. As a consequence, the cognitive model does
not consider it possible to specify competences or their
performance in great detail, nor does it assume that they can be
measured or assessed through simply observing behaviour and
ticking off elements on a check-list. Assessment of 'practical
wisdom' (Winter 1990) must involve interpretation. As McElvogue
and Salters say of a social work programme devised by Winter
along these lines, 'Students are not expected to display precise
behavioural outcomes but rather are expected to act intelligently
and responsibly within the parameters of certain demands and of
an agreed professional framework' (1992: 14).

As was noted above, most of the developmental work for a
cognitive model of competence training has gone on outside the
field of initial teacher education. However, a recent report by a
working party of the Northern Ireland Department of Education
has attempted to apply the framework in our field. The working
party (DENI 1993) argue that professional competences should
be taken to refer to knowledge, understanding and attitudes as
well as to practical skills. They assert that:

> in order to teach satisfactorily certain craft skills have un-
> doubtedly to be learned . . . teachers must in addition to this
> have knowledge and understanding both of the content of
> their teaching and of the processes which they are carrying out
> and be able to evaluate and justify their actions. We would add
> that they also need an appreciation of the broader context in
> which they are working.
>
> (1993: 11)

However, they also assert that no matter how comprehensive and
well structured, a simple list of competences, even if it includes
knowledge and understanding, could not convey all they wanted
to say about the professional competence of a teacher. 'The atom-
isation of professional knowledge, judgement and skill into discrete
competences inevitably fails to capture the essence of professional competence' (para 13). Their strategy for overcoming this
objection is to specify some generic professional competences

which they believe should permeate all of the other specific competences they list. These professional characteristics include professional values, such as liking and caring for children; ability and commitment to engage in professional and personal development; ability and commitment to communicate and handle relationships effectively; and the ability to integrate and apply a wide range of knowledge and skills in practical situations. Their model, whereby they see professional characteristics informing knowledge which in turn informs skills, is set out in Figure 2.1.

From our point of view, the cognitive model of competences is a significant advance on the performance model. Indeed, the framework set out in the DENI report would be a significant advance on most conventional teacher education programmes, covering as it does the skills, knowledge and professional characteristics that need to be developed in the three different phases of professional preparation – initial training, induction and INSET. Nevertheless, as a way of understanding how students learn to teach, the model is still seriously flawed. The critique of the performance model is in reality more sophisticated than the alternative that has been developed. For, although some writers such

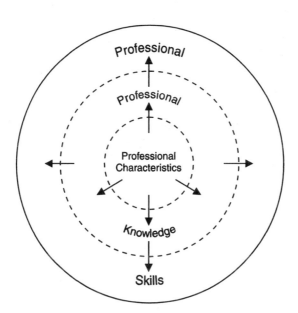

Figure 2.1 Northern Ireland Working Party, model of competences (DENI 1993)

as Elliott (1990) recognise that it is impossible to talk about professional skills in a way that separates them from knowledge or intelligent action, what we are offered, in the Northern Ireland model at least, does not really solve the problem. Skills and knowledge are still seen as separate entities; they are simply held together by the 'glue' of professional characteristics.

As the Northern Ireland working party admit, they had to depend entirely on secondary sources for their work. As a result, little of the content of their framework is new; rather, familiar topics are recast within a competency framework. Neither they, nor anyone else to our knowledge, has as yet subjected the work of newly qualified teachers to the type of analysis that was undertaken by Elliott (1990) in his work on the police prior to developing a competency programme for that profession. Had they been able to do so, the Northern Ireland working group might well have moved away from the idea that 'in order to teach satisfactorily certain craft skills have undoubtedly to be learned'. As Elliott (1990) recognises in his concept of 'intelligent skill knowledge', learning to teach involves students bringing together practical skills, knowledge and judgements in ways that cannot be captured within the constituent elements of a conventional programme, even if they are recast in a novel framework.

One way of characterising our own research question is to see it as an exploration of the 'intelligent skill knowledge' of which Elliott (1990) speaks. That knowledge can only be developed in school, though it clearly draws on forms of learning that take place elsewhere. A clearer understanding of what the intelligent skill knowledge of teaching actually is and the stages through which it develops could help all of us, not merely those interested in competences, develop a more effective curriculum for teacher education. However, before we turn to our own research, we need to consider the other major school of thought that has recently been applied to understanding how students learn to teach – that is, the reflective practitioner model.

Chapter 3

Learning to teach – the reflective practitioner model

There has been a recent proliferation of preservice training courses adopting 'reflective teaching' as a basic philosophy or guiding principle. . . . Terms such as 'reflective practice', 'inquiry oriented teacher education', 'reflection-in-action', 'teacher as researcher', 'teacher as decision-maker', 'teacher as professional', 'teacher as problem solver', all encompass some notion of reflection in the process of professional development, but at the same time, disguise a vast number of conceptual variations, with a range of alternative implications for the organisation and design of teacher education courses.

(Calderhead 1989: 43)

The 1991 national survey of all 317 initial teacher education courses in England and Wales undertaken by the Modes of Teacher Education project (MOTE) (Barrett *et al.* 1992; Miles *et al.* 1993; Whitty *et al.* 1992), revealed that over 70 per cent of those courses that claimed to be underpinned by a particular philosophy of training described that philosophy as being based on the principles of the reflective practitioner. As Calderhead notes, by 1989, an interest in reflective practice was more or less universal among teacher educators. Five years on, the term has achieved even wider currency, and the notion of reflectivity has become incorporated into many teachers' own view of what it means to be a professional.

As McIntyre (1993) has recently reminded us, the debate about reflection is fundamentally bound up with considerations about the role of 'theory' in initial teacher education. In 1986, Alexander pointed to the 'possibility' in British initial teacher education of moving away from a concern with theory to a concern with 'theorising'. Since then, as Furlong *et al.* (1994b) confirm, within the vast majority of British teacher education programmes, notions of 'theorising', 'theory as process' or 'reflecting' have largely displaced the teaching of theory as propositional knowledge.

But the popularity of the idea of reflection has not led to conceptual clarity. Calderhead (1989) has described the notion of reflection as a slogan rather than a principle and indeed, as Furlong (1992) has argued, the rapid rise in popularity of the term in the late 1980s was probably due as much to its apparent political value in opposing the 'technicist' thrust of government reforms in initial teacher education as any serious engagement with the underlying theoretical principles of reflection. It could well be that the popularity of the term was largely dependent on the fact that it was indeed vague – a powerful slogan that could serve as a rallying cry for those determined to preserve some role for 'theory' in initial teacher education. The reflective practitioner 'movement' is therefore a broad church. As Calderhead (1989) points out, 'researchers, teacher educators and other writers in the field hold a range of beliefs about teaching and teacher education into which they have incorporated their own particular notions of reflection' (p. 45).

However, the fact that there is little agreement on the precise definition of reflective practice should not lead us to dismiss the significance of the concept as a way of conceptualising the processes involved in initial teacher education. A great deal of theoretical work on the role of reflection in the professional development of teachers has been undertaken, much of which has been significant as a background to our own work.

Part of the confusion within the debate on reflection stems from the fact that different writers have focused on at least two very different dimensions within the process of learning to teach. One approach to reflection owes much of its intellectual heritage to the philosopher John Dewey (1910, 1933); the other is derived from the ideas of Donald Schön (1983, 1987). As we will see however, both of them are concerned with the *process* of theorising and have a complex relationship to other forms of propositional knowledge.

ROUTINE AND REFLECTIVE ACTION – DEWEY'S LEGACY

The origin of the concept of reflection as an aspect of teachers' professional thinking owes much to the American philosopher

John Dewey, writing in the early part of this century. Central to Dewey's view of reflection was the idea that there is a funda-mental dichotomy between *routine action* – that is, action guided primarily by tradition, *external* authority and circumstance – and *reflective action*.

Dewey presents a picture of people undertaking most of their lives in a routinised almost thought-*less* way. The grounds for their action have not themselves been considered and are based on tradition, instruction and imitation. 'Such thoughts are pre-judices that is, prejudgements, not judgements proper that rest upon a survey of evidence' (1910: 4–5).

By contrast, reflective action, according to Dewey, is fund-amentally different in character from routine action, in that it involves: 'the active, persistent and careful consideration of any belief or supposed form of knowledge in the light of the grounds that support it' (1910: 6). The move from routine to reflective thought is, according to Dewey, based on the need to solve a problem:

> *Demand for the solution of a perplexity is the steadying and guiding factor in the entire process of reflection.* Where there is no question of a problem to be solved or a difficulty to be surmounted, the course of suggestions flows on at random.
>
> (1910: 11)

It is this need to solve a problem, that drives enquiry forward:

> The exercise of thought is, in the literal sense of that word *inference*; by it, *one thing carries us over* to the idea of and belief in another thing. It involves a jump, a leap, a going beyond what is surely known to something else accepted on its warrant.
>
> (1910: 26)

The notion that reflection can be sharply contrasted with more routine, 'technical' action is also one that is central to much contemporary writing in this area. Indeed, as Calderhead and Gates (1993) have argued, part of the appeal of the concept of reflection is that some teacher educators believe that it can chal-lenge what they see as the 'technicist' thrust in contemporary educational policy.

At a time when teachers are increasingly being portrayed in educational policy as technicians or deliverers of the curriculum,

reflective teaching offers promise of an alternative conceptualization that appropriately recognises the thoughtful and
professional aspects of teachers' work.

(1993: 1/2)

The dichotomy between reflection and more instrumental forms
of thought has been taken up in a number of highly influential
contemporary accounts of reflection For example, Tom (1984),
Carr and Kemmis (1986), Handal and Lauvas (1987), Zeichner
and Liston (1987) and McIntyre (1993) all make the same distinction. Each of these authors, however, has gone further than Dewey
in distinguishing different *types* of reflection. Interestingly, many
of them draw on a seminal paper by van Manen (1977) to distinguish two types of reflection. In line with Dewey's arguments,
van Manen describes much of teachers' everyday practical thinking as technical and routine:

> When teachers are involved in the process of daily planning,
> adapting materials, developing courses, arranging subject matter
> content, teaching, evaluating and so forth, they do so largely
> uncritically and unreflectively. This is the attitude of everyday
> work. The practical in this sense is a concern for ordinary life;
> it expresses itself in the routines or taken for granted grounds
> of daily activities.
>
> (1977: 264)

However, van Manen then goes on to distinguish two levels of
reflection, which can lead to a different interpretation of teachers'
'practical' work. At the first level, he suggests that teachers raise
more fundamental questions about the 'educational' aspects of
their work; 'the focus is on an interpretive understanding both of
the nature and quality of educational experience and of making
practical choices' (1977: 226–7); while at a second level they can
address more fundamental moral and ethical questions, concerning 'the worth of knowledge and the nature of the social
conditions necessary for raising the questions of worthwhileness
in the first place' (1977: 227).

Others, such as Zeichner and Liston (1987) express the same
distinctions but in a slightly different way. They distinguish the
teacher as 'technician', the teacher as 'craftsperson' and the teacher
as 'moral craftsperson':

The teacher as technician would be concerned primarily with

the successful accomplishment of ends decided by others. The craftsperson teacher would consider the educational justification for classroom actions and how well the educational goals are being accomplished. The teacher as moral craftsperson would also be concerned with the moral and ethical implications of particular institutional arrangements.

(1987: 27)

Zeichner and Liston recognise that what they refer to as 'educational' and 'moral' issues are always implicit in teaching, even if it is understood as a merely 'technical' process. However, the principle behind the teacher education programme they describe is that without an explicit emphasis on these dimensions, student teachers may well not come to recognise them in their own teaching.

This introduction of a 'moral' dimension to definitions of reflection owes much to use made by van Manen and others of the work of the critical theorist, Habermas (1970, 1974). Habermas' aim is above all to create a moral or ethical social science. As a result of the importation of Habermas' ideas, the ultimate aim of reflection for many contemporary analysts has come to be seen as 'liberation'.

As Zeichner and Liston state:

The stated goals of the elementary student teacher program at the University of Wisconsin, Madison, emphasise the preparation of teachers who are both willing and able to reflect on the origins, purposes and consequences of their actions as well as on the material and ideological constraints and encouragements embedded in classroom school and societal contexts in which they work. . . . Underlying these goals is a metaphor of liberation.

(1987: 23)

They go on to define a liberated person, as someone who is 'free from the unwarranted control of unjustified beliefs, unsupportable attitudes and the paucity of abilities which can prevent that person from completely taking charge of his or her life'.

A similar position is taken by Carr and Kemmis (1986), who call for the development of forms of reflection that will lead to a 'critical educational science' serving the 'emancipatory interest' and promoting freedom and rational autonomy:

'Thus a critical educational science (based on forms of reflection)

has the aim of transforming education; it is directed at educational change . . . [it] aims at involving teachers, students,
parents and school administrators in the task of critical
analysis of their own situation with a view to transforming
them in ways which will improve these situations as educational situations for students, teachers and society.

(1986: 156–7)

In the words of Marx (1941), whom they quote with approbation,
'philosophers have only interpreted the world in various ways
. . . the point is to change it'.

Dewey's idea that reflection is something special and different
from everyday routine action lead him to conclude that reflection
demands special skills and personal qualities on the part of the
teacher. For example, reflection, he suggested, demands that
teachers develop the skills of keen observation, reasoning and
analysis.

Thinking involves the suggestion of a conclusion for ac-
ceptance and also search or enquiry to test the value of the
suggestion before finally accepting it. This implies (a) a certain
fund or store of experiences or facts from which suggestions
proceed; (b) promptness, flexibility and fertility of suggestions; and (c) orderliness, consecutiveness and appropriateness
in what is suggested. Clearly, a person may be hampered in
any of these three regards: his thinking may be irrelevant,
narrow or crude because he has not enough actual material
upon which to base conclusions or because concrete facts and
raw material, even if extensive and bulky, fail to evoke suggestions easily and richly; or finally, because even when these
two conditions are fulfilled, the ideas when suggested are
incoherent and fantastic rather than pertinent and consistent.

(1910: 30)

All of these skills, Dewey suggested, can be developed, but their
deployment in ways that will promote true reflection is dependent on teachers having certain personal characteristics or
'orientations' as well. They must, for example, be committed to
'open-mindedness' 'responsibility' and 'wholeheartedness'
(Dewey 1933).

This idea that reflection is somehow dependent on such special skills and characteristics remains a common theme in much writing in this field (Pollard and Tann 1987; Korthagen 1988; Tann 1993). LaBoskey (1993) provides a contemporary example. In her study of student teachers and their readiness to explore pedagogical thinking, LaBoskey distinguishes between what she characterises as 'Alert Novices' and 'Common Sense Thinkers'. The 'Common Sense Thinkers', she suggests, 'appeared to be unable to engage in the cognitive process of reflective thinking. Others had the necessary cognitive abilities, but seemed to have beliefs, values, attitudes or emotions that prevented or distorted the reflective process in most situations' (1993: 30). By contrast, the 'Alert Novices' seemed to be driven by a 'will to know' they were always on the look-out for something 'better'. In the words of one student teacher in this category, 'If I ever think that I know what I'm doing is right, I really want to step back and check my premise' (1993: 31).

LaBoskey concludes that her research evidence 'tends to support Dewey's proposal (1910) that the attitudes of open-mindedness, responsibility and wholeheartedness are integral to reflective action' (1993: 30).

Most of the writers in the Deweyan tradition argue that learning to reflect in the ways they identify is a central part of learning to teach. As we noted above (on p. 41), writers such as Zeichner and Liston (1987) consider it important for student teachers to engage in systematic enquiry into the moral and ethical dimensions of their own teaching. This type of enquiry, they suggest, will lead to better teaching.

> It is our belief that learning for both pupils and teachers is greater and deeper when teachers are encouraged to exercise their judgement about the content and processes of their work and give some degree of direction to the shape of schools as educational environments.
>
> (1987: 24)

Therefore an underlying concern of the teacher education programme they developed was:

> to enable prospective teachers, both individually and collectively, to develop the desire and ability to assume greater roles in determining the direction of classroom and school affairs

according to purposes of which they are aware and which can
be justified on moral and educational grounds *as well as on
instrumental grounds.*

(1987: 25–6)

An interesting challenge to the Deweyan definition of reflection
in initial teacher education has recently been set out by McIntyre
(1993). McIntyre recognises the significance of reflection defined
as 'systematic enquiry into one's own practice', but sees it as
having only a very limited role in initial teacher education.
'Beginner' teachers, he argues, have much to learn, but given that
at this stage of their development they have comparatively little
experience to 'reflect on', reflection is of limited value to them.
While students need to be taught that in the longer term, reflection
of this sort will be important for their professional development,
McIntyre argues that in initial teacher education programmes,
the emphasis should be on 'suggestions for practice' rather than
reflection.

Certainly, if one does define reflection as 'systematic enquiry
into one's own actions', then we would not disagree. The moral
certainty of writers like Zeichner and Liston (1987) and Carr and
Kemmis (1986), who assume that, by asking students to confront
deeper and more fundamental questions about their own teaching,
will, of itself, produce a better teacher seems unsubstantiated. As
Calderhead notes, 'whether any of the proposed models of reflective teaching . . . offer very adequate conceptions of professional
learning as it occurs in classrooms or of how it might occur, is
largely unassessed' (1989: 45). Equally problematic is the idea
that reflection is something that only occurs when one asks particular sorts of questions – questions with a broader moral and
ethical edge to them. It would seem to us that it is perfectly
possible to ask fundamental questions about all dimensions of
the educational process and from many different points of view.
Moral and ethical questions are important, but, ultimately, they
are not separable from questions about how children learn and
the nature of pedagogy. To prioritise one type of questioning
over all others seems to us inappropriate.

However, our reservations about all of the writers discussed so
far is at a deeper level and stems from their assumption, derived
from the work of Dewey, that there is a fundamental dichotomy
between routine and reflective action. For us, Dewey's notion of

teaching as routine action does not capture the multi-facetedness, unpredictability and sheer complexity of teaching, whether it is reflected upon or not. Moreover, teaching is never 'merely' technical; it always involves educational and moral assumptions as well, whether or not the teacher is aware of them.

Whereas the work by van Manen (1977) and others on the different types of reflection is valuable, a view of reflection that defines itself in contrast to a caricature of teaching as a simple technical following of rules, seems to us entirely inadequate. What is missing from all of this body of work is a careful analysis of the nature of teaching as a professional activity *per se*. In Schön's (1983) words, what we need is an 'epistemology of practice' in teaching. As we will see, Schön's fundamentally different conception of reflection begins by trying to develop such an epistemology.

KNOWING IN ACTION AND REFLECTION IN ACTION – THE WORK OF SCHÖN

[I]n practical performance, 'intelligent' cannot be defined in terms of 'intellectual', [or] 'knowing how' in terms of 'knowing that'.

(Ryle 1949: 32)

Schön's conception of reflection is significantly different from all of the authors considered above. In his two books, *The Reflective Practitioner* and *Educating the Reflective Practitioner*, Schön (1983, 1987) sets out to analyse in some detail the nature of professional practice and how it can be acquired. Traditionally, he argues, the relationship between professional knowledge and action has been understood in terms of technical rationality; professional activity has been seen as a process of instrumental problem solving 'made rigorous by the application of scientific theory and technique' (1983: 21). Professionals have been seen as 'experts' in that they possess a body of abstract knowledge which they 'apply' in a rule-governed way, to the real world.

Schön argues that there is a current crisis of confidence among contemporary professionals which can be attributed to the fact that this is an entirely inadequate understanding of the way professionals actually work. They may have a body of specialised knowledge, but they do not simply 'apply' it in a rule-governed way. Whether or not one's teaching is raised to the level of consciousness, it always involves a complex 'artistry'.

> I have used the term *professional artistry* to refer to the kinds of competence practitioners display in unique, uncertain and conflicted situations of practice. Note however that their artistry is a high powered esoteric variant of the more familiar sorts of competence all of us exhibit everyday in countless acts of recognition, judgement and skilful performance.
>
> (1987: 22)

In his 1983 book, Schön elaborates on the artistic nature of professional action. In an interesting parallel with Chomsky's views on language (1968), he begins by emphasising that professionals (like Chomsky's speakers) constantly find themselves facing situations which are unique. Schön emphasises that teachers will have to cope with the fact that no two groups of pupils they may have to teach are the same; even with pupils with whom they are familiar, the teacher is constantly having to present new material which raises its own unique problems of explanation and understanding. What the experienced teacher (again like Chomsky's 'linguistically competent' speaker) brings to these unique situations is a stock of experiences at many different levels of practical and theoretical sophistication: 'The practitioner has to build up a repertoire of examples, images, understanding and actions [which] includes the whole of his experience so far as it is accessible to him for understanding and action' (1983: 138). Yet Schön argues that it is not a simple process of 'applying' this knowledge to the new situation. The teacher does not try to fit this group of pupils rigidly into some kind of pre-existing pattern of understanding that will simply tell him or her what to do. Rather, past experiences are used as a metaphor or exemplar.

> When a practitioner makes sense of a situation he perceives to be unique he sees it as something actually present in his repertoire. To see this situation as that one is not to subsume the first under a familiar category or rule. It is rather to see the unfamiliar unique situation as both similar to and different from the familiar one, without at first being about to say similar or different with respect to what. The familiar situation functions as a precedent or metaphor or . . . an exemplar for the unfamiliar one.
>
> (1983: 138)

In drawing on his or her past experience the professional imposes a structure or 'frame' on the problem at hand. 'Framing' a problem is an active process. It involves interpreting the situation in *this* way as opposed to countless other possible ways, shaping it to the frame. For example, a teacher may define a standard situation by interpreting a child's behaviour as the result of a combination of the distinct factors seen to be operating in previous cases. To draw on one's understanding and experience is to begin with an interpretation which to some degree shapes the situation one faces.

But this framing process, Schön argues, has to be seen as experimental; one imposes meaning by actually taking action and then evaluating the consequences. The teacher interprets the child's behaviour and responds in a way which leads to many consequences and that may result in the changing of the frame. Imposing a frame therefore leads to a 'web of moves, discovered consequences, implications, appreciation and further moves. Within the larger web, individual moves yield phenomena to be understood, problems to be solved or opportunities to be exploited' (1983: 131). There will also be unintended consequences. The situation 'speaks back' to the practitioner, demanding more reflection and further action.

Engaging in professional activity is therefore always a 'transactional' process. The professional

> shapes the situation, but in conversation with it so that his own models and appreciations are also shaped by the situation. The phenomena that he seeks to understand are partly of his own making: he is in the situation that he seeks to understand.
>
> (1983: 151)

In short, 'the unique and uncertain situation comes to be understood through the attempt to change it and is changed through the attempt to understand it' (1983: 132).

What is clear from the above analysis of professional action is that Schön, in sharp contrast to Dewey and his followers, does not believe that the sophistication of a teacher's action is in principle dependent on whether or not they can articulate and justify their behaviour. The competence of a teacher is revealed first and foremost in his or her ability to work effectively in a particular situation. This 'intelligent action' may be almost entirely intuitive – what Schön calls knowing-in-action:

> I shall use the term *knowing-in-action* to refer to the sorts of knowledge we reveal in our intelligent action – publicly observable physical performances like riding a bicycle and private operations like instant analysis of a balance sheet. In both cases the knowing is in the action. We reveal it by our spontaneous, skilful execution of the performance: and we are characteristically unable to make it verbally explicit.
>
> (1987: 25)

Schön distinguishes this intuitive form of action from two forms of reflection – what he describes as 'reflection-*in*-action' and 'reflection-*on*-action'. Reflection-in-action occurs when a practitioner faces an unknown situation. In these circumstances, the experienced practitioner is able to bring certain aspects of their work to the level of consciousness and to reflect on it and reshape it without interrupting the flow.

> Reflection-in-action has a critical function, questioning the assumptional structure of knowing-in-action. . . . [It] gives rise to on the spot experiment. We think up and try out new actions intended to explore the newly observed phenomena, test our tentative understandings of them or affirm the moves we have invented to change things for the better.
>
> (1987: 28)

Like knowing-in-action, reflection-in-action still largely involves 'situated' knowledge; it is a process we can go through without necessarily being able to say what we are doing. Talking about what we are doing after the event is a different process yet again – it is what Schön calls reflection-*on*-action and it is something that many professionals find it difficult to do. This is because, Schön asserts, whatever language we use, our descriptions of professional practice are always *constructions*. They are an attempt to put into language a kind of intelligence that begins by being tacit and spontaneous. In trying to capture that intelligence through language we necessarily distort its reality because 'knowing-in-action is dynamic and "facts", "procedures", "rules" and "theories" are static' (1987: 25).

For Schön, reflection-on-action is a key process in learning a professional activity like teaching. However inadequate a beginning teacher's verbal reconstruction of events, Schön argues that it is by moving learners from knowing-in-action to reflection-on-action that they can begin to gain control of their developing 'artistry'. They bring to the level of consciousness the ways in which they are 'framing' teaching situations and, in so doing, progressively gain control of their own teaching

> As I think back on my experience . . . I may consolidate my understanding of the problem or invent a better or more general solution to it. If I do, my present reflection on my earlier reflection-in-action begins a dialogue of thinking and doing through which I become more skilful.
>
> (1987: 3)

Schön's ideas have been extremely influential in initial teacher education in Britain in recent years. Many teacher educators have felt that his way of describing the nature of professional action captures something of the complexity involved in learning to teach. Moreover, his ideas have caught the spirit of the times; they legitimise the removal of the formal teaching of 'theory' in teacher education courses (Furlong *et al.* 1994b), and provide a rationale for the move to school-based teacher education that we described in Chapter 1 (Furlong *et al.* 1988). If learning to teach is facilitated by a personalised process of reflection-on-action, then the conventional pattern of training where students use teaching practice to 'apply' the 'theory' they have learned in college becomes inadequate. Schools must themselves become central to the training process, and teachers, who alone have access to the 'situated knowledge' that students must acquire, become seen as key people in the training process.

PERSONAL REFLECTION AND PUBLIC THEORY

A central and unresolved question in all writing on reflection concerns the relationship between knowledge derived from personal reflection and other forms of knowledge. As we noted at the beginning of this chapter, debates about reflection have been centrally bound up in Britain with concerns about the role of 'theory' in initial teacher education. One of the best-known attempts in recent years to explore the relationship between reflection and other forms of 'theory' is the work of McIntyre (1990, 1993) and others associated with the Oxford internship scheme (Benton 1990).

For McIntyre (1993) and his colleagues, reflection is defined as systematic enquiry into one's own practice; a definition that places them (in this aspect of their work at least) in what we have characterised as the Deweyan tradition. However, McIntyre asserts that a concern with this sort of 'theorising' should not deflect us from the fact that students still need to know certain things.

> Our commitment to [reflection] should be equalled by our commitment to making available to our students theoretical knowledge which they will mostly, with refinement, be able usefully to assimilate to their professional thinking. So acceptance of theory as process need not, and should not in my view, limit the importance we attach to theory as content.
>
> (1993: 41)

Like the American curriculum theorist Schwab (1969, 1971, 1973), McIntyre notes that there are many different forms of 'theory' in teaching – speculative theory, the findings of empirical research, the craft knowledge of experienced teachers. But, he argues, none of these different forms of professional knowledge should be presented as having prescriptive implications for practice. Rather, students need to be taught that all knowledge should be tested. Knowledge from university sources should be tested against practicality criteria in the schools; and knowledge from school sources should be tested against more academic criteria.

The strength of McIntyre's work is that it does indeed recognise the importance of different forms of professional knowledge – there is a place for personal reflection as well as other more abstract forms of 'theory'. No one form of knowledge is seen as inherently superior to another – they are simply different. Through the process of testing and questioning, students in the Oxford internship scheme are seen as learning how to decide for themselves what actions to take and what principles to adopt.

While on the surface such an argument seems reasonable, one might still ask, as does Hirst (1990), by what criteria one can judge the results of reflection. Are some forms of professional practice, however they are justified, 'better' than others? The difficulty with McIntyre's work is that in the end it does not help in resolving this difficult issue. With a kind of postmodernist relativism (Wilkin 1993), the Oxford scheme leaves it to the student to make up his or her own mind about what are appropriate forms of practice.

A rather different approach to the relationship between reflection and other forms of knowledge is presented by Furlong *et al.* (1988) in their study of school-based teacher education programmes. Their research began by making a series of case studies of four courses, and from those case studies the research team developed an analytical model in which four different levels or dimensions of training were distinguished. Those different levels of professional training were as follows:

Levels of professional training

Level (a) Direct practice
Practical training through direct experience in schools and classrooms.
Level (b) Indirect practice
'Detached' training in practical matters usually conducted in classes or workshops within training institutions.
Level (c) Practical principles
Critical study of the principles of practice and their use.
Level (d) Disciplinary theory
Critical study of practice and its principles in the light of fundamental theory and research.

(Furlong et al. 1988: 132)

The research team's argument was that professional preparation demands that trainees in their courses must be exposed to *all* of these different dimensions of professional knowledge. Trainees need to be systematically prepared in practical classroom knowledge – they need to be prepared at Level (a) – it is a distinctive form of professional knowledge and training cannot be left to chance. In understanding how trainees acquire this level of knowledge, the authors draw on the work of Schön. They argue that it is mentors working in the school, who know about *these* pupils and *this* curriculum, who are best placed to help student teachers to gain control over their own teaching through a process of 'reflection-on-action'.

However, Furlong *et al.* argue that it is not sufficient for students simply to base their professional knowledge on their own reflection. They also need to develop a broad repertoire of practical knowledge and to subject their own developing professional knowledge to rigorous questioning. It is for this reason that teacher education courses need to incorporate preparation at other 'levels' and to establish course structures so that students can effectively integrate their learning from these different levels.

Because time in training is always limited, it is seldom possible for students to gain direct teaching experience in more than two or three schools. If their repertoire of practical experience is to be extended, then this must to some degree be achieved by 'indirect' practical training – through books, videos, visits and talks. This is what was characterised as training at Level (b).

But if professional knowledge is to be justified, then students' understandings derived from their personal reflections must be subject to questioning. They must be encouraged to question their teaching in the light of established professional principles (Level (c)), and they must also be taught that those professional principles can themselves be subject to rigorous questioning derived from disciplinary theory (Level (d)). In the model of Furlong and his colleagues, the relationship between personal reflection and public knowledge ('theory') is indirect. Established professional principles and disciplinary theory are not a direct source of knowledge to be applied; rather, they are a source of critical questions with which students are required to confront their own developing practical professional knowledge. It is through such questioning, Furlong *et al.* argue, that students' personal reflections are broadened and strengthened.

The model of Furlong and his colleagues therefore implicitly draws on both traditions of reflection we have discussed so far. It recognises the significance of Schön's contribution to an understanding of how student teachers, through reflection-on-action, can gain greater control over their own situated knowledge. But it also recognises the importance of subjecting that personal reflection to systematic questioning in order that professional action can be more adequately justified. However, unlike writers such as Carr and Kemmis (1986) or Zeichner and Liston (1987), Furlong *et al.* do not prioritise one particular type of questioning over others. Any of the 'foundation' disciplines of education – sociology, psychology, philosophy or history – may provide a source of fundamental questions the posing of which may serve to strengthen the principles underlying our teaching.

The work of Furlong *et al.* has not been without its critics. McIntyre (1991), for example, criticises the model for its notion of levels, and certainly, given that the term does carry overtones of a hierarchy, then it would seem inappropriate – different 'domains' of professional knowledge might have been a more appropriate term. However, McIntyre argues that there is an implicit hierarchy in more than the language – he suggests that the model prioritises academic knowledge at Level (d), implying that that is the only route to professional rigour.

More significant from the point of view of the present study is his criticism of Level (a) – direct practice. McIntyre criticises the model for presenting a single, undifferentiated view of school-based learning while more academic kinds of learning are divided into three categories. As we will see in the chapters that follow, it is this area of questioning – the nature of students' practical, school-based knowledge and how it is acquired – that has become the major focus of this present study.

CONCLUSION

As we have seen in this chapter, the conceptions and aims of reflection derived from the work of Dewey and Schön are fundamentally different. For Dewey and his followers, reflection stands in sharp contrast to routine action. It involves the systematic analysis of professional action, and its aim is to help students establish the principles on which their teaching should be based. As we have seen, much of the emphasis of contemporary writers in this tradition is on different types of reflection; they have been concerned to distinguish the different sorts of question student teachers 'ought' to address. Schön's views are very different. For him, reflective action and routine action are essentially similar – both involve the use of complex, 'situated' intelligence. As a result, Schön does not characterise reflection simply as systematic enquiry; rather, it involves the attempt to characterise complex, contextual knowledge in terms of language. It is through this form of linguistic reflection-on-action that students are encouraged to bring their situated knowledge to the level of consciousness and thereby take the process of teaching more directly under their own control.

From our point of view, neither approach, in itself, seems sufficient. We have already indicated that we find Dewey's dichotomy between routine and reflective action inadequate; nor are we convinced by those who argue that the posing of moral and ethical questions about their teaching is the key to becoming an effective teacher. As we indicated earlier, we consider that it is possible and necessary to ask fundamental questions about all dimensions of teaching: the 'technical', the 'practical' as well as the 'moral'. Yet it is also true that the view of reflection put forward by Schön is itself partial. Personal reflection of the sort he describes may indeed help student teachers bring their teaching under their own control, but one is still forced to ask the question as to whether personal reflection, on its own, is sufficient to ensure professional development. Furlong *et al.* (1994b) indicate that many British teacher education programmes now seem to assume that this form of personal reflection is sufficient. Our evidence would support the view taken by Calderhead (1987) and Feiman-Nemser and Buchmann (1987) that it is not. Moreover, as we see later in this book, our evidence also suggests that reflection, however it is defined, is not the only process involved when students learn to teach.

The ideas considered by those writing on reflection are important. They represent a serious attempt to come to terms with the process by which students learn to teach. Their weakness, as Calderhead (1989) suggests, is that much of the work in this area is partial – in both senses of the word. It is analytically rather than empirically derived and presented in a prescriptive form. 'Ideal models of reflection are offered but little is known about how they might operate in practice and how they compare with other forms of reflection or in which context they might be appropriate (Calderhead 1989: 46). As a result, he suggests: 'Our concepts of reflective teaching are at present insufficiently discriminating to take the complexities of students' learning into account.' More positively, however, he goes on:

> Research on teachers' professional learning holds promise for informing our concept of reflection and changing 'reflective teaching' from a general, widely used slogan to a practical, working principle. It is through our understanding of the processes of professional learning that we might begin to provide the structure and support that is needed to facilitate learning to teach.
>
> (1989: 49)

It was precisely with this aim in mind that we undertook our own investigation of teachers' professional learning, and we now turn to a consideration of the aims and methods of our own project in more detail.

Chapter 4

The aims and methods of the project

As we indicated in Chapter 1, school-based initial teacher education is now here to stay in Britain. As a result, the role of the mentor in the professional preparation of the next generation of teachers has assumed great significance. It is for this reason that, in the last few years, research and writing on the role of the mentor has been something of a 'boom industry' in Britain (Jacques 1992; Wilkin 1992b; Hagger *et al.* 1993; McIntyre *et al.* 1993; Shaw 1992; Watkins and Whalley 1993; Furlong *et al.* 1994a; Wilkin and Sankey 1994; Yeomans and Sampson 1994). But, as we have also indicated, we are convinced that although there has been a growing body of knowledge and understanding about the 'process' of mentoring (how to observe students, how to give feedback and so on) there is very little understanding about *what* it is that practising teachers can best contribute to the development of student teachers' professional knowledge. Much of the writing on the role of the mentor has, in our view, been insufficiently based on a clear analysis of the processes of professional learning that mentors should support. Following Calderhead (1989), we would therefore suggest that before the role of the mentor is developed further, we need to have a clearer vision of what is involved in the process of learning to teach; it is only through such an understanding that the processes of mentoring can be illuminated.

Our own research has therefore involved an exploration of students' learning with a view to contributing to the debate on what the role of the mentor might be. In this chapter, we aim to clarify the questions we have sought to explore in our research and to describe the methodologies that we have used.

CONCEPTUALISING TEACHING

As we have made apparent in the previous three chapters, within current political and professional discourse it is possible to identify a number of different conceptualisations of teaching; each of these views implies a different vision about how students learn to teach and, therefore, what the role of the mentor should be in that process. For example, as we argued in Chapter 1, the view sponsored in the most recent government circulars (DFE 1992, 1993a) appears to be a neo-conservative one. Neo-conservatives such as O'Hear (1988), the Hillgate Group (1989) and Lawlor (1990) assert that practical experience in teaching is sufficient in itself. This is because, they argue, teaching is an essentially 'natural' process, based principally on a sound knowledge and deep love of one's subject; beyond that, good teaching is too idiosyncratic and personalised to be analysed. They therefore conclude that learning to teach should be achieved first and foremost through the emulation of an experienced practitioner – a mentor. But for them, mentoring does not involve any specific skills beyond those of being a good teacher. Because teaching is a natural process, mentoring is simply about 'modelling'. All that is needed for teacher education is the definition of a number of broad competency statements, sufficient to focus the attention of student and mentor alike. Much of the thrust of recent government policy in initial teacher education reflects this view. Significantly, for neo-conservative commentators, higher education has little or no role in this process – a position also echoed in the government's most recent policy initiatives (DFE 1993b).

As we indicated in Chapter 1, we consider such a view of what is involved in learning to teach as simplistic in the extreme; moreover, in asserting that we have no reliable research data on the processes involved, neo-conservatives overlook an extensive literature on the nature of professional development. In Chapters 2 and 3, we examined two schools of thought within the professional literature that have tried to conceptualise teaching and the process of learning to teach – they were the competency movement, and the reflective practitioner movement. Interestingly, we noted, that despite the fact that in many ways these two schools of thought are diametrically opposed, there is an important convergence amongst some of the more thoughtful writers in each of these traditions.

Within the competency literature, we identified two very different models – a 'performance' model and a 'cognitive' model. In the cruder 'performance' model, teaching is understood as involving a number of behavioural skills. Learning to teach therefore involves the mastery of these discrete skills, and it is the role of the mentor to act as a systematic 'skills-based' trainer. A more sophisticated approach to competency training, the 'cognitive' model, recognises that competences involve knowledge and judgements as well as practical skills – a view of teaching perhaps best captured in Elliott's (1990) concept of 'intelligent skill knowledge'. Such a view of competence implies a much more complex role for mentors in that they must support students in developing and exercising appropriate knowledge and judgement in relation to their emerging practical teaching skills.

As we noted in Chapter 2, although such an approach may hold promise in the field of initial teacher education, if it is to be developed effectively then it must first be based on an examination of the 'intelligent skill knowledge' that is actually needed by newly qualified teachers; it is from such an analysis that one might derive a 'curriculum' for mentoring. Elliott's own competency-based programme, developed for the police, grew out of an extensive and detailed analysis of policing. To our knowledge, no one has as yet subjected the work of newly qualified teachers to this type of analysis. Although we do not see ourselves as working within this tradition, there is clearly an important overlap between our work on the processes involved in learning to teach and writers working in this 'cognitive' tradition. We too have been interested in the knowledge and judgements as well as the practical skills student teachers must learn in their professional preparation.

The final approach we examined was that of the reflective practitioner. Again we identified two sharply contrasting models within this body of literature, each of which implies a different role for the mentor. On the one hand we discussed those writers whom we characterised as standing within the Deweyan tradition (Dewey 1910). For these writers, reflection is defined as systematic enquiry into one's own and others' action. As we saw, in the last chapter, a number of authors have insisted that this form of reflection is essential if student teachers are to establish a secure understanding of the grounds for their own professional actions. From this perspective, mentoring is different again in that it must involve supporting students in their systematic enquiries. A very different conception of reflection has been that put forward by Schön (1983, 1987), who characterises it as a form of metacognition. It is through reflection-on-action – thinking about their thinking – that students can establish a greater control over the complex processes involved in learning to teach. Here, mentors are seen as having a crucial role, employing their own detailed and contextual knowledge as a basis for 'coaching' students in this reflective process.

As we indicated earlier, what is interesting about the reflective practitioner movement is that, like the competency movement, it too is based more on assertion than on systematic research. Different forms of reflection may well be educative for student teachers and fostering reflection may be a key aspect of the mentor's role. However, at present we have precious little systematic evidence on which to base an understanding of the role of reflection – however it is defined – in the process of learning to teach. Once again we find ourselves urgently in need of more detailed studies of that process.

TEACHERS' PRACTICAL PROFESSIONAL KNOWLEDGE

All three of the different conceptions of teaching we have considered – neo-conservative, competency based and reflective practitioner models – imply a different vision of how students can best learn to teach and therefore what the role of the mentor should be. Each of these models though is theoretically (or even ideologically) driven rather than being based on systematic research. During the last fifteen years, however, an alternative approach to the study of teaching has grown up. This is the approach that focuses on teachers' thinking, their decision making or, what we, following Elbaz (1983), came to call their 'practical professional knowledge' – for reviews of the field, see Clark and Peterson (1986); Calderhead (1987); McNamara (1990). What is distinctive about this tradition of work is that it is neither prescriptive nor reductionist; rather, it asks what it is that teachers themselves need to know; what practical knowledge teachers need to develop in order to be effective practitioners. A study of teachers' practical professional knowledge, and the ways in which students develop it, might, we conjectured, provide an important key to developing a more adequate conception of the role of the mentor. As Elbaz in her classic study of the practical knowledge of one teacher, says: 'The single factor which seems to have the greatest power to carry forward our understanding of the teachers' role is the idea of teachers' knowledge' (1983: 11).

In the British context, the potential significance of such studies for the development of a 'grounded theory' of teaching was first highlighted by McNamara and Desforges (1978). In their article, they challenged what, at the time, was the hegemonic position of the foundation disciplines of psychology, philosophy, sociology and history in initial teacher education, arguing instead for the importance and potential educational value of a different approach to 'theory'. Since that time, studies of teachers' practical knowledge have flourished both in this country and in America.

One of the difficulties facing researchers working in this area is that it is often considered that teachers do not actually possess a body of practical, professional knowledge. As Elbaz explains:

It is hardly surprising that teachers have developed no such articulated body of knowledge if we consider the context of teaching. To begin with teachers are trained in a setting which is rarely seen by them as serious or relevant to their future work; thus, whatever conceptual skills they might acquire during their training would tend to be compartmentalized, rather than applied to the understanding of teaching. In teaching itself, while teachers may often rehash and compare experiences, they in fact have little experience that is shared and there are few opportunities for them to reflect on and attempt to articulate their experience in an organised way. Finally, the view of knowledge as 'empirical' and 'analytical' which prevails in educational thought, tends to place relatively low value on experiential knowledge and thus teachers themselves may be unaware of the value of their own knowledge. Certainly there is little encouragement for teachers to view themselves as originators of knowledge.

(1983: 11)

There also appears to be considerable disagreement between researchers as to the actual definition and nature of this knowledge. Sternberg and Caruso, for example, define practical knowledge as knowledge which is both procedural and relevant to a person's everyday life (1985: 139). Johnston (1992) on the other hand, highlights a *number* of terms researchers have given to this 'knowledge which guides practice' – *practical knowledge* (Elbaz 1983); *practical theories of teaching* (Sanders and McCutcheon 1986); *personal practical knowledge* (Clandinin 1986); *folkways of teaching* (Buchmann 1987); and the *wisdom of practice* (Shulman 1987). Similarly, Brown and McIntyre refer to *professional craft knowledge* which they define as the professional knowledge and thought that teachers 'use in their day-to-day classroom teaching, knowledge which is not generally made explicit by teachers and which teachers are not likely always to be conscious of using' (1993: 19).

Although, as Johnston points out, each of these terms arises from a different set of assumptions and interests, 'all acknowledge that this type of knowledge is built from personal and professional experience, is not readily articulated by the teacher and is used in complex ways during the process of planning for and executing teaching activities, as well as making sense of decisions already made' (1992: 124–5).

Researching teachers' practical professional knowledge was clearly going to be challenging, and our initial review of the literature confirmed the complexity of the task facing us. Existing published work in this area was diverse, fragmentary and dogged by complex methodological problems. Moreover, while welcoming its empirical base, some of the research was, for us, simply too atheoretical. Nevertheless, our preliminary reading convinced us that, whatever the shortcomings of existing studies, the *questions* posed by this body of research were vitally important for those concerned with initial teacher education. As Calderhead notes following a review of the literature in this area,

> It is tentatively suggested that some of [the] difficulties in learning to teach might be attributed to particular models of professional learning which have become implicit in teacher education and which fail to acknowledge the nature and use of knowledge in teaching.
>
> (1988: 62)

By acknowledging the nature and use of teachers' practical professional knowledge and asking how students develop it, we felt we could contribute to the development of a more effective model of professional learning and, in particular, we could throw an important light on what the role of the mentor can and should be in school-based initial teacher education.

The opportunity to explore the issue of students' school-based learning and the role of the mentor in supporting it was eventually provided in a research initiative on the subject of mentoring funded by the Paul Hamlyn Foundation in 1992 (McIntyre and Hagger 1994). Five small-scale projects were funded by the Foundation, one of which was awarded to the authors. Our particular project was entitled 'The role of the mentor in initial teacher education', and, as we have indicated, our way of researching the role of the mentor was to be through focusing on the development of students' practical professional knowledge.

THE RESEARCH PARADIGM

Educational research has in the past often been characterised as being based in one of two competing paradigms; the quantitative, psycho-statistical approach, with its origins in the natural sciences and the qualitative, case-study approach with its roots in certain of the human sciences. In reality, many studies use a mixture of methods, and the divisions between these two paradigms are less clear cut than many text-book writers would have us believe. Nevertheless, it is true that different methodologies are best suited for different types of research question. The nature of our particular research question was, we felt, best suited to a qualitative methodology.

One of the distinguishing characteristics of qualitative research is its emphasis on 'progressive focusing'. Research of this sort deliberately starts out in an open-ended, exploratory fashion; only slowly does the questioning become progressively more focused during the course of the study. In qualitative work, the nature of the questions being asked, and the direction of the research, are therefore in part informed by the results of the study itself – both the empirical work and one's continued reading. Such an approach is particularly valuable in research that is intended to be exploratory in nature. Our initial review of the literature on the nature of student learning and the role of experienced teachers in supporting student development revealed a fragmentary picture. What was needed, we therefore felt, was indeed an exploratory study 'mapping the territory', raising questions, suggesting new directions for future research. We were therefore keen to maximise the opportunities provided by our small-scale project to learn as much as possible about the nature of student learning; too early a narrowing of our exploration in order to produce the forms of research instruments that would have been necessary for a more systematic, statistical methodology would, we considered, have been inappropriate.

THE RESEARCH STUDIES

We divided our project into three interrelated research studies (they are each reported in the next three chapters). In accordance with the principles of progressive focusing, each of our studies took the form of empirical fieldwork combined with an on-going review of the literature on different aspects of teachers' professional knowledge. In each case, the analysis we provide is therefore equally derived from our theoretical as well as our empirical research.

Our first study, which served as a pilot for our later work, focused on the developmental learning needs of student teachers as they change over time. The empirical part of the work began in March 1992 and was carried out in five schools (two comprehensives, one junior school and two primary schools). Fieldwork in each training 'site' involved the development of a single 'triangulated' data set. Planning meetings between the student and the supervising teacher were observed and recorded; the subsequent lesson was observed; follow-up debriefing sessions between the student and the supervising teacher were recorded; in-depth interviews were then conducted separately with the student and the supervising teacher. Recordings of approximately twenty-five hours of interviews and observation sessions were subsequently transcribed.

From the analysis of these sessions and our reading, three broad areas of interest emerged. First, it became apparent that teachers' knowledge base and their 'thinking' is extremely complex and difficult to articulate and pass on to students. Nevertheless, as we describe in Chapter 5, we have suggested that teachers have practical knowledge that relates to a number of different areas or domains. These include: knowledge of pupils; knowledge of context; knowledge of subject matter; and knowledge of strategies. Each of these domains seems to be held as actual or specific knowledge as well as typificatory or generalised knowledge. In addition, we maintain that teachers will have knowledge of 'self-as-teacher' and of the 'values' inherent in schools today.

The second area of interest concerned the different stages of development through which students typically move in their professional development. Each of these different stages of development were found to be associated with its own 'focal concerns'. These were characterised as: early idealism, personal survival, dealing with difficulties, hitting a plateau and moving on.

A final area of interest concerned the different issues that mentors saw fit to raise with students. These too seemed broadly developmental, focusing first on classroom management and control, then on teaching skills and strategies and last on lesson content.

The next two studies were designed only after the pilot study was complete and written up in a preliminary form (Maynard and Furlong 1993). Our purpose in designing them was to follow up on what we had learned so far about what students need to learn from their school experience and the complexity of that learning. Given the potential size of that task, we chose to focus on two particular topics that we had come to recognise typically assume importance at different stages of students' development. The first concerned 'classroom management and control' – an issue of overwhelming importance to students in their early stages in the classroom when their greatest concern is 'personal survival'. The second issue to be investigated, lesson content, is more typically addressed at a later stage of students' development once they have established effective classroom control. Here, the concern was with understanding what teachers meant by 'good ideas' for teaching.

For our second and third studies, which took place in the following academic year (1992/3) fieldwork was undertaken with primary PGCE students, during their first and second block teaching practices. In all, the eleven students, working with sixteen different teachers during their two block practices, were studied. Seven of the students were visited weekly, the remaining four students were visited fortnightly. Each visit was of several hours' duration and, where more than one student was placed in a particular school, lasted a whole day. Data were gathered through a variety of techniques, including observation, interview, group discussions with supervising teachers and students. Documentary evidence, such as student teachers' teaching-practice files, written plans and evaluations of activities, were also consulted.

During our interviews with students we asked them both about the intentions behind their teaching and what they had learned from their debriefing. Teachers were interviewed about their interpretations of students' 'performance' and their intentions behind the debriefings they had given. From this methodology it was therefore possible to produce a series of 'triangulated' data sets. Our own observations and interpretations of students' teaching and the forms of feedback they were given could be carefully compared and contrasted with both the teachers' and the students' own views. This methodology became particularly important in exploring the differences between what the student 'knew' and what experienced teachers 'knew' in relation to each of the two topics we chose to investigate. In all, over thirty hours of interviews and discussions were recorded and transcribed. What we learned about students' school-based learning in relation to classroom management and control and 'good ideas for teaching' is set out in Chapters 6 and 7, respectively.

ACTION RESEARCH

As we have indicated, the methodology we adopted was significantly influenced by the nature of the questions we wished to ask. It involved in-depth, exploratory observation, semi-structured and sometimes unstructured interviews as well as documentary analysis. But our methodology was also influenced by the fact that Maynard had a double role within the project in that she had a joint appointment as both research associate to the project and as a lecturer on the University College of Swansea primary Post Graduate Certificate of Education (PGCE) course. Given that it was the students from this course who became the major focus for much of the study, Maynard's joint role had the effect of introducing an element of action research into the project.

Action research is now a well-established tradition within the qualitative paradigm. What is distinctive about action research is that, unlike more traditional forms of 'objective' methodology, the researcher is *in* the field of study. Rather than trying to remain a neutral 'outsider', the researcher deliberately tries to change the context in which he or she is studying. Through a carefully monitored process of intervention, the researcher hopes to gain a deeper understanding of their field of study.

The action research element of our project became particularly important in the later stages of our work, especially when we came to focus on how student teachers develop appropriate forms of pedagogical knowledge. As we will discuss in more detail in Chapter 7, we came to recognise that if students are to focus on pedagogy, they need to 'de-centre' – they need to stop worrying about their own 'performance' as a teacher and pay more attention to pupils as learners and the quality of their learning. Moreover, we, like others before us, came to recognise that if students are not explicitly encouraged to 'move on' in this way, many student teachers are unlikely to engage systematically with the question of pupils' learning. As their tutor, as well as a researcher, Maynard therefore felt that she had to intervene in their learning process at an appropriate stage; not to do so would have been to deny her role as their tutor. Moreover, the knowledge she had gained from reading and research encouraged her to make much stronger and more systematic interventions than she would have done previously. As we will describe in Chapter 7, at what she judged to be an appropriate stage in their development, the questions Maynard posed to students about what they were teaching were experienced by the students as challenging and unsettling. They were intended to be. Following her interventions, she was then in a position to monitor their continued growth.

THE RESEARCH CONTEXT

As has been implied above, the context for most of our research has been the early years and upper primary Post Graduate Certificate of Education course at the University College of Swansea, though in our pilot study we also undertook a limited amount of fieldwork with BEd and secondary PGCE students as well. The PGCE is a one-year initial teacher education course for graduates. In the UK, PGCE courses have traditionally been associated with the training of secondary teachers. For primary teachers, the BEd degree has been and remains the main entry route. Nevertheless, in recent years the number of primary PGCE courses has increased considerably. In 1991/2 (when our research began) 44 per cent of all PGCE courses in England and Wales were for primary teachers (Barrett *et al.* 1992b).

At the time of our study, the pattern of training in this particular primary PGCE course was relatively conventional. Following a preliminary two-week attachment to a primary school in their home area, students spent four days a week in their first term in college-based study. However, throughout the term, students would spend a fifth day working in groups of ten in a local primary school on a programme of structured observations and small-group teaching. On these school-based days the students would be accompanied by a university tutor. During this term students therefore had the opportunity to become familiar with a second primary school and follow up a number of predefined investigations and activities. However, because of the large numbers and limited time, at this stage, they had relatively little opportunity to engage in whole-class teaching. Despite having had approximately four weeks in school during term one, students would therefore begin their first full teaching practice in term two as relative novices to teaching itself.

During terms two and three, students would undertake two periods of block school experience in a third school. These periods of teaching practice, which lasted approximately six weeks each, were interspersed with other periods of full-time study back at the university. Even though both of these periods of teaching practice were spent in the same school, students would be attached to different teachers for each practice – ideally, at least, experiencing teaching with contrasting age groups. The focus of most of our work with students and their teachers was in connection with these two sustained periods of teaching practice in terms two and three.

At the time of our study, the role of school teachers in the Swansea primary PGCE was still fairly conventional too. They were not at that stage formally designated as mentors to their students; rather, they were supervisory teachers. Training and assessment formally remained the responsibility of the university. During the first teaching practice, most of the teachers would remain in the classroom working alongside the student; during the second practice, teachers would progressively withdraw, giving the student more and more responsibility for the whole class.

Given the character of the PGCE course at Swansea at the time of our study it is important to emphasise that we were not researching a fully developed, school-based model of teaching education. As we have said, the course was in this regard fairly conventional. This, however, was not in our view an important factor in our particular research design. Rather than studying the work of mentors *per se*, we were more interested in deducing what the work of the mentor *should be* from a study of how students learn to teach. Given that this was the nature of our research question, the fact that teachers undertook a fairly conventional supervisory role in relation to their students was of little relevance. Because of the role they took, we refer to the teachers whom we worked with in our study as supervisory teachers rather than as mentors – this is what they were.

This then is the background to our empirical and theoretical work. In the next three chapters we present the results of our three studies; in Chapters 8 and 9 we explore the implications of our findings for the role of the mentor.

Chapter 5

Stages of student development

It is almost twenty years since Fuller and Bown stated that when learning to teach, students feel 'stimulated, apprehensive, exposed, endangered, confused, discouraged, touched, proud, and lost – not necessarily in that order' (1975: 47). Although our research took place nearly two decades later, and in another continent, it appears that nothing much has changed! For our students, learning to teach was still a complex, challenging and, often, a painful experience.

The purpose of this chapter is to set out what, through our research, we found out about the ways in which students develop during the course of their professional preparation – the different 'stages' they go through and the difficulties they face at each stage. But before turning to our own work, we must ask what is already known about the developmental processes involved in learning to teach. What is known of the difficulties faced by student teachers and of their responses to those difficulties?

One of the most influential studies in this area remains that of Fuller and Bown (1975). They maintain that researchers have essentially identified and labelled three discrete 'stages' of student teachers' development: survival, mastery and, finally, a stage where student teachers *either* settle into routines and become resistant to change *or* they become 'consequence orientated'; that is, concerned about their impact on pupils and responsive to feedback about their teaching. In short, there is a progression from 'survival concerns' to 'task concerns' to 'impact concerns'.

In his research, Calderhead (1987) also recognises three 'phases' in the process of learning to teach: 'fitting in', 'passing the test' and 'exploring'. In the first phase, he suggests that students view the task as one of fitting in to the school and in particular to the class teacher's routines. Even where these practices conflict with students' ideals, they take a pragmatic survival approach. Towards the middle of their placement, according to Calderhead, students begin to view the placement as an assessment task in which they have to adopt particular types of behaviour that signal competence and will please the supervising tutor. Later, students begin to experiment with classroom organisation, subject matter and different types of lessons, although 'The quality of reflection upon this experimentation . . . was again shallow and did not seem very effective in promoting professional learning' (1987: 276–7).

Another study is that of Burden (1990), who presents a comprehensive summary of research into teacher development at both the 'pre-' and 'in-service' phases. He cites research by Adams (1982), whose five-year longitudinal study generally supports Fuller and Bown's stages of concerns about self and instructional tasks, although Adams found that years of experience produced no significant differences in impact concerns. The work of Sitter and Lanier (1982) further broadly supports the idea of development through different 'stages', in that the students in their study showed commonalities of concern at different times. However, their research also indicated that 'Concerns about self, survival, teaching tasks, pupil learning, materials and curriculum development occurred simultaneously and were dealt with concurrently by the student teachers' (Burden 1990: 314).

Similarly, a study by Guillaume and Rudney (1993) notes six broad categories of concern expressed by student teachers: lesson planning and evaluation; discipline; working with pupils; working with cooperating teachers and adjusting to their classrooms; working with others in the profession; and transitions from student to professional teacher. Like Sitter and Lanier, Guillaume and Rudney found that these concerns were held simultaneously by student teachers throughout their school experience, but that the *nature* of these concerns shifted as students began to take on more responsibility as a teacher – as they moved towards independence. Guillaume and Rudney maintain that their study shows development to be a general process in which students move towards more complex thought patterns as their learning, experience and responsibility as teachers increases.

Progress, it seems, is therefore far from linear. It may also be that these stages are, to some extent, revisited at a 'macro' level during teachers' post-qualification teaching experience. Katz's (1972) study, for example, of pre-school teachers, reveals four developmental stages during the first five years or so: survival, consolidation, renewal and maturity. Within these stages, Katz suggests, teachers go through a number of different experiences and forms of learning, including: feelings of anxiety; gaining 'typificatory knowledge' about children; beginning to see and respond to individual differences; experimentation; and finally to 'a more meaningful search for insight, perspective and realism' (Katz 1972: 53).

Broadly, then, characterising student teachers' development as a passage through various 'stages' or 'phases' or through a series of 'concerns' seems to have been adopted and accepted by many researchers. While, in our research, we also adopt the notion of 'stages' – these should not be viewed in a crude or simplistic way. We do not suggest that student teachers simply progress along a narrow, linear pathway, moving smoothly from stage to stage. This is far from the case. Our research indicates that development from 'novice' to 'professional educator' is dependent on the interaction between individual students, their teacher education programme, and the school context in which they undertake their practical experience. As a result, a student's learning and progress is complex, erratic and in one sense unique to them as an individual.

However, we did find that there appeared to be a discernible pattern to students' development that was reflected in their changing concerns and in their behaviour. The main purpose of this chapter is therefore to set out this pattern of student development. However, before describing our findings it is necessary to consider the character of student learning underlying these different stages and some of the factors that seemed to exert a particular influence on the emergence of this pattern we describe.

Forming concepts – learning to 'see'

Student teachers often appear to begin their school experience with simplistic and idealistic understandings about, for example, their role as a teacher, the relationship they may have with the children in their class (they often see them as children rather than pupils) and the nature of teaching and learning. As we will demonstrate in this and the next two chapters, over a short space of time students need to develop more appropriate and complex understandings about the nature of teaching and learning; they must also develop a more appropriate, 'professional' relationship with their pupils.

However, if students are to make sense of teaching and develop their own body of practical professional knowledge, then it is vital, as Copeland maintains, that they begin to 'see' classrooms in conceptual terms. This will reduce the complexity and allow them to 'gain a measure of control over the happenings within them' (1981: 11). Concepts, Copeland maintains, may be held at the level of personal theory, such as what counts as acceptable pupil movement or noise; alternatively, they may be generalisations about *typical* pupils or ways of representing subject knowledge that are *likely* to elicit understanding. Following Schön (1983, 1987), we would suggest that it is these concepts which allow student teachers to 'frame' what is happening around them; to interpret the significance or insignificance of events or behaviours; and to know what to expect. But the formation of concepts will also enable them to think and act in ways in which the complexity of their decision making is reduced – it therefore helps them to gain control over their own practice.

Others have characterised this development of concepts in different ways. Leinhardt and Greeno (1986) for example, talk of the formation of 'behavioural routines'; Carter and Doyle (1987), and Berliner (1987), describe 'schemas' and 'scripts', while Brown and McIntyre (1993) talk of 'Normal Desirable State of Pupil Activity' in the classroom. Each of them, we would suggest, is pointing in the same direction – towards the importance of developing ways of 'seeing' in classrooms; a process which is essential if students are to gain some control over the complexity of the teaching and learning process.

Influences on student learning

However, the ease with which students are able to develop and to use these concepts – these ways of seeing – is, as we will demonstrate, influenced and possibly constrained by a number of different factors. Hollingsworth (1989), in her study which investigated changes in pre-service teachers' knowledge and beliefs about reading instruction, explored three types of influence that affected student teachers' concerns and their change over time: they were what she called 'personal', 'programme' and 'contextual' factors. Our study also acknowledges and encompasses all three of these factors, to greater and lesser degrees; indeed, these influences are an important underlying theme for our research.

The influence of personal factors on the formation of students' concepts was clear throughout our study. Certain beliefs and expectations held by individual students either enhanced or militated against the development of what were seen as 'acceptable' or 'useful' practical knowledge and skills. Particularly significant were students' existing beliefs and understandings about the nature of teaching and learning, and their vision of what the role of a teacher should be. It may be, as our study suggests, that if students hold simplistic or what are seen by teachers and tutors as 'inappropriate' views of these issues, then students will need significant help if they are fully to appreciate the complexities and demands of becoming a professional educator in contemporary British primary schools. As we will demonstrate later in this chapter, if this is the case, then at a certain point in their development, students may need a mentor or tutor to 'guide their seeing' so that they may adjust or redefine their concepts in 'appropriate' ways.

The influence of 'programme' factors on the development of students' concepts was also apparent. As we indicated in Chapter 4, the main focus of our work has been with students on the University of Swansea Primary PGCE programme. Our research has been primarily concerned with students' development and learning while they are on their block school experience; we did not have the time or the resources to explore the whole of the programme. However, the structure, aims and content of the course were probably highly influential in terms of the concepts students formed in their school-based learning. Moreover, as we will see below, the interventions from the university tutor while the students were on their school experience were of particular significance.

Finally, we found that 'contextual' factors were also highly influential. The *content* of students learning was clearly influenced in a myriad ways by the overt and covert 'culture' of the school and classrooms they were in. But the context also influenced their *opportunities* to learn as well. Particularly important here was the attitude and approach of their class teacher. Supervisory teachers hold power in complex and subtle ways and may be reluctant to relinquish their power to the student teacher. As we will also demonstrate below, students' negotiation and gradual acquisition of power, and their developing understandings about how to use that power, appears to have a fundamental influence on the progression of their thinking and behaviour.

In summary, then, we can say that our research has adopted a notion of 'stages' to characterise student teachers' development in learning to teach. These stages are set out in the remainder of this chapter. However, we would re-emphasise that we do not see them as discrete or fixed; rather, they are, in our view, inter-related and mutable. The focus of student learning, throughout these different stages is the formation of ever more sophisticated concepts or 'ways of seeing'. It is through the development of such concepts, we argue, that students begin to gain control over their own teaching. In describing and understanding how these concepts develop, we also highlight the importance of certain personal, programmatic and contextual factors. The influence of these factors is explored in each stage of development that we describe.

STAGES OF STUDENT LEARNING

From our research, we were able to discern five broad stages in student teachers' development while on their school experience. We have characterised these as: 'early idealism', 'personal survival', 'dealing with difficulties', 'hitting a plateau' and 'moving on'.

Stage 1: early idealism

Expectations

Research into the concerns of students at the very beginning of their training suggests that they are often idealistic, both in terms of their feelings towards the pupils and the image they hold of themselves as teacher. They tend to identify with 'the pupils' (whom they tend to see solely as 'children') rather than the teacher, and are unsympathetic or even hostile to the class teacher. They have not, as yet, to use Fuller and Bown's term, 'gone over to the enemy' (1975: 38).

Our research generally corroborated these findings. At the beginning of their first block teaching experience (term two of their one-year course) the students in our study appeared to have clear, if idealistic, ideas about the sort of teachers they wanted to be, the kind of relationships that they would develop with their pupils, the physical appearance of their classrooms and the classroom atmosphere that they would create.

Initially, students maintained they wanted to be seen by their pupils as 'warm', 'friendly', 'caring', 'enthusiastic' and 'popular' teachers. One student teacher maintained she was terrified of 'ending up like that miserable old cynic in the corner of the staffroom'. A balance, often an uneasy balance, of friendship and respect frequently summarised the relationship they wished to develop with pupils. For example, one student commented, 'I'd like to be someone who they could come to . . . but they know I'm in charge.' Others maintained, 'I'd like a friendly interaction between us . . . but respect, mainly, so they would listen to me' or 'I'd like them to see me as a friend and feel like they can talk to me. But they have to see me as someone they've got to respect . . . but not be afraid of me.' Several students also referred to the importance of the children 'feeling really comfortable and known'.

Students maintained that the classrooms they wanted to work in were 'large with lots of space to move around in'. One student stated that, 'As you stepped through the door, it would take your breath away . . . the amount of things in it.' Several others referred to the 'brightness' of their classrooms. One student in particular described her ideal classroom as having 'lots of windows with lots of light coming in'. She maintained that this was because, 'you can see the outside world and feel less cut off'. Similarly, students often referred to the colourful display work they would have on the walls. For example, students maintained, 'I think I'd like quite a lot of display work on the walls, pictures and posters to make the classroom look exciting'; 'Lots of nice displays, colourful, so you'd be attracted to looking at them'; 'The walls have got things the children have done all over the place'; and simply, 'It would be really brilliant in terms of display work'.

Many students described the 'happy', 'caring' atmosphere they hoped to create. One student maintained,

I want people to come into my classroom and automatically feel it was a really happy place to be. The kids know exactly what to do and are enjoying it and everyone is getting on with it. I hate silence. I like lots of buzz and children chatting away and getting on with their work and you're having a bit of a laugh at the same time. I like lots of life going on.

Students also maintained the importance of teaching the value of cooperation and creating a 'community spirit' – 'that we care for each other, look after each other and are there for each other'. This student added, 'I'd like to be part of that sense of belonging.' Another student commented that, 'Although you're the teacher . . . not to be really separate so they can come to you and ask you questions.'

'Significant' teachers

These idealised beliefs or images (see Clandinin 1986, Calderhead and Robson 1991) about teaching and learning at this point, are, it seems, often influenced by students' own histories, including their own experience as a pupil – what Lortie (1975) calls their 'apprenticeship of observation'. Calderhead (1988) similarly maintains that student teachers frequently begin their teacher preparation with the belief that they already know a lot about teaching.

The students in our study had clear memories of what were for them, 'significant' teachers – either for positive or negative reasons. However, students appeared not to be viewing or evaluating these teachers in terms of their effectiveness as *teachers*. Indeed, several students commented that it was difficult to remember anything about what or how they had actually been taught. Rather, it was the teacher's personality and the relationship they had established with them as pupils that was deemed to be the significant factor. Where teachers were remembered as terrifying, moody or unpredictable, students often maintained that 'I want to be everything she wasn't'. In particular, students often reiterated that they didn't want *their* pupils to be scared of them. One student commented that one very strict teacher probably had no idea of how frightened she was of her. This student felt that she was now aware and concerned about how she might affect children.

Several students had more positive memories. Teachers were remembered fondly because they were particularly caring or encouraging or 'because they had such strange mannerisms and used to make up silly rhymes'. For one student, it was the fact that one teacher 'used to read to us, and tell us about her own life outside school' that made her significant. This student claimed it was also because, 'she used to talk to us like an equal'. As well as fundamental ideas about the importance of their relationship with pupils, it appeared that students had also internalised ideas about the way teachers act, what teachers should and shouldn't do – snapshots of teachers' behaviour, even if the implications and consequences of these were not fully understood.

Teaching and learning were therefore, commonly seen in a simplistic way. Students maintained that it was their relationship with pupils that would be the crucial factor in terms of their effectiveness as teachers. Whether students believed that pupils were blank slates waiting to receive information and that teaching was essentially a matter of 'telling', or whether they maintained that their role was more of a facilitator, and were concerned to develop pupils' independence as learners, the learning *process*, and their *role* in this process was viewed as something that just happened without a great deal of effort on their part! As Feiman-Nemser and Buchmann point out, 'Looking at teaching from the perspective of a pupil is not the same as viewing it from a pedagogical perspective, that is, the perspective of a teacher' (1987: 257).

Stage 2: personal survival

Once student teachers began their school experience, their idealism appeared rapidly to fade in the face of the realities of the classroom, and they became obsessed with their own personal survival. Personal survival meant detecting and 'fitting in' with the teacher's routines and expectations, being 'seen' as a teacher and, in particular, achieving some form of classroom control. As Fuller and Bown (1975) recognised, this stage, which may last only one or two weeks, is a period of great stress for students.

Feeling vulnerable

In these early days, not only were students unable to 'see' – to make sense of what was happening in the classroom – but without a clear understanding of the rules, routines and rituals of the class, they were also utterly powerless. Students were not able to ascertain, for example, the teacher's expectations of the pupils or what the teacher defined as 'acceptable' behaviour – both for pupils and of themselves! If children behaved in a way that the student found unreasonable, they were unsure if it was appropriate or even expected that they intervene; if they did intervene, they were also unsure how to deal with the problem. As one student commented, 'You don't know whether you can assert your authority or not . . . when the teacher went out of the room whether you can say, 'A bit too much noise over there' or whether you ought to sit there and let them get on with it.'

Behind the students' worries about whether and how to intervene lay a deeper concern that if they *did* intervene and the pupils did not respond to them, their self-esteem, and any status they had as a teacher, would be further eroded. As a result, in the very first days in the classroom, asserting their authority was a risk that many students preferred not to take.

In our study, the classroom, initially at least, was clearly seen by the teachers as their 'domain'; one teacher in our study described it as 'my own little world'. The early years teachers, in particular – possibly because of the nature of the relationship with 'their' children – appeared highly protective of the pupils and were often reticent to relinquish their power to the student teacher.

But it was not only the class teacher who held power – the pupils were felt to be powerful too – assessing and testing the students' authority. Indeed, in all their dealings with the pupils, students at this stage tended to be 'reactive' rather than 'proactive' – leaving the children to define the situation. As one student in our study commented, she felt that the children were actively 'trying to test her out to see if she was going to be on *their* side or on the *teacher's* side'. This process must have been of some significance for those students who had initially identified themselves with the pupils.

Being 'seen' as a teacher

That the pupils recognised them as a teacher quickly assumed enormous proportions for the students in our study, particularly in a classroom where there were several adult 'helpers'. Students, who had initially begun their teaching experience by being given a group of pupils to work with, found this a particular problem. They maintained that this approach worked to their disadvantage when they were eventually required to become a 'real' teacher and address the whole class. For example, one student commented,

> I feel like in my class, because I've only done group work, the children don't see me as a teacher, and then there was a point when the teacher said, 'Introduce your activity to the whole class' and . . . panic. I couldn't speak. I kept looking at her . . . for her to help me. I didn't know how to address the whole class, what words to use and how to explain it.

Another student commented, 'Even if you've planned all the work, if the teacher is there the children go to her.'

'Fitting-in'

A common response to the need for 'survival' was to try to copy the teacher's 'style' – particularly in terms of her or his relationship with the children. One student teacher commented 'I think it's quite important to keep a similar sort of interaction with the children otherwise they get a bit confused as to who is a teacher. If you teach them together perhaps they won't see the join.' Another said, 'While in her class I want to emulate some of the things she does for the children.' And a third explained:

> To be seen as a teacher you've got to follow what she does, her rules. And also know what the lesson is going to be about, so if the children come up to you and say 'What shall I do next?' you *know*. Otherwise you have to say, 'I don't know, go and ask the teacher' . . . and then they know.

Fitting in with the teacher was therefore a source of conflict for many students, and appeared to cause particular difficulties where there was a recognised difference in approach. For example, one student maintained, 'I'm naturally quiet and she's louder than I am, so I'm disappearing. They [the pupils] need someone loud because that is what they're used to.' While students stated that they wanted 'their own personality to come out', many maintained that if they didn't emulate the teacher's style, the children would not respond to them. For example, one student stated, 'If your personality isn't like the teacher's, it's quite difficult because . . . you don't really want to behave like the teacher but if the children are used to the teacher they're going to respond to that.'

Fitting in with the teacher was also seen by students as a way of achieving some measure of stability for the pupils. As one student commented, 'While you're on "T.P." you have to fit in with that routine and keep the rules up so that the goal posts don't change.'

Challenging the 'ideal'

Students' relationship with pupils was obviously of crucial importance to them throughout their school experience. As we have noted, before starting on their teaching practice it is often of great significance to student teachers that the pupils *like* them – several students commented that they wanted to be seen as approachable. For some students, this expectation was balanced by an understanding of the need to retain a distance, whereas others still essentially wanted to be seen as a friend. For the majority of students in our study, however, the first attempts at teaching the whole class revealed or emphasised that if they were to become a teacher then they did need to establish their authority. As one student commented, 'I'm more interested at the moment that the children get on with their lessons than like me.'

This realisation (which we consider in more detail in the next chapter) often brought with it a fundamental challenge to their idealised image of themselves as teacher and the sort of relationship it was possible to have with the pupils. Some of the students felt real anger towards the children for making them become the sort of teacher they did not want to be. The 'ideal' teachers they initially *wanted* to be had been replaced by the teachers they felt they *had* to be if they were to survive. However, this did not mean that students relinquished their ideals entirely; rather, they appeared simply to put them 'on hold' while they tried to survive.

As should be apparent by now, 'idealism' for many of our students implied a child-centred view of teaching, but this was not always the case. One student maintained:

I allowed the children to carry on being more noisy than I would have originally thought to allow. The teacher assures me that although the children talk in class this does not mean they are not working. I must learn to be more realistic and not have an idealistic view of children regimentally sitting in rows and working quietly.

Classroom control

Given students' concern at this stage with their own survival, the content of the activities they set for their pupils were often devised, or modified, primarily as a way of keeping control. As one student put it, 'Keeping the children busy – heads down doing something'. Another maintained, 'I wanted to give them work I knew they could do, but where they wouldn't have to move around', while a third later reflected that, at this time, 'the content of the lesson was judged sufficient if the pupils were occupied for the set time'.

Lack of control not only influenced the content of students' activities, it also influenced their actual practice – their 'performance'. Several student teachers maintained that, at this stage, all their effort was put into keeping the class quiet, and when they did have the children's attention, it was a case of 'quick tell them everything I know'. Many students recognised that they had left the pupils bewildered and confused, as they rushed through instructions or explanations. As one student commented, 'I had intended to go through the worksheets, but the noise level was such that I gave up trying to make the whole class listen to me.' Most students agreed with the comment, 'I didn't have time to stop and think what I was doing', and that often, they felt 'out of control, out of your depth'.

As they were besieged by so many problems, and their performance and understanding was so fragmented, students, in this first period in the classroom, appeared to find it difficult to know just what to focus on – what 'teachers' would do. For example, one student stated that,

> When working with the whole class a couple of pupils started chatting. I told them to stop and even moved one of them. The one I moved started talking to the person she was now sitting next to, but I was concentrating so hard on keeping the pupils interested in the story and asking the right questions that I ignored her. I am now worried that because I wasn't consistent

with her she will be hard to control in the future but if I had made a big thing about it, it would have disrupted the flow of the lesson at a time when I thought it was quite productive.

Quite often, students who felt particularly uncomfortable about control, and were 'battling to get attention', tended to try and maintain a one-to-one interaction with the pupils. Students were seen scuttling around classrooms, repeating the same instructions on thirty different occasions to thirty different pupils rather than, as one student maintained, 'competing against the children' to get their attention. Another student reflected in desperation, 'I wonder whether I should use some kind of whistle or hooter to initially get their attention when they're making a noise?'

When things did go wrong, student teachers appeared to become consumed by a mixture of fear, anger, frustration and exhaustion. In particular, the feeling of being ignored seemed to cause real stress and indignation. One student commented, 'At the end of the lesson I felt out of control as the children were packing away at their own speed and in their own way rather than waiting to be told what to do.' Another said, 'The children started calling out suggestions. I tried to stamp on this behaviour, but as soon as I turned my back to write a suggestion on the board they started to call out again.'

While students appeared able to rationalise both the children's and their own behaviour *outside* of the classroom, this appeared not to be the case *inside* the classroom when faced with children who did not conform to their expectations. As one student humbly reflected, 'I believe that the children misbehaved because the work was not demanding enough for them.' Her real feelings may have been more clearly revealed, however, by her next comment, 'I must ask about what punishments are available to give children.'

Not only did students appear to be constrained by the class teacher, the pupils and their own lack of knowledge and skill but also, in a sense, by their lesson plans. Students often appeared frightened to deviate from what they had planned. One class teacher commented that she had noticed that student teachers, in their first few weeks in the classroom, would pursue discussions, explanations and activities even when it was painfully obvious to all concerned that it was heading for disaster – rather like 'holding onto the back of a runaway horse'.

Stage 3: dealing with difficulties

Establishing themselves 'as a teacher'

Fortunately, the confusion and sheer panic brought about by their first taste of teaching did not, in most cases, last more than a week or so. Slowly, the 'survival' stage gave way to a second stage where students could at least start to identify some of the difficulties they faced.

After a week or so, therefore, students commonly voiced their concerns that, 'You know there is so much to grasp, to get under your belt – it's just like a mountain.' One student teacher later reflected, 'You can't see the complexities . . . but you know it is much more complex than you are doing.' And another commented, 'I keep seeing things I'm doing wrong all the time. I know what I should be doing but I just can't get there.' As they began to 'see', to make personal sense of what was happening in the classroom, and gain some measure of classroom control, their concern therefore shifted from personal survival to their survival as a 'teacher' (or at least, their perception of what a teacher should be).

A common reaction to this difficulty was for students to try to replicate, or 'mimic' what they *believed* to be teachers' behaviour. If they did not understand the complexities of teaching or the 'thinking' of teachers, then they could at least adopt the outward appearance of being a teacher. Indeed, for many students, it is likely that this was all they considered teaching was about. Like Calderhead (1987), we found students starting to 'act' like teachers but without necessarily understanding the underlying purpose or implication of those actions.

Meadows has recently commented that 'adult and child may act alike and talk alike but have different underlying types of concepts and conceptual reasoning' (1993: 107). She goes on, 'Because children need to function and communicate adequately, they seek to understand and to talk as adults do, taking on ready-made meanings without necessarily understanding their conceptual basis' (p. 107). Both these statements seem to us to reflect the behaviour of students in relation to their classroom teacher.

Multiple pressures – trying to impress

This attempt to gain at least a 'procedural' understanding of what it meant to be a teacher understandably left students feeling vulnerable. This vulnerability was often made worse by the fact that for many students, influenced as they were by their own memories of school, teachers were still seen as someone to be feared. For some students, this fear had implications for their relationship with the class teacher. Certainly many of them were very concerned about what the teachers thought about them.

One student teacher expressed the feelings of many when she explained how she was constantly worried about failure and that this led to an enormous sense of 'pressure' – 'from college, from the teacher and from yourself'. She stated, 'The little things panic you, the trivial things like if you don't choose the right book then you'll fail.' Several students talked about their anxiety, particularly when the class they were teaching got noisy. As one commented, 'you are conscious that another teacher will come in and tell you off.'

At this stage in their development the students in our study constantly referred to the pressures they felt that they were under. For example, one said, 'You want to make a good impression on your class teacher, the school, the rest of the staff. You want to look different from the rest.' Another said, 'You feel under pressure to think of exciting and new things to do with the children and that overtakes what you want to teach . . . it has to be something . . . no one has ever done before.' However, this was not always easy. As a third student explained, 'I think I'm coming up with brand new novel ideas to find out the teacher's been using exactly these methods for years and years.'

Students maintained that despite assurances from the teacher and tutor and attempts to help them view this as a 'learning experience', the dominant question in their minds at this stage was often 'Will I pass?' For student teachers, such a concern is perhaps unsurprising. Learning to teach is a very 'public' affair; students' successes and failures are visible to a great many different people – teachers, tutors and pupils. Moreover, other people's opinions about them as a 'teacher' are often understood as opinions about them as a 'person' (see Squirrell *et al.* 1990). This, we would suspect, is because teaching is very much a personal activity and as such it exposes and makes calls upon the personality.

As Nias (1989) suggests, teaching is an occupation that is *felt* as well as experienced; as a result, learning to teach, is as Fuller and Bown suggest a process of 'constant, unremitting self-confrontation' (1975: 48). Given the visibility of students' learning and given the personal nature of the experience, it is unsurprising that they felt it so important to impress those involved with the assessment of their competence as a teacher.

Students also spoke of their feelings of inadequacy when the teacher altered or criticised their activity – however sensitively this might have been done. Although, as one student recognised, 'The teacher has had the experience, they know what's right and wrong – they're used to the class and those children,' students still admitted to feeling upset and foolish when their ideas were criticised and that they 'wished they hadn't bothered suggesting anything'. Even when the teacher didn't make comments, students were often themselves painfully aware when their activities were not successful. As one student explained, 'You plan so carefully and were so confident and it seemed so good. And then it doesn't work and that brings home to you all the time that what you're doing isn't good enough . . . and how are you going to get there?' Another commented, 'I'm really aware of wanting to be a help rather than a nuisance. When the children get noisy, I don't know how to say I'm sorry.'

But it is not only the class teacher's opinion that matters to students, for they are also, to an extent, reliant on pupils for feedback as to their effectiveness as a teacher. But the response from pupils can be particularly painful for students, for pupils will also let student teachers know how they feel about them as people. Certainly, for many students, their worth as a teacher *and* as a person appeared to be judged by how far the pupils appeared to 'like' them.

However, at this stage, it was the college tutor who was commonly seen by students as the person they most needed to impress; it was the tutor who appeared to have the greatest influence in terms of their assessment. This attitude was often supported, indeed often appeared to be generated by the supervisory teacher, based on their own experiences as a student. The tutor was seen to represent and to be evaluating students on the 'ideal' rather than the 'real'. As a result, teachers frequently colluded with the student by, for example, removing disruptive children from the classroom when the tutor was visiting, or telling the student about 'good activities to impress your tutor'. Students, therefore, not only tried to mimic teachers' behaviour but appeared to try to ascertain what ways of behaving would gain most approval from tutors. Calderhead (1987) similarly reports that the students in his study reached a point where they felt they had to teach in a particular way to 'pass the test', after which they would be able to teach in the way they really wanted to.

As a result of these different pressures, many students at this stage believed they were caught between the demands of the teacher and of different tutors. For example, one student complained,

> One said if you didn't understand something admit it, say 'I don't know, shall we look it up together' and another one said, 'You should never let them know you don't know anything.' So with those two approaches if you follow one lecturer's advice, and you come to school and the teacher had a different approach . . .

The vulnerability of students, caught as they often were between the demands of teacher, tutor, pupils and their own feelings of self-worth as a teacher and person, were well expressed by one student when she stated,

> You get college saying don't go too mad – so mad that it's going to go wrong. Make sure the children know what they're doing. On the other hand you're trying to impress the teacher and tutor and trying to get the children's attention. You want them to say, 'Wow she's a good teacher!' And the teacher is saying, 'Go on, have a go. If it goes wrong it doesn't matter' . . . but it does to you.

Teaching strategies and classroom organisation

Given their limited understandings about teaching and learning, the students in our study often tried to establish themselves as a teacher, to 'impress' and to gain control through focusing on their 'performance' – in particular, on teaching strategies and classroom organisation. For example, one student maintained that *whatever* the content, 'If I make it interesting then a lot of problems just disappear because they'll just sit there and listen.' Students commonly began to worry about the clarity of their explanations and their use of questioning. One student spoke of her difficulties with 'using the right language' and how 'you can really confuse the class by saying "divided" rather than "shared by"'.

Many of the students, particularly those in 'early years' classrooms, were, after the first few weeks of their school experience, asked to take on more responsibility for organising pupils working in groups. This seemed to present a major difficulty for them. Whereas in the 'personal survival' stage students tended to rush through whole-class explanations and instructions with the consequent confusion and disruption, at this stage students seemed to want (and even enjoy) activities where the pupils' attention was focused on them. If given the choice, students therefore tended to keep the class together for as long as possible and appeared much more reticent about beginning group tasks. Having just begun to gain some power and control, it seems that our students were reticent to relinquish it. As one student commented, 'I had to read a story to the whole class and I couldn't stop shaking but there again I feel like I had more control because they were all listening to me. You could hear a pin drop.'

Students also appeared to try to compensate for their lack of knowledge and control by elaborate preparation (see Lacey 1977). In our study, this often took the form of a heavy reliance by students on the use of worksheets. For students, worksheets appeared to keep the children 'occupied and in their places'. In addition, they gave visible evidence at the end of the session of work completed. One student admitted, 'I'd get home and think I've got to think up a new activity – it had to be different and it had to be a worksheet.' However, devising several worksheets every night put an enormous strain on students. One student later spoke of her frustration that they 'took several hours to make . . . and the children would whiz through them in five minutes'.

Interestingly, even though hours were spent on planning, students seemed reluctant to differentiate the work they devised in terms of pupils' abilities. Several students admitted that they knew certain children were having difficulty with the work they were being given but they were concerned that they should 'not feel any different from their friends'. As one student stated, 'With "special needs" children I've found that they don't like to do separate worksheets. I've tried that twice. They don't like being given what they call "baby work".' Seeing them as 'children' and worrying about what they perceived to be their feelings of inadequacy appeared, at this stage, to be a more powerful influence on their planning than any consideration of pupils' actual learning. As one student later reflected, 'If [for any pupils] there ever was any progression of learning it was more by luck than judgement.'

Where there were difficulties with control or organisation some students appeared to blame these on the constraints of the situation – the way the classroom is arranged, lack of resources or having to 'fit in' with the teacher's method of organisation, or routines and so on. This observation supports Lacey's finding; he too noticed that when problems were encountered in the classroom, students tended to 'displace' the blame – either on to the 'system' or on to the children (Lacey 1977: 85).

Socialisation

Many commentators have pointed to the fact that students are socialised into their supervising teacher's ways of working (Lacey 1977). We found that socialisation was particularly powerful at this 'dealing with difficulties' stage. As we have indicated, at this stage, students focused much of their attention on teachers' outward teaching strategies and organisation; they therefore became particularly sensitive to their class teacher's methods. Students, it seems, may well adopt and adapt the strategies their teachers use for a number of reasons – as an attempt to disguise their lack of understanding, to gain approval, or because they lack knowledge of alternative approaches. Students may also find that emulating the class teachers is a useful strategy in maintaining classroom control – they discover that pupils respond better to *known* ways of working (see Copeland 1981).

However, by this stage the students in our study had adopted not only their teachers' ways of working; some students had also adopted some of their teachers' more obvious forms of 'teacher talk'. Several early years students, for example, noted that they had begun, like their teachers, to refer to themselves in the third person – 'Does Mrs Jones look happy?' – or begun asking the children to 'sit nicely'. One student commented, 'A lot of teachers do that and now I've started doing it myself. I'm not really sure why.' Sometimes students seemed unaware of having listened to or adopted another teacher's 'tactics' or approach. One student explained, 'I was saying something and then I heard the teacher next door and I realised where I had got it from.'

However, although we would argue that the students in our study *did* go through a powerful form of socialisation at this stage in their development, this is not to suggest that they were 'passive' to institutional forces. Our observations would support Egan's findings (cited in Zeichner and Tabachnick 1985: 10) that, under common institutional constraints, students react different-ly. Student teachers are no more 'blank slates' than their pupils.

Adapting to and adopting their class teacher's 'ways of work-ing' did not, therefore, necessarily mean that students adopted their teachers 'perspective'. For example, one student maintained:

> My teacher has very set ideas on education. He doesn't talk about these directly but you can tell what he thinks by what he says and from the way he teaches. I can see his point all the time because he argues things very logically . . . but it hasn't changed what I think about education, it's just helped me develop my own ideas.

This observation is backed up by other research. For example, Goodman maintains the school experience 'merely reinforced what was already there; its power to shape or mould individuals was secondary to earlier influences' (1985: 47). Similarly, Tabach-nick and Zeichner comment that, 'For the most part, students became more articulate in expressing and more skilful in imple-menting the perspectives that they possessed in less developed forms at the beginning of the experience' (1984: 33).

Moreover, although students did tend to adopt their teachers' ways of working, it did not mean there were not 'felt difficulties' or that working in this way did not create tensions. One student, for example, maintained, 'If you've got an innovative teacher it's OK, but if you've got a teacher who just likes to use the board all the time . . .'

However, while the students in our study often became in-creasingly 'quietly critical' of their host teacher, most of them did not want to do anything that appeared overtly to criticise the teacher's practice. The relationship students had with their class teacher was one that most of them tried to nurture. As we have already noted, even in a reasonably 'friendly' environment, for the student teacher there are inevitably serious tensions between pleasing the teacher, pleasing the tutor and pleasing themselves: between fitting in and finding themselves as a teacher. While stud- ent teachers may be striving for personal autonomy this can only be achieved within the constraints of what is considered 'accept- able'.

Stage 4: hitting a plateau

Having gained basic competence and confidence in management and organisation, often towards the end of their first block teaching experience, there was a noted tendency for student teachers to 'relax' a little; their learning seemed to 'hit a plateau'.

Most students by this stage gave the impression that, from their teacher-centred perspective, teaching had begun to look manageable. They identified strongly with their class teachers and, by copying their teacher's behaviours, they felt that they had themselves begun to be real teachers. At last they had gained some control, and they, at least, thought they were sounding and behaving like a 'proper' teacher.

However, much of an experienced teacher's expertise is not visible in his or her behaviour. Replicating that behaviour without a full appreciation of the professional knowledge that underlies it can lead to difficulties. As we will demonstrate in this section, for our students, this lack of real understanding behind their newly found teaching strategies was revealed in the fact that their teaching still showed little appreciation of the relationship between teaching and how children learn. Despite having achieved some success, their teaching therefore remained shallow. In some cases it even started to 'slide' – they took inappropriate short cuts, their planning and evaluations became weaker and their enthusiasm to try out new strategies waned. Having found one way of organising their teaching that worked for them – they were going to stick to it!

Growing in confidence

At one level, students started to gain confidence in their abilities to manage classes. For example, several commented on the fact that their expectations, particularly in terms of the pupils' behaviour, had changed; they became more relaxed. One student stated that

> It always amazed me, if I was in a class on my own I would keep on at them to put their pens down and the teacher would come in and she'd be totally oblivious and I'd think I'll try that next time. I'll ignore it.

Another commented,

> At first you expect complete silence (before starting an explanation) but now if 80 to 90 per cent are ready . . . the rest will come into line. At first you're waiting and waiting, but now if most of them are quiet . . . that's good enough.

One student justified this approach by maintaining, 'You've got to remember what it's like to be a child. I can remember resenting teachers telling me not to fiddle all the time.'

Many students commented at this time that they felt they were 'turning into a teacher'. For some, this identification was 'personal' as well as 'professional'; it appeared to 'leak' into their out of school lives. For example, one student commented that she found it difficult to 'switch off' and had been told, 'that I've become bossy when I'm at home'.

However, most students we felt were merely 'going through the motions of teaching' (Feiman-Nemser and Buchmann 1987: 257); they were still 'acting' like a teacher, rather than 'thinking' like a teacher. The *content* of student teachers' activities continued to reflect what teachers, tutors as well as we ourselves considered to be simplistic and naïve understandings about the nature of teaching and learning. Students, it seemed, were, in the main, still not engaging with the quality of the learning experiences they were devising for their pupils and their lesson evaluations remained superficial. For most students a lesson was thought to have 'worked' if the pupils enjoyed it or seemed interested.

Problems with teaching and learning

At this stage, then, it was the content of activities (factual knowledge), and the method of their teaching (aimed at 'remembering' rather than 'understanding') that was frequently criticised by teachers and tutors. As in previous stages, it was not that students did *not* think about what the pupils were to learn, but that what and how students were teaching was not considered acceptable, appropriate or effective.

These criticisms of students' practice made by teachers and tutors, inevitably reflect value judgements about what children need to learn and how they best learn. As we discuss more fully in Chapter 7, there was broad agreement among teachers and tutors involved with this course as to what constituted good primary practice in this regard, and, for the most part, despite superficially acting like a teacher, these students were not achieving it.

Why was it that, despite having gone through two terms of their course and with clear expectations from teachers and tutors, students still failed to teach in an appropriate way? We would suggest that there were a number of different reasons. For some students, whose beliefs were considered particularly simplistic or 'traditional', the difficulty seemed to be rooted in their own experience as a pupil. For example, some maintained that the idea of 'teacher as transmitter of knowledge' was 'natural' because 'That's what we've experienced; the teacher tells you and you listen'. For these students, their beliefs appeared to be deep-seated and linked not just to their educational values, but to more fundamental values as well. For other students, there was a sense of self-interest: factual knowledge – knowledge 'that' – was considered easier to understand and to teach than, for example, conceptual knowledge – knowledge 'about'. As one student teacher admitted, 'It's a lot easier just to sit there and spiel things off. "I want you to know this. I'm going to tell you that."'

By contrast, a few students in our study did appear to hold a greater understanding of the complexity of teaching and learning. Nevertheless, they often appeared unable to achieve sufficient control of the teaching situation to be able to put their beliefs into practice. This finding is supported by Pigge and Marso (1987), who found that students may have worries about meeting the individual needs of their pupils but may be unable to act upon them. Similarly, Fuller and Bown comment that, 'Flooded by feelings of inadequacy, by situational demands and conflicts, they may have to lay aside these concerns until they have learned to cope with more urgent tasks, such as being heard above the din' (1975: 39). For our students, such difficulties became particularly apparent in relation to practical activities.

Practical activities are seen by many primary teachers as a fundamental aspect of 'effective' teaching. However, many of our students, irrespective of their beliefs about children's learning, saw practical work as far too risky to contemplate. For example, one student teacher commented,

> You naturally shy away from practical work because it's messy and much more difficult to control. You think 'I'll manage – the kids will understand.' I've been sitting at home thinking they'll be able to do this and knowing deep down that they won't.

Another student recognised that 'No matter how long or hard you explain it to them they can't see it because it's on paper.'

For all the students, then, whether due to values and beliefs about how children learn, or because of their lack of control, there was at this stage a difficulty with actually devising and giving lessons that reflected a detailed engagement with children's understanding and their learning over time. The challenge for their teachers and tutors at this time was therefore to help them 'move on' to a fuller, more professional understanding of what is involved in effective teaching.

Stage 5: moving on

Although Guillaume and Rudney (1993) maintain that the student teachers in their research *were* able to reflect 'on the purposes and implications of education' (p. 76), other research has shown that without challenge or support, while student teachers *may* go on to analyse their teaching critically, experiment with different ways of teaching and show concern for children's learning over time, it is very much a 'hit and miss' affair (Calderhead 1987; Fuller and Bown 1975). Feiman-Nemser and Buchmann, for example, maintain that 'by themselves, student teachers can rarely see beyond what they want or need to do or what the classroom setting requires' (1987: 272).

Certainly, in the teacher education programme with which we were involved, it was felt that this risk was untenable. Student teachers needed to be 'moved on' to understand the role and responsibilities of being a professional educator. For the students at Swansea, this involved the attempt to get them to consider the quality as well as the value of what and how children learn. Whereas, up to this point, the teachers and tutors responsible for students' school-based learning had been 'teaching with the tide' (Fuller 1969: 223), it was now necessary to become much more 'interventionist' when working with the students; from this point on, therefore, our research took on more of the character of an action research project. Slowly, as a result of these interventions, the students learned that there was still much more to learn. As one student commented, 'It's kind of opening up a bigger and bigger area of the unknown, taking one step at a time. You can cope with that . . . but if you had this great big expanse . . .' And another student said, 'If you hadn't challenged me it might have dawned on me but it certainly wouldn't be such a dramatic change.'

Challenging students

As we indicated in the last section, it is our contention that student teachers' expectations and beliefs often exert a powerful influence on their classroom learning and on their practice. As a result, simply 'telling' students about the complexities involved in effective teaching and learning is unlikely to produce anything more than strategic compliance. It is only when students are forced to face and to reconsider their own value position, what that means in terms of their practice and in particular in terms of children's learning, that there is likely to be any 'movement'. Students, we would suggest, have to understand the *need* for change.

While student teachers may well feel challenged about their practice throughout their school experience, we felt that the challenges at this stage of their learning appeared to be the most fundamental and difficult, in that they attempted to force students to evaluate their whole understanding of the role of the teacher, and their understandings about teaching and learning. The interventions from the tutors, pushed – and were intended to push – the students to change their ways of seeing and working, and to relinquish and redirect some of the power they had only recently acquired.

Student teachers were, therefore, asked to re-evaluate their planning and reflect on the broader implications of the activities they devised in terms of pupil learning; they were asked 'to look beneath the familiar, interactive world of schooling and focus on [pupil] thinking and learning' (Feiman-Nemser and Buchmann 1987: 257). For example, students were asked questions such as: 'What, exactly, are you wanting the children to learn?', 'Why do the children need to learn this?', 'What "use" will this learning be to them?', 'What is the best method of teaching this?', 'How will you support and differentiate this learning?', 'Why are you using this method of organisation?', 'What are the implications of this?', 'What is the children's present understanding of this "topic"?', 'How do you know?', 'How does this lead on from, use or extend the children's present understanding?', 'How does this contribute to their greater understanding of this subject area?', 'What processes and skills are you developing?', 'What "hidden messages" does this learning convey?' and 'How will you evaluate and monitor the children's learning and your teaching?'

For the majority of students in our study, being asked, at this stage, to devise and implement activities in ways that reflected an engagement with children's learning over time, represented an enormous challenge and was met with varying degrees of resistance. As we have already stated, for many student teachers, after the first arduous weeks of survival and confusion, having now attained basic control, competence and confidence in teaching skills and strategies, teaching had begun, at last, to look manageable. Perhaps unsurprisingly therefore, many were reluctant to be pushed any further.

Most of our students recognised that they were being challenged to re-evaluate their beliefs and to see in new and more complex ways. One student described it as being asked to 'think of a lesson for them [the pupils] rather than a lesson for me'. Another student later reflected, 'I needed that kick up the backside in a way because I hadn't thought about it before and it was that that made me think.' A third said, 'I've just never thought about teaching like that before . . . it's a different channel of thinking altogether.'

Whereas for many students it was the tutors' interventions at this time that were influential in challenging their views, others pointed to different influences. For example, one student maintained, 'Some sessions at college started me thinking but I can't remember where. I can't remember a big bang, it just kind of emerged.' Another student teacher maintained that her change in perspective was essentially pragmatic – practically and experientially driven; a realisation that her work-sheets were taking far longer to make than for the children to complete led her to question the purpose of her activities and of teaching.

Resistance

The students who had the most difficulty in accepting the need to re-evaluate their ideas were, perhaps unsurprisingly, those who appeared to have strongly held but simplistic beliefs about the nature of teaching and learning. These students felt they were often being asked to reassess fundamental and deep-seated beliefs based on their own experience. As one student teacher commented, 'That's the way I've always learned, so for me I had to challenge my own way of learning.' This student maintained that up to this point she had

> felt quite happy. I didn't think I knew it all but I felt confident I would get there in the end. . . . And then you realise how much you don't know. At that point (when I was challenged about the quality of the activity in terms of the children's learning) I thought I'm never going to make it. I was very depressed . . . but I did start questioning my teaching.

For these students in particular, developing and using a more sophisticated understanding of the processes involved in teaching and learning was something that emerged only very gradually. As one student commented, 'I had some lessons that went disastrously wrong after that but then I started to realise what the tutor meant. But even when I knew what she was getting at I didn't know how to do it.' Similarly another student maintained,

> The idea may be a flash of light but you've got to work on it – I don't think you can just change. It is gradual. The more you learn to 'let go' the more you realise that . . . talking to them . . . they're not going to take it in. They have got to go through an experience. I've got to let them do it.

Evidence of understanding

A few student teachers in our study maintained they had always *understood* the complexity of teaching and learning, but had not been able to *use* this understanding. For example, one student commented, 'I think it's hard to put your ideas into practice. I think my ideal was there all along but it was difficult. So many things got in the way . . . there is so much to think about.' Another explained, 'I might have known about it but I couldn't connect the two up very well because I was thinking about children running around and quickly give them something to do.' While a third maintained, 'You have to take one step at a time. You know what the ultimate goal is but you can't do it all at once.'

Once again, it was classroom control that seemed to be the fundamental factor in inhibiting their development. Student teachers who did not feel 'comfortable' with classroom control needed a great deal of encouragement to put into practice their developing understandings about children's learning. Teaching in ways that reflected more appropriate understandings about how children best learn – for example, allowing the children to engage in enquiry and investigation – requires students to relinquish or soften their control. But the students in our study were often reluctant to take this risk. As one class teacher commented, her student still felt she had to be formally didactic in her teaching because 'it keeps everything under tight wraps' for her.

Constraints

Some students maintained that there were contextual factors within their school that inhibited them from engaging with pupil learning. Although in the earlier stages students had stated that they were desperate for the class teacher to give them 'ideas' for activities, there was now a belief that it was because they had not been given control of the planning in the past that they had not had to think thoroughly about how and what the children were learning. One student commented, 'Over the last five weeks I feel different – more in control. All the ideas come from me.' Another said, 'With teaching one hundred per cent I've been thinking more about a development of learning.' A third maintained,

> Now if you have a lesson where you think they didn't quite grasp it then you can do another lesson – because it's up to you now. This time we're more in control of what we're doing. You can put in an extra lesson or take one out. It's like being a classroom teacher rather than just being in the classroom.

Other students maintained that they were now more willing to experiment and work in ways which they felt were more consistent with their own ideas about how children should learn because, at this point in their teaching practice, the class teacher was not in the classroom so often and there was not so great a pressure to 'fit in'. As one student put it, 'You can really let yourself go when you're not being watched.'

When students began to teach in a way that did reflect an engagement with children's learning, they maintained that they gained approval and encouragement not only from the teacher and tutor but also from the pupils. As one student explained, 'I could see it in the children's faces . . . I must have been doing something right.' Other students agreed: 'I now feel I am progressing as a teacher – whereas before I felt stagnant really.'

Obviously, the degree of challenge and support given to the student to make this move is dependent on the perspective, understanding and skill of the tutor and class teacher or mentor. However, we would maintain that the importance of helping student teachers to evaluate their beliefs about the nature of teaching and learning is fundamental if students are to develop into fully professional teachers.

CONCLUSION

Unlike Fuller and Bown (1975), who emphasise a development through a series of *discrete* stages and concerns, we found that the students in our study expressed a range of concerns *throughout* their school experience. Our findings would therefore support Guillaume and Rudney, who state that the student teachers in their study 'did not so much think about different things as they grew; they thought about things differently' (1993: 79.) Thus the student teachers in our study initially viewed pupils as 'children', and as allies. Later they viewed pupils *en masse*, as a class and even as enemies, before they eventually came to see them as individual pupils and learners. Similarly, their view of the content of activities changed over time. Initially the content of activities was viewed, primarily, as a medium of control, then as a chance to impress, before it finally became a vehicle for learning. In both of these dimensions of professional knowledge, students, it seemed, swung between extremes before they eventually achieved a more balanced perspective. Overall, we would suggest therefore that our study lends support to Guillaume and Rudney's conclusion that this pattern of learning mirrors human development in general. Like the pupils they are teaching, student teachers move from concrete and undifferentiated ways of thinking to thinking that is 'more integrated, flexible and holistic' (1993: 78).

We would emphasise that the stages and the associated concerns we have described represent no more than broad patterns of development. Students' progress from novice to professional is, we maintain, very likely to be fragmentary and erratic. For example, students may develop and be able to use understandings in one context but not generalise these to the whole of their practice. They may also, on occasions, 'revisit' stages. When faced with disruptive pupils, even experienced students may be plunged back into focusing on their personal survival.

From our study of student development, we also came to recognise some of the factors that affect that development. As we indicated in the introduction to this chapter, we discovered that students' ability to develop appropriate forms of practical knowledge, and the speed of their progress through the different stages from 'novice teacher' to 'professional educator', is profoundly influenced by personal factors. It is influenced, for example, by the attitudes and beliefs they hold and the way these interact with the attitudes and beliefs of their supervising teacher and the university tutor. In particular, where students hold strong, traditional or simplistic beliefs about the nature of teaching and learning – for example, that teaching involves no more than 'telling' – they need a great deal of support and challenge if they are to move on in the ways we have described. For many students in our study, it was only by being challenged that they came to appreciate the complex nature of teaching and learning and could begin to develop what teachers and tutors considered to be more 'appropriate' practical knowledge.

Also important were contextual factors. These included the class teachers' ability to articulate their knowledge, their ability to support as well as challenge students and, interestingly, the 'mix' of teacher and student's personalities. In this respect it was apparent that in some cases students' development appeared to be impeded by a lack of communication when both teacher and student were naturally quiet and unwilling to 'impose'. Similarly, where teacher and student both had 'strong' personalities, students maintained that they were not being given enough room to develop or 'let their personalities shine through'. However, perhaps most important of all was the teacher's willingness to relinquish their own power over 'their' class. Students' development, is also, we came to recognise, affected by their particular teacher education programme; for example, how tutors work with students on their school experience, how they respond to students' needs and their willingness to challenge students' beliefs.

In the next two chapters, we will explore some of these issues in more detail as we report our case studies of student learning in two key areas. In Chapter 6, we explore what it is that students need to learn in the area of classroom management and control, an issue of particular importance to students in the early stages of their development. In Chapter 7, we look in more detail at an issue that assumed more significance for students in the later stages of their development: how they develop what the teachers in our study called ' good ideas' for teaching.

Chapter 6

Learning for classroom management and control

As we indicated in the Introduction to this book, the ultimate aim of our research was to throw light on the role of the mentor in supporting students' school-based learning. From our initial review of the literature, it became apparent that while some research had been carried out into the practical and organisational demands of mentoring and mentoring strategies and techniques, few researchers had grappled with the more confused, problem- atic, yet fundamental aspect of 'what' is mentored – the practical knowledge base of teachers, how it is used and how it develops. Until we had a clearer grasp of *these* issues, we argued that we could not begin to characterise the process and content of effective mentoring.

Having completed our preliminary investigation into the 'stages' of development that students go through during the course of their school-based experience, we therefore chose to use the second year of our project to undertake two case studies of the 'content' of students' school-based learning. Drawing on what we had learned during the first year of our research, we chose to investigate two topics that we had found were of particular importance to students at different stages of their development. These were 'classroom management and control' – a topic of overwhelming importance to students during their early days in school – and what teachers called 'good ideas for teaching' – the content of their lessons or activities. Although students were clearly concerned with both of these issues throughout their school experience, we noted that it was not until later in their PGCE year – and not until they had achieved basic classroom control – that the issue of lesson content became a central focus of attention. In this chapter we describe what we discovered about the forms of school-based learning associated with achieving classroom management and control; in Chapter 7 we turn our attention to what they had to learn in relation to lesson content – 'good ideas' for teaching.

As we indicated in Chapter 4, our methodology in this aspect of our work involved a mixture of classroom observation and interviews both with the students and with their classroom teachers. On numerous occasions, students were observed teaching, their follow-up discussions with their supervising teachers were recorded and then both teacher and student were interviewed separately. During these interviews, students were asked both about the intentions behind their teaching and what they had learned from their debriefing; teachers were interviewed about their interpretations of the students 'performance' and their intentions behind the debriefing they had given. From this methodology it was therefore possible to produce a series of 'triangulated' data sets. Our own observations and interpretations of students' teaching and the forms of feedback they were given could be carefully compared and contrasted with both the teachers' and the students' own views. This methodology became particularly important in exploring the differences between what the student 'knew' and what experienced teachers 'knew' in relation to each of the two topics we chose to investigate.

CLASSROOM CONTROL AND THE NEED FOR A 'PROFESSIONAL' RELATIONSHIP

Our initial discussions with teachers on the nature of classroom management and control revealed a commonly held belief that classroom control was essentially to do with confidence. When pushed, most teachers acknowledged that, in reality, it had to involve more than confidence but found it difficult to articulate what that 'more' was.

Student teachers, as we have stated in Chapter 5, appear to come into teaching with their own beliefs about the role of the teacher, the sort of teacher they want to be (and do not want to be) and the kind of relationship they want to develop with their pupils. This, as we indicated, is in part formed through their own memories of school (Lortie 1975). In addition, though, their beliefs may be affected or re-affirmed by the child-centred ideology which is fundamental to the culture of today's British primary school.

This child-centred ideology is often characterised by the slogan, 'We teach children not subjects'. Within this ideology, the teacher (usually, and probably significantly, a woman) is seen to provide for the innocent child, a refuge, a haven against the hostile world outside (Alexander 1984). Alexander points out how this ideology even permeates through to a child-centred vocabulary: we 'nourish' and 'nurture' as opposed to 'restrict' and 'impose', we talk of children's learning and not of our teaching (1984: 16).

As we have indicated in Chapter 5, most of the student teachers in our study revealed both their own needs and expectations, and a common perception of this ideology, when they talked about the sort of teacher they wanted to be and the classroom climate they wished to establish. Their descriptions, as we saw, centred on such qualities as 'warm', 'friendly', 'caring', 'enthusiastic' and 'popular'. For many of our students, it seems it was the promise of personal, close encounters, and importantly the chance to be themselves, to be 'natural', that attracted them to the profession of primary teaching in the first place.*

However, as the students themselves quickly realised, these needs and expectations had to be balanced by the professional demands of having to teach. The students became aware that in order to teach, to 'survive' as a teacher, they had to establish and maintain their authority, and this necessitated asserting their power and retaining a distance from the children. But as teachers they could not simply *demand* compliance – this would be at odds with both their own teacher self-image and what they believed to be the basic tenets of the child-centred ideology. In order to teach effectively, they recognised that they must 'motivate' as well as control.

The dilemma faced by students in the early stages of their school experience was therefore fundamental and urgent – how to reconcile their own, often deep-rooted, expectations and aspir-

* In our pilot study, we found that a number of secondary student teachers also seemed drawn into teaching because of its potential to provide close and personal relationships with young people. However, unlike our primary group, there were also significant numbers of secondary students who seemed attracted to teaching because of the possibilities it offered to teach their own specialist subject. The implications of these differences in the initial motivations among different groups of secondary student teachers is clearly worthy of further research.

ations with the immediate professional demands made upon them. How could they maintain their teacher self-image and meet their own needs in the face of having to control and teach the children? Feeling, exploring and learning to balance these conflicting demands appeared to be extremely painful, frustrating and exhausting for our student teachers.

For experienced teachers, the solution to this dilemma appears to be the development of a 'professional relationship'. It is this relationship which, we believe, underlies teachers' practice in terms of classroom management and control and which student teachers have come to understand and develop for themselves. This relationship, we will suggest, has four broad, inter-connecting dimensions. They are:

- 'awareness of self' – discovering me-as-teacher
- 'self-control' – managing your feelings
- 'self-protection' – maintaining your authority
- 'satisfaction of self' – bringing 'the personal' back in.

Our approach to classroom management and control is therefore fundamentally different from that commonly put forward in books on learning to teach (for example, Kyriacou 1991), in that it is not 'skills'-based. Although we came to recognise that there were many practical skills students had to learn if they were to manage their classrooms effectively (where to stand, how to use their voice and their eyes, how to establish clear rules for the beginnings and ends of lessons and so on), we concluded that unless students developed an understanding of these other forms of knowledge, they would not be able to deploy these skills in the classroom. Students could be taught to recognise the skills of classroom management and control relatively easily; learning how to use them in the establishment of an appropriate 'professional relationship' was a far more complex matter.

As the categories are broad, and are our attempt to impose a structure on a complex reality, there is necessarily some overlap between them. Some aspects of teachers' practice, for example, can be seen to fit into several categories – teachers' practice may, at any given time, hold and reflect several purposes and intentions.

Within each of the dimensions of this professional relationship, we will discuss what the teachers in our study appeared to 'know' and the difficulties student teachers experienced in the process of developing this sort of knowledge themselves. Before doing so, it is important to point out that we do not intend these categories to be understood as either discrete, or sequential, stages of development. Although classroom control does appear to be a particularly pertinent issue in the early weeks of students' school experience, 'awareness of self' and 'self-control', for example, appear to develop *throughout* students' school experience and possibly throughout teachers' professional careers. Nevertheless, within the early weeks of students' school experience there does appear to be some form of generalised progression; the *primary* focus of the students with whom we worked seemed to move from an initial awareness of themselves as teachers and the professional demands of teaching, to what this meant in terms of the need for self control, to learning ways of 'protecting' their own self-interests and needs before they were able to achieve any measure of 'personal satisfaction'.

We now turn to consider each of these different dimensions in detail, contrasting what experienced teachers as opposed to student teachers 'know' about them.

AWARENESS OF SELF – DISCOVERING 'ME-AS-TEACHER'

One of the most challenging issues for students in achieving a 'professional relationship' with their pupils was that they had to develop a different persona; they had to discover a new person – 'me-as-teacher'. Teachers, we discovered, however natural they appeared, were not always 'themselves' in the classroom – particularly when they were in the process of establishing their authority. In the early stages of working with a new class, teachers would use a variety of resources, including their own personalities, to establish themselves as this 'other person' – this teacher who commands respect and has a right to control the class. As we will demonstrate below, students found the development of this new 'self' – me-as-teacher – both difficult and personally challenging to achieve.

Establishing their authority – teachers' views

I want them to understand that I'm in control. You don't rule me, I rule you and the learning will come from that. Because if they're all doing what they want to do and they can walk all over you . . . if they think they're in control then they won't get any work done.

(Classroom teacher)

The first fundamental step to attaining a 'professional relationship' with pupils occurs within minutes of meeting a new class; when teachers strive to establish their authority – some kind of 'dominant presence' (Wragg and Wood 1984, cited in Robertson 1989) – and convey their expectations in terms of pupil behaviour. This was seen by the teachers in our study as a prerequisite of pupil learning.

Teachers established their authority in different ways. Generally, teachers stated, 'The first thing is to lay a ground plan . . . what you expect', and maintained the importance of 'getting to know the children's names as quickly as possible'. The age of the pupils appeared to be a pertinent factor in terms of teachers' practice. Teachers of older children maintained that establishing one's authority meant 'not letting them move, breathe or do anything'. They wanted the pupils to be 'slightly unsure of me and of how I would react'. One teacher commented, 'I don't want them to think I'm harmless to start off with.' Another teacher noted that she was 'Louder, noisier, a bit of an actress.' This was because, 'I think if you go in very quiet . . . they'll take advantage. I don't go in shouting . . . perhaps not being a clown . . . but being . . . perhaps a little bit unpredictable.' Another teacher maintained that she would 'Lay the law down . . . wouldn't let them move, talk . . . do anything'.

However, the teachers in our study did not maintain this level of dominance. For example, as one explained, 'There's no joking around for the first ten minutes and then slowly it comes round but they know once I say it then . . .' Another teacher stated 'After a while I relax a little but the children will know that I can get them whenever I want to.'

Teachers maintained that becoming this 'other person' initially gave them a feeling of confidence with a new class. One teacher maintained, 'I think that's why I tend to be a bit more dramatic in the beginning . . . I feel the confidence thing, because if a student gives the impression of being nervous the children will pick up on it. They will always find your weakness.' This teacher further commented, 'Even now if I'm asked to look after a new class I tend to walk in and ... "Look, I've arrived". It's just a bit of an act again to walk in. Because if I crept in quietly through the door ...'

At this point, if children – particularly children with a reputation for disruptive behaviour – did 'test' their authority, teachers maintained that

> Straight away, if they put a foot out of line then I come down hard on them. It depends on what they were doing. I wouldn't be harder on them than the rest of the class but knowing that they're the sort to go a step further I wouldn't allow it to go a step further ... I would chastise them straight away.

The ease of establishing authority appeared, in part, to be linked to teachers' personalities. Teachers' practice, as we noted on many occasions, is built around and constrained by their personalities. One teacher, for example, considered that she ought to begin the year being seen as 'strict' but admitted that she found this difficult. 'I always find it quite hard, I always go in and say I'm going to be really strict but I find it really hard to stick to being like that. ... I don't know why I just do.' However, this teacher maintained that because she had a 'strong' personality, establishing her authority was not a problem for her. She stated: 'Because I'm quite an extrovert person, I'm just like that all the time. It's just my personality ... because I am so loud.'

Teachers of younger children were also careful to establish their authority but, in an 'oblique' (King 1978) or 'mitigated' (French and Peskett 1986) way. Early years teachers appeared to try to find 'softened' or indirect ways of conveying their expectations and controlling children's behaviour. The teachers in our study used a variety of oblique strategies. Two reception class teachers, for example, both used puppets to establish their authority. One maintained,

> Initially when I come into a class I always talk through a puppet, interact through a puppet and we get to know each other that way ... and they are attentive because their attention is focused on the puppet and puppet tells them what to do. And gradually, through that, they become aware ... as they come to know me I wean them off that.

The other reception teacher commented that, 'When the children are sitting together on the carpeted area, the puppet looks round to see who's not looking, the puppet tells me, "Oh, James is not ready, Mrs Williams."' These teachers maintained that they used puppets, as 'children respond better in a play situation rather than in a telling situation'. Further, it was maintained that 'while establishing your authority . . . could be done without the puppet, it wouldn't be as easy. It just makes it more fun, more enjoyable'.

Another early years teacher commented that she established her authority and conveyed her expectations though telling the children that they had a 'magic finger' that could keep their lips still. This teacher maintained that with young children in particular, 'You don't want to be too negative', and that 'You need to treat them gently or they won't want to come to school'.

However 'indirect' their strategies, teachers all appeared to recognise the need quickly to establish their authority. However, as several teachers recognised, this was not always easy in terms of their personal 'needs'. As one teacher commented, 'I know it would be nice . . . ideally you want to go in and get them to like you and have a lovely rapport and a nice relationship . . . but it doesn't always work like that.'

Establishing their authority – student teachers' views

Early on in their teaching experience, certainly when they began whole-class teaching, the students in our study also quickly realised that if they were to 'survive' then they, too, would have to gain control. While many students were able to act as teachers when working on a one-to-one basis with pupils, establishing their authority and 'making their presence felt' with the class as a whole appeared extremely difficult for student teachers for several reasons. First, as their class teachers had established their authority in the early days and weeks of the school year – well before students began their school experience – the students had not had the opportunity to observe this process. As Robertson (1989) comments, students may try and emulate what they see as the teacher's warm, close relationship with the children even though this may bear no resemblance to the relationship teachers were able to have on their initial meeting with their pupils. In addition, the students appeared not to appreciate either the understanding on which this relationship was based or that the teacher was not, in reality, being 'natural', however natural and easy his or her performance may have looked. Indeed, even if students had been given a chance to observe this process of establishing authority, it is unlikely, at this stage, that they would have understood the *significance* of the teacher's comments and actions.

A second problem is that, in order to establish their authority, teachers have to convey their expectations in terms of behaviour. Our student teachers initially had neither the knowledge of what their expectations were, nor the knowledge of how to convey them. Teachers' practical knowledge is practical – it only develops through actual 'participation' in teaching. It is only with experience that students appeared to come to 'know' their expectations and what they considered 'appropriate', in terms of, for example, pupil noise and movement.

Moreover, students lacked any 'typificatory knowledge' of how the children were, for example, *likely* to react, or of any strategies that were *likely* to work for them.

Finally, while teachers maintained the need to become 'larger than life' and 'unpredictable', when establishing one's authority for the first time, students, because of their lack of experience, felt inhibited. These inhibitions that arose because of lack of experience were also exacerbated by students' lack of power and control. One student maintained, 'You're conscious of asserting your authority all the time because the teacher's there and you think – that's her responsibility.' Another inhibiting factor was their awareness that they were being assessed: 'there's another adult in the room who may or may not be judging you.'

Whereas teachers complained that, in general, 'Students don't let themselves go enough,' there was a great deal of sympathy for their difficulties. Teachers maintained,'Thinking back to my own practice, I didn't mind making mistakes in front of the children but I certainly didn't like making mistakes in front of the teacher . . . it's very intimidating. It would be now.' Another teacher commented, 'Students have difficulty because they're very nervous and I think it's very intimidating being in a class with a teacher who might have been teaching for a long time. You feel inhibited from putting your authority on the class.' Yet another said: 'You're not going to go into this strange situation where the teacher is watching you and the nursery nurse is watching you and the head could walk in and the tutor could walk in . . . you're not going to become this other person straight away.'

Discovering 'me-as-teacher'

Above all, establishing their authority appeared to be dependent on an understanding of the *need* for a professional relationship and the ability to become this new person, 'me-as-teacher'. While student teachers may be armed with advice that they should not, at least initially, be too friendly with children ('Don't smile until Christmas'), they lacked an understanding of the underlying principle that being a teacher meant that they could not also simply be a friend.

However, becoming this other person was a slow and painful process. As we stated in Chapter 5, in the early days of their school experience the student teachers in our study became concerned that the children should identify them with the teacher and not with other adult helpers. They recognised the need to be seen as holding power. Student teachers commented that they often felt the pupils were 'trying it on to see whose side we were on'. It was through the process of asserting their power, however difficult this might have been, that student teachers began to discover this other person, 'me-as-teacher'. One student commented, 'I'm not the same. If I went in as 'me', I'd be different . . . not completely different . . . I don't know why.'

Me-as-teacher – anger and frustration

It was at this stage that students confronted their 'ideals' and the impossibility of living up to them. Student teachers were heard complaining to bored, restless children that they considered them ungrateful after all the hard work they had put into preparing this activity – as if they believed that the children had a responsibility at least to pretend they were enjoying the work. As they found out, children are rarely party to social 'niceties' when giving their opinion about their teacher or their work!

Student teachers seemed, on occasions, to feel real anger towards the children, particularly when they felt they were being ignored. One student commented, 'Your heart is beating fast. I'm thinking, "What do I do now?" I'm thinking "You're not going to beat me, I'm going to get you back." You think, "Right, you're not doing it this time."' Another student commented, 'I feel very insecure and angry . . . it's because you're being ignored. It's the fact that you're there – you're speaking to them and they're all carrying on and . . . they can't do this to me.' A third student maintained, 'After six weeks they should *know* that I am the authority in the classroom as well as the teacher and they still don't listen to you when you tell them something. The teacher goes out of the room and they start talking.' Another explained,

> You feel this panic rising in you because they won't do what you want them to and it comes out in this enormous voice and it takes you a couple of seconds to realise that you've made the sound. And the children are all sitting there looking at you as if . . . oh my God she's going to explode or something. And all your frustration has come out in that enormous shout.

Students maintained that their reactions to the children at this time were often surprising and sometimes frightening. Several students mentioned the disembodied feeling of almost listening to their own voice, and that they had not been aware that they could speak so loudly. For example, one student said, 'It's your voice taking over . . . it's my voice coming out in a great big boom.' While another said sadly, 'It's quite scary to come out with all this . . . but they make me so angry.'

Me-as-teacher – retaining their ideals

Students also felt anger towards the pupils for making them become someone they did not want to be. One student commented, 'I knew I would have to change slightly going into the classroom because you can't be as natural as you want to be. I accepted that, but then . . . you do scare yourself sometimes with what you can do.' The teachers students had initially *wanted* to be – for example, 'warm' and 'friendly', had been replaced by the teachers they *had* to be – 'firm', 'organised', 'calm', 'efficient' and 'fair'. However, as we stated in Chapter 5, this did not mean that students let go of their 'ideal' teacher self-image; rather, it was put on hold while they attempted to survive.

Students would therefore justify their actions by stating that 'ideals are to be worked towards' and 'At present I can't have the ideal but it doesn't mean I won't in the future'. One student commented that she had to find a way of accommodating the sort of teacher she wanted to be into the sort of teacher she had to be so that she could feel comfortable with her teaching style. Another student maintained, 'When I have my own class, my own personality will come out, I expect.'

Me-as-teacher and personality

While we have maintained that students need to discover this other person – 'me-as-teacher' – this is not to suggest that it is not greatly influenced by who students are 'as people'. Rather, as we have already stated, students appear to learn ways of teaching that exploit their strengths and minimise or compensate for the weaknesses of their personality. One teacher commented that while you can teach people about 'teaching',

> You can't change personalities, I don't believe. Some people say you can make people different teachers. I think you've got to stick with your personality, you've got to live within the constraints of that, otherwise you will be found out and end up being a mess. I think you can grow strong if you are weak and if you're frightened slightly you can put on a face and get away with that. But I think it is important . . . I think all students want to be themselves. I want students to be more competent teachers but based on their own personalities, the limits of their personalities, and working out what those are.

SELF-CONTROL – MANAGING YOUR FEELINGS

> It's easy to fall into the trap – react to something they've done. . . 'Miss, my pencil's gone,' 'He's taken my book' . . . to get involved at their level. You've got to keep them at arms' length to keep control. You are their teacher not their parent and you've got twenty seven of them.

> Sometimes I want to cuddle them, run after them in the play-ground, but I can't do that. I find that difficult.

In order to control the children, student teachers found that they also had to control themselves: their natural, personal and instinctive reactions. Students seemed to find withholding the personal 'self' painful and exhausting. For example, one student teacher commented,

> I've had so much trouble that I've gone in as someone completely different . . . at least a side of me I've never thought about. You've got to go in . . . don't smile . . . you know. Well I smile all the time – it's natural. I just walk in 'Oh hello' . . . and you can't do that. And every minute I've been thinking, keep

it together and don't. . . . It's been difficult. All the time I'm
aware you can't do that. . . . I should say this.

Another commented, 'Some of the children are really cute and
sometimes you feel like you just want to give them a hug . . . or
play with them . . . just play.'

The problem of withholding their natural reactions was particularly visible for students when involved in whole-class teaching.
Although once through the survival stage students often found
whole-class teaching easier to manage than when the children
were working in groups, in that the children's attention was, at
least, focused on them, it was in this situation that students
realised the danger of trying to maintain a personal, individual
relationship with the children. This was particularly difficult as
students felt that the children were 'fighting for attention to be
focused on them'.

When dealing with children on a one-to-one basis, students
also spoke of their instinctive desire to help the children with, for
example, tying their shoelaces or doing up buttons even when
they knew the children could do this for themselves – they appeared
to be drawn into and flattered by the chance of what they saw as
a personal encounter. One student commented,

> The children are trying to get your attention – as much as they
> can. A lot of them don't want to be independent. Like doing
> their coats up. But you couldn't teach if you paid attention to
> everything they said they couldn't do.

Another student maintained, 'Sometimes it's quite hard when
you hear a teacher saying, "Now you must do your coat up" – but
you couldn't respond to them all like that.'

It may be that when experienced teachers are addressing the
whole class or using their public voice (King 1978) they structure
their comments and questions in a particular way in order to ensure
that these indicate a professional rather than a personal relationship.
It is also likely that, despite their demands for attention, children *do*
expect their relationship with teachers to be different – that is,
distanced – particularly when the teacher is dealing with the whole
class or working within the classroom situation. After several exhausting weeks, most of the students realised, 'You learn what to
ignore' and 'You've got to keep them at arms' length to keep control'.

Students, of course, were beginning to learn what is of significance and what as a teacher you need to ignore.

Self-control and feelings of anger and frustration

As well as controlling their desire to form close relationships,
student teachers found that they also needed to control their
anger or frustrations. The student teachers in our study initially
seemed in awe of their teachers' ability to remain calm. One
student commented, 'My teacher doesn't ever get angry. At times
I felt my patience running out, but she's hardly raised her voice.'
Another student complained that the children 'would start crawl-
ing around on the carpet when she was trying to talk to them' and
voiced her frustration that shouting at them was ineffective. She
commented, 'I can't keep getting angry at them.' However, as
teachers understood, 'There's no point shouting. It's better to
keep calm and control the situation.'

Self-control and the use of 'oblique' strategies

Learning to control their frustrations can be linked to the teachers'
use of oblique or mitigative directives in terms of control. Being
indirect reconciles the demands of control and motivation, and it
may also lessen the pain of having to behave in ways that do not fit
in with their teacher self-image. While oblique strategies were most
obvious in the infant classrooms, they were also used by junior
teachers but in more subtle ways, for example, by the use of humour
or, in our area, the use of commands in the Welsh language.

In the early years classrooms, in line with the studies of King
(1978) and French and Peskett (1986), indirect strategies constituted a real performance, with each teacher having their own
'sayings' and 'tactics'. One teacher in our study seemed to have
perfected this 'act' and always appeared positive, patient and
professional. She continually distracted and refocused the children with comments such as 'Are your brains working well today?'
or 'Are you going to sleep over there?' When children's school
bags had been kicked into the classroom, despite her (possible)
annoyance, she brightly asked the likely 'culprits' if they would
'pretend they were bulldozers and push them all out of the way'.
The children instantly responded. Of course messages were not

only conveyed in the language teachers used but also in the intonation, body posture and in the overstated gasps and sighs.

Interestingly, neither the teachers nor the students were aware of the use of oblique strategies. Once pointed out to the students, they began to 'collect' these sayings, but many students were reticent to use them in 'that' teacher's class. They saw them as personal rather than 'personalised' – that is part of the teacher's professional relationship – and maintained that these tactics were 'hers'. One student commented,

> It won't be the same, her strategies coming out of my mouth. And I don't know whether to use her strategies or make up my own. I don't want to use her strategies in front of her. I'll use them with another class.

Even though the students appreciated why these strategies were used and that as the children were familiar with these sayings they would be more likely to respond to them, they felt they needed the teacher's permission to use them. When they eventually did try them out, they were delighted with the results – they worked! However, in terms of mentoring, it is interesting to note that student teachers commented that they could only appreciate the need for oblique directives in terms of control when they had found out for themselves that a direct approach did not work. Moreover, even when they could see and understand the need for and significance of oblique strategies, they still had difficulty 'using' that knowledge in the immediacy and urgency of the classroom situation. As one student stated, 'on the spur of the moment it's difficult to remember.'

French and Peskett(1986) note not only teachers use of oblique strategies in terms of *control*, but also their use of bare imperatives in terms of *pedagogy*. Teachers, it seems, want to make sure that pupils have clear instructions about the work they are being set. This was often in sharp contrast to students. Student teachers, we noticed, were direct, and negative, in terms of the children's behaviour when this was seen as personally threatening. However, perhaps in the desire to be liked, to uphold their teacher 'self-image' and possibly also through a lack of knowledge of children, students were often unclear in giving directions about work. For example, students would often give too many choices to pupils, and comments such as, 'What would you like to do?', 'Well, the children could do this, but if they don't like it then they can always . . .' and 'I decided not to dictate . . . they can choose' were initially fairly common among the students in our study.

Self-control and feelings of panic

We also became aware that students need to control their feelings of lack of confidence and of panic. For example, in the early weeks of teaching, students would often begin explanations or introductions before the children's attention was focused on them. When students *did* gain the pupils' attention, as we stated in Chapter 5, they were often so concerned that the children would begin talking again that it sometimes appeared to be a case of 'quick tell them everything I know', before they lost control again. Consequently, pupils who were often left confused, and not understanding the demands of the task tended to become even more disruptive. One teacher sympathised, 'It's a strange situation . . . you don't want to stop and wait. It takes courage to wait. Silence can be very, very long.'

Self-control and the desire to dominate

Students also need to learn to control their desire to dominate the children: if the children are to *learn*, then students, as we will describe in the next chapter, need to relinquish their power. The teachers in our study often complained that students' practice was too 'teacher-led' – students were concerned only with what they had to say and were afraid that if the children became 'partners' in the learning process then they would lose their authority. One teacher commented, 'Initially the student didn't spend a long enough time with the children and extract things from them, getting them to think about the issue. Instead she would tell them all about it.' Another teacher told her student, 'You fell into the trap of actually doing too much for them . . . you didn't give them enough room to get their own skill going.' A teacher maintained that

> Kids need to generate a lot of ideas for themselves. Stuff that's 'teacher-led' doesn't often achieve what students hope it will do. Which is, they don't remember it necessarily because it hasn't come from them. . . . Real learning involves working alongside other people, finding solutions to problems as you work with them.

Yet another teacher put it a different way; she maintained that her student 'needs to listen to the children more and feed off their responses'.

Whereas initially this behaviour may reflect the students' stage of development and their simplistic beliefs about the nature of teaching and learning, at some stage students do have to 'let go'. Students, as we stated earlier, have to learn the relationship between 'effective' control and 'effective' teaching. However, being able to relinquish some of the power they had only recently gained seemed to be extremely stressful for our student teachers. The ability to control their instinctive reactions appeared to emerge slowly and gradually. Classroom control *can* be gained through domination, but as one teacher commented about her student,

> She can control the children very well considering she hasn't got their interest. But you don't want to control them like that. You want to control them through giving them the right kind of things. If you can capture children's interest then you don't have to discipline them.

Becoming this other person – 'me-as-teacher' – remaining calm and positive and relinquishing their power can be stressful and exhausting, even for experienced teachers, yet this is what students have to learn to do. As one teacher in our study commented, 'You can come in feeling like death on legs, but you can't react like that . . . you've got to make it fun.' She added tellingly, 'and sometimes it's hard . . . so hard.'

SELF-PROTECTION – MAINTAINING YOUR AUTHORITY

The desire for a personal relationship is for many prospective teachers a natural reaction; however, it also can make teachers rather vulnerable. Becoming this 'other person', being slightly detached, keeping calm and learning what to ignore may, however, help to protect the teacher from such stress – protect the self. One student teacher commented sadly that she believed that if you did not protect yourself, if you *were* 'yourself', 'some of the children would walk all over you'.

Creating a distance between the personal self and the professional self may also make it easier to cope with failure and disruption. As Calderhead (1987) notes, students are then able to reflect on difficulties with their 'performance' rather than seeing their failures in more personal terms. They may, therefore, be less likely to feel that it 'must be something wrong with me that I can't relate to these children' (1987: 272).

Self-protection and strategies for pupil management

In his research, Pollard (1985) defines four major strategies that teachers use in managing the classroom – 'open negotiation', 'domination', 'routinisation' and 'manipulation'. Like Pollard, we came to recognise how some of these strategies are used by teachers in ways that ensure that their self-interests are maintained and enhanced.

The first of these, 'open negotiation' – where there is a balance of 'friendship and respect' and each party recognises and respects the interests of the other – may be the sort of relationship that student teachers had *expected* to have with children. However, such a relationship is not common in the classroom, at least for extended periods.

At the other extreme, 'domination' does not seem to fit in with the desire to balance self-interests and the professional demands of teaching, although it is a strategy, as we have seen, that many students seem to resort to out of anger and lack of self-control. This strategy is, as Pollard comments, 'overtly confrontational – the strategy of last resort' (1985: 189).

The students in our study often appeared to make demands which were not considered acceptable by their teachers – threatening to keep the whole class in at playtime for a week, for example, or 'If you say something when I'm talking you're out'. Moreover, making threats when they had not established their authority often ended in disaster. One student threatened to write 'offending' pupils' names on the blackboard. Within minutes, the student had a blackboard covered in names, and a class full of giggling and jeering pupils. As Pollard comments, rebellion is not an uncommon reaction to this strategy! As one teacher advised, 'Never threaten children with something you're not able to carry out. If you can't do it, don't say it.'

Teachers in our study also recognised that, 'Coming down hard has a negative effect. They don't want to be good for you then. They don't respect you so much somehow . . . perhaps they think you don't care for them.' Further, 'You mustn't back them right up. You must always leave them space so they can get out of it without losing face in front of the others. There's got to be room for negotiation.'

However, Pollard's concept of 'routinisation' appeared to play a large part in our teachers' classroom control and in their 'self-protection'. As Pollard comments, routinisation not only 'provides a straightforward way of giving children practice at learning activities but also . . . provides a highly dependable way of coping with the complexity of classroom life' (1985: 187).

However, we would maintain that the idea of 'routine' and 'routinisation' can be interpreted in different ways and on different levels. First, with experience, teachers' *thinking* appears to become routinised. The teachers in our study appeared to understand their professional role and the implications and responsibilities of that role – their ways of working reflected that in their dealings with children, they were aware of 'what it is they needed to know' and 'what it is they needed to do'. Experience appeared to have enabled them to develop the most efficient and effective ways of thinking about their work, and 'seeing' and 'interpreting' what was happening around them. Routinised thinking therefore had helped to bring their own practice under control and protect them from excessive demands.

In addition, teachers' *practice* itself appeared to have become routinised. Teachers often established a pattern or rhythm to their day and to the school year. One teacher commented that she 'measured out her year' by festivals – Christmas, St David's day, Mothers' day and Easter. As we will note in the next chapter, teachers also appeared repeatedly to use 'representations' or ways of working that they knew were likely to elicit understanding. Once again, routinisation acted as a form of self-protection.

Teachers also seemed to gain control through conveying patterns of behaviour or expectations to the children in their class. Through their use of routines, pupils came to understand the likely format, demands and expectation of the tasks they were given. Teachers also established routines in terms of pupils' behaviour – children *knew* what they were supposed to do at the beginning of the day, where they were to hang their coats, where they were supposed to sit. They would also have clear ideas about what would happen if they didn't comply with these routines. In this way, teachers' routines reinforced expected ways of behaving.

The importance of establishing behavioural routines was

particularly visible when observing students' practice in the early weeks of their school experience. Without established routines, they felt particularly vulnerable. For example, one student admitted,

> I felt like I was losing control with so many things going on at once and so many problems needing to be sorted out at the same time. There was always such a queue behind me that there wasn't time to go round and see what the other children were doing.

Another said, 'When the class is ending a piece of work, I find I am bombarded by pupils holding pieces of paper under my nose.'

Teachers also, on occasions, appeared to make use of routine *activities*. While the teachers in our study appeared to have clear understandings about pupil learning and their 'best' activities (see Chapter 7), they also recognised the constraints of the teaching situation. Teachers maintained that they could not always work in ways they felt they should – for example, when they had large classes and were overloaded with content they felt they had to cover. Again teachers used routine activities; generally these were unchallenging tasks which the children could complete with little or no help from the teacher. Teachers maintained that these activities, which were most often used when the children were working in groups, 'freed them' to work with small numbers of children on more challenging or demanding tasks. Teachers also admitted that when they were having a 'bad day' they tended to rely on activities where the children were engaged in routine activities that they could 'just get on with'.

Undoubtedly, routines and routine activities are used by teachers as methods of control and as strategies for self-protection, although obviously a fine balance is needed if teachers' self-interests are not to dominate.

The final teacher strategy described by Pollard is 'manipulation', which he characterises as the 'attempt to get children to want what the teacher wants them to want' (1985: 187). We would suggest that it is this strategy that seems to relate most closely to the professional relationship that teachers in our study had with their pupils. It was through 'manipulation' that teachers used their power in sophisticated ways in order to balance and meet professional demands and their own and pupils' personal needs and interests. As Pollard comments, 'the gap between what a child is interested in and what a child is deemed to need has to be bridged' (1985: 188). Interestingly, Pollard comments that the success of this strategy lies in the teacher's acting ability, their skill in communicating and the way they are able to use praise, flattery and appeal.

At the most obvious level, the teachers in our study manipulated situations so that, for example, they were seen to 'win' – to be in control. An example of this is teachers' frequently heard directive, 'I want everything tidied away by the time I count to ten', which is usually followed by 'nine, nine and a half, nine and three quarters'. However, most of our teachers' practice was a good deal more subtle than this. For example, they would make use of pupils' desire to please: 'Before they do any work I'll say "Right, hands up who's going to do nice work, who's going to do the best work." And they'll all put their hands up and I'll say, "Right, let's see".' Another form of manipulation occurred when teachers shared the responsibility of upholding order by the use of peer pressure. One teacher commented,

> In the story bay if someone has damaged a book I'd say, 'Nobody wants to read this book now, do we, children? . . . because you've damaged it and it's ripped and it's not nice to look at any more.' Then the other children are cross, they'll say, 'I'm cross with you now'.

Moreover, it was also apparent that teachers paid attention not just to what was said but also to the *way* in which it was said – ensuring that answers were given within the boundaries of the rules and expectations that were set. For example, one teacher maintained that when children 'called out' answers she would comment, 'Please put your hands up, don't shout at me, I don't shout at you. Just wait your turn and put your hand up nicely. I'll ask you next time.' She added, 'They've got to learn to take their turn.'

Self-protection and the use of tension

In order to maintain their authority and protect their self-interests, teachers, it was found, make use of 'tension'. Nias (1989) talks of teachers living with tension, and their ability to handle tension. Galloway and Edwards similarly comment that 'It seems impossible to get away from the tension that lies at the bottom of teacher-pupil interaction' (1991: 57). Tension is central – teachers create tension and dissipate, defuse or resolve it. They use tension to establish their authority, maintain control and gain the children's interest. One teacher commented,

> Like you bring something slowly out of your bag. You don't say, 'Look what I've brought in, I've brought this clown in to show you,' you'd say (whispered), 'Look what I've got' . . . you'd use your voice. Or show one child. You're trying to get their attention essentially. And I'd say to the nursery nurse, 'I'm going to read this book to myself because it's a really good book . . . look, Miss John.' They all want to know, they're nosey . . . naturally inquisitive.

We noted that many teachers introduced even quite routine tasks as 'something special' or 'something important'. One teacher maintained,

> I've seen teachers say, 'Tidy-up time', and nobody moves. It's not interesting enough and everybody is engrossed in what they're doing. But if you say, 'Stop! Listen to what I'm going to say. It's responsibility time and I'm going to see who does their job best' – there's a challenge there. They know what their jobs are and they do it.

Self-protection through preventing and dealing with disruption

If teachers are to protect their personal selves, then maintaining a state of 'normality' by preventing disruption or, if it does occur, not allowing it to escalate, is of the utmost importance. As the students in our study were only too painfully aware, when a class, or even an individual pupil does become disruptive, it is an extremely unsettling experience.

Effective teachers, it has been noted (Munn *et al.* 1992), stand out in their ability to be pro-active – to recognise the danger signs and defuse any possible disruption before it builds up. Eye contact and scanning are fundamental to this ability. Teachers constantly scanned and 'read' the class, looking for and defusing possible disruption. One teacher maintained that she was constantly aware of 'Whether they're listening . . . their eye contact . . .

whether their fingers are fiddling with pencils or whatever'. As one teacher stated, 'It's easier to prevent problems than it is to cure them.'

Awareness or 'withitness' (Kounin 1970) seemed to be especially difficult for student teachers to achieve, particularly when they were asked to take responsibility for children who were involved in group work. Our students appeared to become so involved with one individual or group of children that they lost sight of the rest of the class. Partly, this may be that, as beginners, it was hard for them to concentrate on more than one thing at a time. In addition, they may not have understood the significance of pupils' comments and gestures – they did not know what it was they were supposed to be looking for, what was of 'use' to them *as a teacher*. As one teacher commented,

> It's so easy when you're dealing with people, you tend to focus in on the people you're dealing with, don't you, whereas when you've got thirty people around you, you can't do that and need to be awake, alert to everything else. So somehow you need to learn to communicate with a small group and at the same time be aware of everybody else around. It isn't easy.

Dealing with disruption – teachers' views

When problems did arise, teachers appeared to have a range or hierarchy of strategies or sanctions they used to restore order. One teacher explained, 'If something's going wrong, you mustn't be afraid to stop. Things do go wrong. What you need are strategies to get out of trouble.' These could be as simple as, 'raising your voice initially but then bring it back . . . talk in your normal voice'. Another teacher commented that,

> If one child starts having a little chat it spreads. That's the start of lack of control. I think something's wrong, they're not listening to me . . . and you wonder why and change the tone of voice, change the tactics. Once that happens you're on a downward slope if you don't do something about it soon.

A third stated that,

> If a child is not disturbing anyone I would leave it alone. If he was poking or nudging others I would bring his name into the story, 'James, do you know what happened next?' I would ease

my way in and if that didn't work, 'Come and sit next to me'. If that still didn't work . . . I would come down like a ton of bricks.

One teacher maintained that if a child did challenge her authority, she would 'put them somewhere else – behind me, beside me, but not with the other children'. While another explained that 'I'd take them out and have a talk with them – not in front of the class. I wouldn't want the rest of the class to hear what I was saying and I wouldn't want to draw attention to that child.' Teachers of older children also referred to the 'line of command' within the school and the importance of knowing the school policy on discipline.

Importantly, when dealing with disruption, teachers saw children as 'individuals' and responded to them as individuals in terms of control. Teachers appeared to try to recognise and meet children's individual needs. As one teacher noted,'Gradually as you get to know the children you realise they are all so different.' Another commented,'Your control varies with different kids. Some kids need that sharpness, some kids can't handle it and are more sensitive. Although you've got to have that control you don't want to put them off for life.' A third maintained,

I've got a good book and a naughty book. I had it for one particular child and then I put another child in the naughty book and I didn't realise how devastating it was for him. Again . . . it was through parental contact that I found out how devastated he was. He went home and cried all night and I felt awful. I didn't realise what a powerful tool this naughty book was. . . . For the two particular children I started it for I don't think they could give a toss, but this other child who was also put in there . . . he was devastated. So we had a ceremonial ripping out of the page and he threw it in the bin. But that was really early on and I didn't really know him.

Dealing with disruption – students' views

When student teachers felt that pupils were challenging their authority, they maintained they felt 'panicky . . . heart beating fast. I'm thinking what do I do now?' One student commented, 'You're on the spot and you can see something rising and you think you've got to do something about it and you try all your methods'(laughter from the other students as she counted on her fingers).

Often students attempted to ignore pupils who were misbehaving. One student commented, 'One little boy disappeared behind the bookcase and I thought the best strategy is just to ignore it, but when I did the kids were, "Miss, Miss, Lee is behind the bookcase." It just collapsed all around me.'

Towards the end of the second practice, most students did come to see and treat children as individuals. Sometimes students seemed to learn this through watching their teachers. For example, one student commented, 'My teacher . . . there's always an attention-seeking child, but if you make a big deal out of it they'll love it. But a really shy child she shouted at and she burst into tears.' Another student referred to her own experience,

> You find you can be more of a friend with some children – you can have a joke with them and when you say get on with your work they'll do it. Some children accept your authority straight away and you can chat to them on a friendlier basis. Whereas other children are testing you and you've got to be firm with them – you can't have a joke.

Further, students learned ways to deal with behaviour that was more supportive of the pupils' learning. One student commented,

> You use different techniques. At first I'd tell them to put their pens down. Now I just go over and pick the pen up. You carry on with the lesson – you just go over and pick the pen up and carry on. And everyone else stops. You've made an example.

Perhaps most important of all in terms of protecting their self-esteem, as they gained in experience, students learned to ignore and to rationalise some pupils' potentially disruptive behaviour. For example, one student stated, 'With nursery and reception children, they're so young they're naturally disruptive, I don't think it's me though.' Another stated,

> At the beginning of the teaching practice, any little thing the kids did – fiddling with their pens etc. used to niggle me . . . it used to really get to me and I'd say stop that. Put it down, put it down. At night I'd get home and think, 'I'm going to kill someone.' And by the end of the practice you just have to ignore it.

SATISFACTION OF THE SELF – BRINGING 'THE PERSONAL' BACK IN

Of course, in highlighting teachers' professional relationship with their pupils we are not suggesting that teachers' personal selves do not ever enter the classroom. The personal interaction teachers have with children appears to be of great importance to them and a source of deep personal satisfaction.

This 'personal self' appeared to be used most often when teachers were talking to pupils on a one-to-one basis. It was in this situation that they seemed to make the most use of endearments. However, even when talking to the whole class, teachers sometimes made use of their personal selves, shared something of their lives with children in order to gain the children's interest and strengthen their relationships with them. One teacher commented, 'Showing yourself makes you more approachable – gets them to like you as a person.' It was through this personal interaction that teachers appeared to meet their initial ideal of being the children's friend, to 'play' with them.

Students were also aware of the benefits of showing themselves as 'people'. Comments such as, 'It gets them on your side,' 'It's natural,' 'They can see you as someone they can talk to, someone they like', and 'I like showing my sense of humour to them because it makes me feel better about teaching' were fairly common among the students in our study. Similarly, students maintained that, 'Some children come up and chat to you on a personal basis . . . say something personal. If someone tells you about themselves, it's special because they're telling you.'

However, teachers were also able to sense when children were becoming too close, when their authority was being threatened and would then distance themselves – draw back. Their professionalism and skill enabled them to switch instantly and fluently between their personal and professional selves (Nias 1989). As Nias comments, teachers often find themselves 'shifting between instruction and affection' (1989: 198). One teacher in our study maintained, 'With experience you can feel the "temperature" of the class – how far you can go with them.'

In the later stages of their teaching experience students also spoke of this shift between the 'personal' and the 'professional'. One student maintained, 'You've got to get involved – show your own personality, but you get to a certain point and then withdraw from them. You feel them going . . . and you bring it all back down.' This student, referring to this process, and illustrating the 'unconscious' or 'intuitive' nature of this knowledge, added, 'You don't think, "I've come to the point where I say settle down" . . . it just happens'.

The need to make this switch also seemed to emerge from a gradual understanding about the role of the teacher, the teacher's professional 'interests', and the complexity of pupil learning. One student commented that while she would like to continue 'with the jokey bits, that would defeat the object of teaching'. She maintained that she now 'used' the personal as, 'After a joke they're more ready to settle down to work'.

In this way we came to recognise that being personal is *part* of being professional. One student teacher in our study maintained that she found making this 'switch' so difficult that she had stopped showing anything of herself. She felt it was far too dangerous – the children were able to go 'too far'. She commented,

> I can have a joke with them – that's fine – but when that's finished I've had problems switching back. So I couldn't go in with the jokey bits so much because it's too dangerous. So I've thought quick, hold back . . . and that's difficult.

By the end of their course, students, like their teachers, had come to recognise that the personal self could only be used when their authority had been established. For example, one teacher commented, 'I think I'm always a different person for the first few weeks of the term with a new class . . . but then . . . I come out myself.' Similarly, a student maintained,

> Some children you can chat to and then tell them to get on and they will get on, they won't mess around, whereas with others you've got to be more distant, you can't have a joke, come down to their level until you've established your authority.

This may have fundamental implications for the possibility of satisfaction for student teachers who have difficulty in this regard.

Satisfaction of self and the belief in children's 'ultimate goodness'

Teachers also increased their satisfaction of self, and appeared to meet their own needs by their belief in pupils' 'ultimate goodness'

(King 1978). Their commitment to this belief was a source of high professional ideals for many teachers. For example, teachers maintained they would not 'prejudge' a child they were going to teach. One teacher commented, 'I think you have got to go in and judge for yourself. Some classes you go in and someone has said watch so and so and it's someone else who gives you the trouble.' Another explained,

> I think first of all you need to get to know the children for yourself because I know that you have expectations and that can affect the way you work with the children. . . . But I think you've got to try not to have an expectation, but to take them as you find them. How you interact with the children can affect their behaviour. Some teachers will say I couldn't do anything with that child, I just don't like that child, but another teacher may be able to develop a rapport with the child.

Moreover, when children did misbehave, teachers were reluctant to condemn, but were eager to find a reason for this behaviour. In this way, teachers could be seen to view the situation 'professionally', and in line with child-centred beliefs, rather than seeing pupils' disruption as a personal slight or threat. One teacher commented, 'If a child was misbehaving, I'd say, "What's the matter? Why are you behaving like this? Has something happened at school? Has something happened at home?" And try to get to the bottom of it.' Another teacher commented,

> I always think there's a reason why they aren't behaving. It might be because they want attention . . . it doesn't really matter if it's negative attention as long as it's attention. But there's usually a reason behind why they're misbehaving. Nines times out of ten there is.

Teachers felt they were there to 'Bring out the best in a child', and this entailed 'looking behind the behaviour . . . why a child is behaving like that'.

Viewing pupils' behaviour in this way not only fulfilled teachers' high professional ideals but also served to meet teachers' own personal needs and ideals. Teachers maintained that it was important, particularly with 'difficult' pupils, to find something that they could like about them. One teacher maintained, 'I couldn't teach them if I couldn't find something, some aspect of their personality that I could warm to.'

Initially, as we have seen, 'understanding' pupils in this way was often problematic for student teachers, particularly when they were having difficulty in establishing or maintaining their authority. Occasionally, understanding children's disruptive behaviour proved problematic even for experienced teachers. Where there were extreme difficulties, teachers maintained that these children 'were not run of the mill' or 'could not be "normal"'. One teacher recalled,

> I had a little one who was so disruptive . . . his language was . . . oh, disgusting and I knew his background and I knew his problems but you can't put up with that in the class, it's not fair on the other children . . . four-year-olds learning language like that . . . I had parents complaining about him every night. I knew educationally that I was there to socialise him. . . . There was nothing I could have done. I appealed to his better nature and he just called me disgusting things. I understood him but it didn't make any difference . . . he was schizophrenic.

CONCLUSION

In reality, achieving and maintaining a professional relationship with pupils is not easy, even for the experienced teacher. As the teachers in our study were only too ready to admit, there were times when the children 'got to them'. What our research highlighted for us was the fact that teachers *do* want to be liked – they do care about the children and care about the children's opinions of them as 'people' as well as 'teachers'. However, unlike many students, they know that they don't have to be 'nice'. Children *will* like them as long as they are a fair and effective teacher. One teacher spoke of this realisation, that came after a year of teaching, as being 'a great release'.

The importance of effective classroom control and management has been widely accepted. It is not just a separate strand of teachers' knowledge and skill, nor an end in itself. Rather, it is a means to an end and that end is effective pupil learning (Feiman-Nemser and Buchmann 1987). As such it is a prerequisite of effective teaching (Robertson 1989).

For student teachers, the importance of quickly establishing their authority cannot be minimised, for without this understanding, it is the pupils who will define both their own and the students' learning. But achieving classroom control cannot be achieved until students accept the need for and the implications of a 'professional relationship' that has the character we have tried to describe.

In order to establish and maintain effective classroom control, what student teachers have to do is therefore essentially 'personal'. They must learn how to balance their own personal and professional needs and interests alongside the children's individual and collective needs and interests. They must learn what is possible and what is appropriate, how to gain and how to 'use' their authority. Developing a professional relationship with the pupils therefore involves students in becoming a 'new' person – 'me-as-teacher'; learning to control their natural instinctive reactions and how to protect and satisfy their self-interests. It also demands that they gain actual and 'typificatory knowledge' of pupils, strategies, content and context. This is a momentous and on-going challenge and requires tremendous effort, adjustment and courage on the part of student teachers.

In the next chapter, we move on to consider another form of learning that could only be addressed by students once they had established effective classroom management and control. The focus of that learning concerned the devising and implementing of what teachers considered to be 'good ideas' for teaching.

Chapter 7

Learning about 'good ideas' for teaching

In our pilot study, we noted that many teachers, in both secondary and primary schools, referred to the need for students to have 'good ideas' for teaching. Indeed, teachers often maintained that initially, all that they expected from student teachers was 'plenty of enthusiasm and plenty of good ideas'. Just as teachers had maintained that classroom control was essentially to do with 'confidence', so they maintained that the ability to produce 'good ideas' was 'natural' and simply 'common sense' to those students who had the potential to become effective teachers.

From our preliminary studies, we were aware that the issues surrounding the 'content' of teaching, although of course relevant throughout a student's school experience, often did not become a central focus for student learning until later on in their course. We therefore felt that an exploration of this topic would provide a useful contrast with our work on classroom management and control reported in the last chapter. What experienced teachers 'knew' about 'good ideas' for teaching and therefore what students had to learn in this regard therefore became the second area for our detailed investigations.

The issue of the 'content' of teachers' activities was of particular interest to us for other reasons too. In recent years, there has, in the UK, been a growing body of opinion which highlights and berates primary teachers for their inadequacies in one aspect of their teaching – that is, what is seen as their lack of subject knowledge. Indeed, it has been a central concern of those close to the government (Alexander *et al.* 1992; Lawlor 1990; Bennett and Carre 1993) and others that primary teachers' subject knowledge is inadequate for effectively teaching the National Curriculum. Moreover, it has been argued (McNamara 1991) that 'promoting the importance of subject-matter is seen as a way to reform teacher training and foster the quality of learning in school'. As we indicated in Chapter 1, we would broadly agree with this interpretation of recent policy initiatives in the field of initial teacher education. Given the topicality of the issue, we were therefore keen to take the opportunity provided by our project to explore the content of primary teachers' activities for ourselves.

WHAT ARE 'GOOD IDEAS' FOR TEACHING?

By 'good ideas', it seems that the teachers in our study were referring to what Shulman (1986) has called 'pedagogical content knowledge'. This aspect of teachers' knowledge has been a central focus for a growing body of research in recent years (Shulman 1986; Wilson *et al.* 1987; McDiarmid *et al.* 1989; Ball and McDiarmid 1990). According to this research, pedagogical content knowledge is essentially built from two distinct forms of professional knowledge. One is teachers' knowledge of the subject they are trying to teach, and the other is their knowledge of children and how they best learn.

Subject knowledge

Following the work of Schwab (1978), there appears to be a general consensus among researchers that subject knowledge can be grouped under two broad headings – substantive knowledge and syntactic knowledge. Substantive knowledge, according to these researchers, is knowledge of the subject – for example, facts, concepts, key ideas. Substantive knowledge also includes an understanding of how a particular body of knowledge is structured and organised. Syntactic knowledge, on the other hand, is knowledge *about* the subject; it involves an understanding of the way a particular body of knowledge is generated and validated. In science, for example, this would involve an understanding of the significance of scientific investigation, and in history, an understanding of the nature of historical enquiry.

McDiarmid *et al.* (1989) develop these views by arguing that teachers need to have a *flexible*, thoughtful and conceptual understanding of the subject area or discipline if they are to teach it effectively. By this they mean that teachers need to know about relationships between 'given phenomena' both inside and outside their field, how knowledge in the field is generated and validated, and fundamental ideas and relationships that underlie interpretations of particular phenomena (p. 198).

Shulman (1986) similarly maintains that teachers, 'must not only be capable of defining for students the accepted truths in a domain. They must also be able to explain why a particular proposition is deemed warranted, why it is worth knowing, and how it relates to other propositions, both within the discipline and without, both in theory and in practice' (p. 9). Moreover, it is argued that teachers may need to hold understandings about the 'nature' of a body of knowledge. For example, Sanders (1994) argues that teachers' beliefs about mathematics profoundly influence the way they teach.

Pedagogical content knowledge

Nevertheless, having a *personal* understanding of the substantive and syntactic knowledge of a subject area, although important, is not enough. Teachers, it is claimed, also need to find ways to transform and represent that knowledge in order to make it 'accessible' to the children in their class. McDiarmid *et al.* (1989) maintain that the teacher's role is to 'connect children to the communities of the disciplines' (p. 194) and that appropriate activities will 'emerge from a bifocal consideration of subject matter and pupils' (p. 194).

Subject knowledge for teaching – what Shulman (1986) terms 'pedagogical content knowledge' – therefore involves more than substantive and syntactic knowledge; it is also dependent on an understanding of children and how they best learn. Shulman maintains, therefore, that it includes 'an understanding of what makes the learning of specific topics easy or difficult: the conceptions and preconceptions that [pupils] of different ages and backgrounds bring with them' (p. 9).

Shulman describes pedagogical content knowledge as 'the most useful forms of representation of those ideas, the most powerful analogies, illustrations, examples, explanations and demonstrations – in a word, the ways of representing and formulating the subject that makes it comprehensible to others' (1986: 9). According to Shulman, there is no single, most powerful form of representation; teachers must have a wide range of ways of making knowledge available to pupils. Certainly, actual representations are not, at least initially, generalisable. As McDiarmid *et al.* (1989: 195) put it, 'Learning to represent subject matter in ways that will help pupils learn depends on the subject.'

McDiarmid *et al.* also suggest that teachers' instructional representations derive from two primary sources, 'one outside themselves and the other within' (1989: 196). What they mean by this statement is that teachers may refer to existing curricular materials, gain ideas from 'In-Service' courses or college lectures, even from what they did when they were at school – these are 'external'; they will also invent their own. Sometimes their own ideas are original and sometimes they will be a modification of another existing activity. But, as Wilson *et al.* (1987) emphasise, pedagogical content knowledge cannot be gained simply by copying 'a repertoire of multiple representations of the subject-matter'. Rather, it is built up through the process of pedagogical 'reasoning' – through planning, teaching, adapting instruction and reflecting on classroom experiences.

What our teachers referred to as 'good ideas' would therefore be characterised by these researchers as involving effective forms of pedagogical content knowledge; that is, accurate and effective ways of 'representing' knowledge to children. 'Good activities' for teaching are the 'realisation' of the dialogue teachers have held between their knowledge of children and children's learning and the subject knowledge they are trying to teach.

So much for what contemporary literature tells us about the structure of teachers' knowledge in this aspect of their work. In the sections that follow, we will use this framework to explore what the teachers and the students in our study understood by 'good ideas' for teaching; what they understood about how children learn, how activities could be structured to support pupil learning, as well as their substantive and syntactic subject knowledge.

TEACHERS' KNOWLEDGE OF PUPIL LEARNING

The vast majority of the teachers in our study had clear if fragmentary ideas about how activities could be structured that supported and reflected their beliefs about how children best learn. While they were able to articulate these in a generalised sense – often in terms of a simplistic, child-centred notion of 'children learn best through first-hand experiences' – it was when talking about specific activities that the richness of their thinking was most apparent. Moreover, it was often through talking about what they saw as the 'inappropriateness' of their students' activities that their views became particularly clear.

Several key issues emerged and could be drawn together from teachers' descriptions. However, it should be noted that teachers stressed that what they were referring to were what they saw as their 'best' activities; they maintained that they were not able to incorporate all of these understandings into all of their everyday teaching. Rather, these were seen as their ideals, their guiding principles for 'effective' teaching.

A search for meaning

What seemed to underlie teachers' descriptions was that the best teaching centred on 'creating meaning' – helping children to 'make sense', conceptually to understand what it was they were being taught. Teachers therefore maintained the importance of initially exploring and understanding what children already knew about the idea or concept to be learned, in order to enable them to 'connect' the learning to the children's present understanding. One teacher commented, 'You have to make links to their own understanding, otherwise children won't feel it's meaningful.' Another teacher referred critically to her student's activity, maintaining, 'She had made no attempt to find out what they understood. She didn't understand that it's important to know what they know to start with.'

Teachers also maintained the importance of an appreciation of the way children view the world – the content should be 'something that they can relate to' and be 'within their interest level ... their world'. Further, 'It should be within their compass, something they feel confident with.' Several teachers referred to the fact that 'We're looking at things as adults, we really need to break back into how we felt as children'. Children, it was maintained, should also be able to see the purpose of the activity – they should consider that it was 'useful' to them. As one teacher commented, 'It is important we look at ... what they want to get out of it.'

In order that children felt connected to the work they were doing, teachers believed that their activities had to be 'open' enough so that children were able to contribute; 'there has to be a chance for the children to feel that there was something of them in the activity.' This did not mean that the children's interests defined the content of their learning – this would, anyway be impossible considering the demands of the National Curriculum; rather, it meant that the teachers were skilful at manipulating the situation to stimulate children's interest and desire to engage with the specified learning.

Striving to make learning meaningful for children also affected the way teachers viewed and used subject matter. Teachers regarded 'useful' knowledge as knowledge pupils could use to 'make sense of' their experiences. For example, early years teachers spoke of the need to start from the senses, because 'working from the senses gives the children something to hook the learning on to'. They were also aware of the importance of practical experiences, particularly for young children, in order for them to achieve real understanding. National Curriculum statements of attainment, therefore, were seen as an end point, an accumulation of understandings. Teachers would consider what lay beneath the concept to be taught and devise appropriate practical experiences for the children. Teachers maintained that giving the children information was useless on its own. Information was only seen as valuable when it was used as a way of articulating or labelling experiences in which the children had participated – when it helped children to represent and gain control of their understanding. Teaching children that, for example, bends in rivers are called 'meanders', was regarded, in itself, as 'useless learning'. It would only become useful when children had experienced and understood a great deal about rivers and the paths of rivers. It was then that the information would capture or develop their understanding of that experience. Similarly, a student's activity on two-dimensional shapes centring on teaching the children the *names* of the shapes was regarded as 'pointless' unless pupils already understood something about the attributes and *properties* of those shapes – for example, how many straight sides and corners they had, and whether they would roll.

As one teacher commented about one of her student's activities,

They now know a garment is made out of polyester. What does it mean to them? Why do you want six and seven year olds to know what is written on labels. I can't see it's any use to them. Just giving them labels when they don't know anything else about the fabrics isn't right – where does it go? They haven't got anywhere to put those understandings. I don't find information in isolation helps me, it just sits there.

Where teachers were dealing with concepts or ideas that children could *not* experience in a first-hand way, they maintained that they recognised the power of discussion. In addition, where the learning was 'abstract', teachers were careful to find analogies which would allow children to make sense of their new learning by relating it to a previous understanding. In these different ways, teachers strived to help children 'to see' to 'build up a better picture', often cognitively to visualise it. One teacher described this as 'bringing it to life'. Another teacher illustrated this point by referring to a lesson where she had been

talking about bees and insects seeing things in different ways – not as a bright colour necessarily, but in an ultra violet light there are actual lines channelling into the centre a bit like a runway. So the children could then associate an aeroplane landing with a bee. They can participate at their level in their own minds – they can be a part of it.

Another teacher described an activity with older junior children concerning punishment in Tudor times. This teacher had initiated a class discussion on what the children considered to be good and bad behaviour in order for them to clarify their understanding of these concepts. She then discussed with the children what was considered 'good' and 'bad' in terms of the law, and what happens to people if they commit a crime. This understanding was then related to crime and punishment in Tudor times. Afterwards, the teacher maintained that this activity had worked because,

The children can relate to it themselves as they had all had some kind of experience of being good and bad. In terms of good and bad there was no right answer, so the children were all able to contribute and could draw on their own experiences. The discussion stimulated ideas and encouraged the children to make choices . . . they were thinking for themselves . . . thinking about the consequences of actions. They were learning what is acceptable in different times and how society has changed.

Another teacher, talking about a similar activity maintained, 'They are thinking what they would do in a situation, so their learning is becoming personalised. If it's relevant or pertinent to yourself you're going to internalise it and store it better.'

Structuring activities

The initial stimulus for an activity or series of activities was seen as very important. What teachers saw as the 'best' activities were those which provided a challenge, a real problem, and it was through the process of solving the problem that the specified learning took place. Instead of the teacher defining the investigation, a situation would be contrived where the children would themselves be led to understand the need for the investigation; they would *want* to find out. Further, as in the activity concerning crime and punishment in Tudor times, the initial stimulus appeared to bring children's 'thinking' or understanding about the idea or concept to the level of conscious thought. Teachers commented, 'You have to stimulate that response,' 'You have to signal to the children what you are going to be looking at' and 'As a first activity, it's got to be "zappy".'

Teachers maintained there was a necessity to be clear and explicit about the actual purpose of the activity – exactly what it was you wanted the children to learn – and then define a small 'tight' focus. One teacher commented, 'It needs to be a small thing from which you get lots of different learning experiences or even the same learning experience in a different way.' The activity was then structured in a way that would support the specified learning – either in terms of feeding the children small bits of information as they were needed, or by technically supporting the learning – for example, by using a framework or providing a model. For instance, one teacher talked about a poetry writing activity where the children were given a structure to work from. This teacher maintained,

> These children have not got a great wealth of language, they need a model to work from. This way they didn't get tied down with thinking about rhyming words or format or structure . . . they could think about the language they wanted to use. All their effort was put into carefully selecting . . . choosing the appropriate words to put into the model.

The specified learning was also explored in depth through developing it or transferring it to different contexts; for example, using different senses, processes and skills and in different curriculum areas. One teacher commented that it was important that 'It can be extended, things come from it. It's important they move off onto other things.' Activities were often devised in which the children connected several pieces of learning – drawing them together for a new purpose. For example, in one activity that was observed, as part of their topic of 'food' early years children were asked to make a bag that would be suitable for carrying apples back from the shop. Through considering the strength of different materials, whether they needed to be waterproof, the shape and size of the bag, and also the actual construction and decoration of the bag, these children were being asked to utilise previously developed understandings within a new context and for a different purpose.

Ways of working

Teachers also felt, even within each activity, that the children themselves needed to 'use' and transform their learning. When they made this claim, teachers were not simply referring to some kind of unaided 'discovery' learning. Rather, they were referring to the fact that children need to be *active* in the learning process. They need to be given a certain amount of 'knowledge' or information but then 'need to react back'. One teacher, referring critically to her student's activity, maintained,

> Asking them to make a drawing of the dress and copy the label isn't an activity that enables children to learn – it's a copying activity. It doesn't feed into any of the systems – they aren't reinterpreting something they've found out. And at some level children need to reinterpret, whether it's drawing or talking about it or thinking internally. In order for anybody to learn, something comes in and connects to something and by coming out again in some form – writing, modelling, drawing, talking – you are reaffirming [that learning] to your brain.

Learning was therefore seen as an interactive process. Teachers constantly framed and re-framed pupils' 'learning', altering their approach or ways of working in response to the children's reactions in order to ensure understanding. As a consequence, teachers talked about the importance of being able to 'read' the children's responses. As one teacher explained,

> I must be picking up signals, asking or challenging the children to think somewhere else. When you're picking up those signs you must react to them. It comes back to knowing where their understanding is and the next bit they can go to and that interface is where the learning takes place. It's not linear . . . you have to keep sensing where the gaps are and how far the jumps can be.

This dimension of teaching rested on what, on the surface, appeared to be a contradiction; activities, teachers maintained, had to be 'open' to allow children to make their own connections, yet at the same time they had to be tightly structured. One teacher explained that, while she was always sure of the destination she wanted the children to arrive at, and would guide, support and structure children's learning, ultimately, she asserted, the children must be allowed to 'take their own route'. She therefore maintained, 'Partly it's a matter of believing in children and if they 'meander' they will come round in their own way.'

However, teaching of this sort (teaching for meaning) takes time. Teachers, particularly those whose pupils were at the stage of having to undertake government Standard Assessment Tests, maintained that their teaching had been affected by pressure to cover National Curriculum attainment targets. One teacher commented, 'We did translation and rotation in two days . . . that was it. I think it's appalling, but I was running out of time.'

Teaching for meaning may also necessitate (as with classroom control) controlling what appears to be a 'natural' reaction to simply 'tell' the children. Striving to create meaning for children is likely to place considerable demands and frustrations even on experienced teachers. Some teachers may never totally develop these understandings; others may understand, yet through pressures of time or self-interest choose not to implement them. One student teacher commented in this respect that, 'I fear when I am teaching that I might just think of nice activities – it's so much easier and comes much more naturally.'

At one level, therefore, the teachers' understandings of how children learn were therefore essentially centred on a neo-Vygotskian idea of 'scaffolding'. Yet to characterise their strategies in this way underestimates the richness, complexity and sophistication of their thinking. Moreover, while it could be argued that these teachers' views essentially reflect a contemporary view which sees cognition situated within both the physical context and the social context (Butterworth 1992), it would be impossible to ascertain whether their understandings were derived from the adoption and adaptation of particular learning theories, or whether they arose primarily from teachers' own experiences. Either way, this 'knowledge' is likely to have been filtered through teachers' own attitudes and beliefs and influenced by their understandings of the child-centred 'culture' inherent in the primary school.

The child-centred culture of primary schools

The influence of the child-centred culture was particularly apparent in teachers' comments about the attitudes and values they wanted to engender in children. Teachers maintained the importance of developing certain processes and skills (for example, problem-solving and social skills) and of developing positive attitudes – confidence, self-esteem and enthusiasm for learning. For example, several teachers commented that, 'children need to feel good about what they're doing'. One teacher maintained that, 'I enjoy things. I think knowing about things is exciting and I want to share my excitement and wonder of the world with the children.' Another said, 'I'd want to show just how intricate one little plant is and compare it back with human beings. I want them to know what the parts do but it's *more* than that . . . it's the wonder of life.' This teacher went on,

> The most important part of teaching is to make children want to do things on their own afterwards. As teachers, as well as facts and figures we want to develop a desire to learn. . . . If you can develop a desire to learn, that's so much better than trying to push things in.

There was also an emphasis – often seemingly rooted in deeply held beliefs – on the importance of developing children's independence as learners. Activities, teachers believed, should encourage children to 'make choices', 'think for themselves' and think logically. One teacher maintained, 'I want to give them the tools so they can go out and find out for themselves without having someone show them how to do it.' Another explained,

There are things I still try to do . . . despite the National Curriculum. Things like independence and co-operation and ways of finding out things they don't know – all those basics. They need to read and write and all those sort of things, but as an adult once you've got those skills . . . they need to be in charge of whatever they learn. That's what I think I need as an adult.

Teachers also maintained they sought to teach the 'whole child' – they did not consider children's learning as only taking place within the classroom but took account of their learning outside school and aimed to give them understandings they could adapt and use in their everyday lives. One teacher commented that, 'If they've been interested, they can transfer that knowledge to other things they see.'

Therefore, while teachers were – to use McDiarmid *et al.*'s (1989) phrase – attempting to 'connect children to the communities of the disciplines', it was the children and not the subject knowledge that was their primary focus. Moreover, it also appeared that many primary teachers did not see children's *intellectual* learning as their sole, or even arguably their main concern, but considered other aspects – for example, the children's emotional, social and moral development – to be of paramount importance. Interestingly, these particular understandings that were implicit in teachers' conceptions of what constituted 'good ideas' for teaching were not specifically addressed by any of the teachers in their student 'debriefings'; they were merely 'inferred', as if these values were *already* understood and accepted by students.

From our analysis of teachers' accounts of their teaching, it became apparent that their child-centred beliefs did not represent a single strand of their thinking; rather, they had profoundly influenced both 'how' and 'what' they taught. We would assert that for primary school teachers, how they see and use subject matter knowledge is framed or filtered by their understanding of children and how they best learn. It is from *this* perspective that, for example, judgements are made about the 'usefulness' and 'value' of aspects of subject matter. 'Good activities', according to the teachers in our study, were not therefore constructed from what McDiarmid *et al.* (1989) describe as a 'bifocal consideration of subject-matter and pupils'. Rather, it seems, subject matter was viewed through the 'lens' of child-centred values.

As our research was primarily focused on the process of students learning to teach, we were not able to ascertain how far individual teachers did actually incorporate what they said about pupils' learning into their day-to-day practice. Although it would have been interesting to explore how teachers used these understandings in their own teaching, this was beyond the scope of this present study. What could be ascertained was that, in general, although held with different degrees of conviction, these were the principal criteria by which teachers judged the value of their students' activities; they therefore reflected the understandings they wanted students to gain.

STUDENTS' KNOWLEDGE OF PUPIL LEARNING

The majority of our student teachers found it difficult – even when talking about specific activities – to articulate what they believed or what they understood about how children 'best' learn and how to structure activities to support children's learning. As one student explained, 'It's very hard to put into words. I don't think about it consciously.'

Students' understandings of how children learn, while broadly reflecting the same aspects as those of the teachers, were tentative, stilted and often contradictory. It was also apparent that those student teachers who had maintained an underlying belief in the teacher as facilitator of children's learning were more 'open' to developing this understanding than those who held more 'traditional' beliefs about the nature of teaching and learning.

Making connections?

Initially, as we have stated, students appeared to have very simplistic views about pupil learning, and their role as a teacher in the learning process. In marked contrast to the sophistication of teachers' views, students often regarded teaching as 'telling', and learning as 'remembering'. One student commented how she had initially thought, 'Teachers – they teach English, maths and geography – they just get on and do it.' Similarly, another student said, 'I thought teaching was about standing at the front because that's what I remembered.' A third acknowledged, 'I'm doing pollution, so I'll look it up in all these books and now I'm an expert on it, so I'm going to tell you . . . it's definitely there!' Moreover, students initially appeared to find it difficult to focus on what the children were 'learning' as opposed to what the children were 'doing'.

Interestingly, we noted that both teachers and students constantly referred to their knowledge of children's learning in terms of their personal beliefs about how they learn. As we have indicated, students often interpreted this process as being 'told' and asked to 'remember'. For example, one student said, 'Telling is most natural because that's what you've experienced – Mum telling you things you didn't know . . . and that's how my learning was at school.' Teachers similarly referred to gaining understandings from their own experiences; for example, one teacher said, 'I've looked at the way I learn best' and 'That's the way I learned so that's the way I think others learn.' Teachers, however, held different and much more complex understandings about their own learning – they appeared to be able to see their own learning in more complex ways.

One consequence of students' inadequate understandings was that they initially did not appear to take account of pupils' prior knowledge or understandings. However, by the end of the second period of school experience, most students had made progress in this regard and had started to think in general terms about what the children already knew. For some student teachers this was linked to a developing appreciation of the need to differentiate, and to the relevance of well-matched subject matter in achieving classroom control. As one student teacher stated, 'If I don't give them something that matches their ability they're up and off. You can see them thinking, "I can't do this – so I'm just not going to try."'

However, where students did try to evaluate pupils' prior knowledge, this was often through simple 'tests' or questioning. Requests for student teachers to 'find out what the children already *know*' might therefore better be worded 'find out what the children *think* and how they "*make sense*" of this'.

Only a few students talked of the importance of 'giving children knowledge that they could adapt outside school' and of understanding children's 'culture' and 'perspectives'. One student maintained she tried to 'draw on something the children had done – to make it relevant so the children can relate to it'.

Because they did not appreciate the need to create meaning, students initially did not appear to recognise the differences in their own and the children's ways of seeing. They therefore

attempted to impose their own structures or ways of understanding on the children, and side-stepped the experiences that
were underlying a concept. For example, pupils were taught (that
is, 'told') about the water cycle, without any knowledge of their
present understanding or without any actual experience of water
in the environment. Drawing a diagram of water moving from
mountain to sea might have made sense to the student teacher,
but copying this diagram from the blackboard did not appear to
help the pupils achieve much in the way of understanding.

Similarly, students appeared unable to break down a concept
in appropriate ways; they did not initially recognise the complex
understandings on which concepts are based. They were, unsurprisingly, unaware of how they 'came to know' – about simple
fractions, for example. One student commented that

> We see things as one over four – that's a quarter. We cut the pie
> into four and say that's quarters . . . but they don't know what
> quarters are. You write one over four and they say 'a half'.
> We've bypassed all of that – thinking it's simple. But it's not.

By the end of the second practice, however, another student was
able to comment, 'Now if you're building up a concept you've got to
think where one activity is going to get them by the end in order to
go on to another one, what knowledge they must master first.'

Another difference between students' and experienced
teachers' teaching was that analogies were not commonly used
by students as a way of helping the children make sense of their
learning. In classroom discussions, the development of ideas often
appeared, from the children's perspective, to be unconnected;
there was no attempt to provide a structure or overall plan in
order to help the children cognitively to represent their thinking.

Moreover, whereas teachers were careful to contextualise pupils'
learning and tried to provide a real or valid purpose, students
tended to isolate and decontextualise learning. For example, if
teachers had wanted the children to learn how to write a letter,
they would have contrived a situation where the children *needed*
to write to someone. By contrast, when two students delivered a
simple lesson where 'learning the correct layout of a letter' was
the given purpose, the procedure was 'learned' through copying
from the blackboard.

Even where students did claim to understand that 'children

learn best if they know it's going to be useful for them', they did not always interpret 'useful' in the same way as their teachers. For example, one student took the view that 'useful' meant helping the pupils to feel that they were 'really intelligent and brainy . . . doing something that they were going to be doing at the "Comp" [secondary school]'. Another student teacher reflected that,

> During my first teaching practice I thought the children can't know anything before [they come to school]. I'm now thinking more about what they are doing at home. You've got to think it's not all in the class and giving them knowledge they can adapt outside school is important.

Because they viewed teaching and learning in simplistic ways, students, at least initially, also tended to focus their teaching on conveying information. Having themselves learned about a topic, the inclination was for the students to tell the children everything they knew. For example, in one activity on 'teeth', a student talked to the children about different parts of teeth, different types of teeth, dental hygiene, dentists, food that is good and bad for your teeth, and the orthodontist!

Most students, therefore, at least in the early stages of their teaching, failed to appreciate the ways in which children come to accommodate new knowledge and the importance of helping them make 'connections' for themselves. But not all students lacked this understanding. One student in particular did seem to have what her teacher considered an 'appropriate', if tentative, understanding of 'useful' knowledge even in the early stages of the course. As this student argued,

> There's no point in just giving them facts – it's too abstract, it will just go. It's not personal to them. These facts are just things they might be able to quote. It's more important, in terms of history that they understand consequence and cause – the processes. What is the point of education? It isn't facts . . . sometimes it is knowledge . . . it isn't just skills. You're teaching them the skills through the knowledge.

Structuring activities

Most of the students developed an understanding of the need to be 'tight' in terms of the focus of each activity – to be clear in what it was they wanted the children to learn. One student teacher commented that this had stemmed from a realisation that, 'If you are very small in your purposes, the children are more likely to understand'. However, a few students had continuing difficulties with this. One student said that, whereas she could think of things for the children to 'do', she found it difficult to focus on the actual 'learning'. Her teacher maintained there tended to be 'a hundred things wrapped up in one activity rather than one idea and a hundred ways of doing it'.

While several students supported the view that, 'To learn something you've got to get them interested in it first – if you're not interested, you'll have no enthusiasm for learning', the importance teachers placed on motivating pupils and the effort they made in this respect in order to 'stimulate a response' was not always recognised by students. One student illustrated her understanding of motivation by her comment, 'This week the children have all been looking forward to Friday because they know they're going to be making bread and so the motivation is there, and by Friday they should be ready to have a go.'

Although none of the student teachers referred explicitly to the need to structure pupils' learning in the sense of supporting the specific concept or skill, there was an awareness that the technical demands of the activities they devised sometimes got in the way of actual learning. What was more readily articulated was the need to 'feed' instructions or information to pupils a bit at a time. 'The better lessons are the ones that are tightly structured – you give them a bit and then you give them a bit more.' As one student teacher maintained, 'The children feel more secure knowing they're going to come back to you for the next bit.'

Another difference in their understanding was that there was no reference made by students to 'using' or transferring the knowledge pupils had acquired to other contexts, although this did appear to be developing in some student teachers' practice. More commonly, student teachers simply gave pupils 'more of the same' – understanding, it appeared, would come after plenty of practice! However, this approach did at times lead to difficulties. As one student commented, 'With four and five year olds you can't keep on with the same thing – "Oh we're doing that again" – they'll get bored.'

Ways of working

Differences between students' and teachers' understandings also emerged in their ways of working. At times students were what teachers considered to be over prescriptive, while on other occasions they seemed to be *laissez-faire*. For example, students quickly learned that if they were to be effective, tasks to be learned had to be broken down into 'steps'. Yet, having broken them into steps, students seemed reluctant to 'let go' and allow the children to gain understanding in their own way. Several student teachers maintained, 'There has to be a connection between each step.' Another commented, 'I wouldn't let them move until I knew they'd got it.' This reflects Goodman's comment that to students,

> the existing curriculum and nature of instruction seemed natural. If one wanted to learn something, it would be 'just common sense' to break the knowledge up into discrete parts; drill individuals until they mastered these parts; and then test them to make sure they knew it.

> (1985: 37)

One teacher maintained that her student didn't trust the children to get out of it what she wanted them to and saw that the only way to learn was to follow 'a little concrete path'. This teacher maintained, 'As a new teacher you don't let go enough of the children. You take them each step at a time and you don't allow them to jump over the steps you've thought out.'

Over time, most of the students also came to recognise the importance of 'active learning' – although what they meant by this term varied considerably. Indeed, their changing interpretation of 'active learning' appeared to illustrate their development in terms of seeing and understanding in more complex and 'appropriate' ways. One student teacher, for example, saw active learning as important because, 'After you've been telling them, the children get bored and you have to let them get on with it'. More positively, another student commented, 'Instead of doing maths we do a maths investigation. It means more because it belongs to them.'

As stated, the notion of 'active' was open to wide interpretation. Several students interpreted 'active learning' as doing 'practical work' – particularly in maths. Indeed, for many students, it was

interpreted solely as being *physically* active: children were believed to be actively learning as long as they were, for example,
busy cutting and gluing. Student teachers needed to come to
understand that while practical experiences are often an important feature of active learning, what was essentially being referred
to was pupils' cognitive engagement with the specified learning.
As we have seen, this did not happen by chance but was dependent on teachers' professional knowledge and skill.

It is also unsurprising that students initially felt that 'active
learning' threatened their classroom control. One student teacher
referred critically to an activity she had devised earlier in her
practice. She maintained:

> The learning was 'water in the environment'. I thought of
> doing the water cycle. I thought 'How am I going to do this in
> a simplistic way?' I could have used a mountain of sand and
> water but they're so 'hyper' I couldn't do it. They would have
> just got really excitable – started messing around. It just isn't
> worth it. I wanted to show what happens to the water when it
> gets to the ground – stream, river, water, sea. They had to copy
> a diagram from the board. They had statements to cut out and
> put in the right place.

As with the teachers, the pressure (real or imagined) of time
seemed to be a factor in the activities they devised. One student
commented, 'I was telling them about pollution. I didn't do an
investigation as I had limited time so I gave them an information
sheet.' Another student referred critically to her activity, but
maintained, 'It was the quickest way of getting it done.' A third
said,

> The children were so busy sticking the labels on that they
> didn't read them. I think the knowledge got lost in the labels
> and the drawing and the colouring. I knew when I was doing
> it, it wasn't right . . . the actual concept got lost in the doing.

In her later activities, this student stated that she tried to ensure
that 'the experiment *enhances* the concept because it demonstrates
exactly what I'm trying to get over. The actual hands-on doing
means they'll remember it.'

For many students it was the influence of their beliefs about
teaching and learning that appeared to affect their interpretation
of what constitutes active learning. For those students who held

a strong view of teacher as 'expert' and 'transmitter of know-ledge', the idea of 'finding out', for example, was often interpreted solely as looking things up in books – supplanting the 'teacher as teller' with the 'book as teller'. Similarly, the terms 'finding out' and 'investigation' were often considered to be interchangeable. For example, one student describing her activity stated, 'In a scientific investigation, when they're looking things up in books. . . .'

One teacher said that her student teacher 'thinks she ought to investigate but doesn't know what investigation means. Although she knew she shouldn't tell them she wanted to, so she wrapped the activity up in a pseudo-investigation.' At the other extreme were student teachers who held what could be termed as crude 'Piagetian' views; they initially maintained that the teacher should not intervene at all. Active learning was seen as somehow 'natural', particularly for younger children: 'Children aren't designed to sit in rows and listen to someone spouting off facts to them.' Another student teacher described 'hands-on' experience as 'letting them come to their own conclusions before stepping in'. Further, 'You leave them with the task for five minutes to do themselves and then come back and see. And if they're not going anywhere you give them little bits of help along the way.' However, the student teachers themselves usually realised that this approach was not always effective! One student teacher admitted that while she had initially worried about telling them too much, she was now aware that she was not giving them *enough* instruction or explan-ation and the children could sometimes get confused.

Attitudes and values

As we indicated in the last section, teachers aimed to do more than just focus on children's cognitive learning; they had 'other agendas' which also placed considerable emphasis on the non-cognitive aspects of teaching. For example, they took for granted that 'good ideas' for teaching should support social and emo-tional development as well as promote a positive attitude to learning. By contrast, only one of the eleven student teachers in our study referred specifically to the importance of additional aims. This student maintained that she was not only giving the pupils knowledge but also 'facilitating a way of thinking'.

However, although such attitudes and values were not widely articulated, they were generally apparent in students' practice.

However, the key difference between students and teachers in this regard was that the main 'other agenda' for students was, at least initially, their own survival. As we indicated in Chapter 5, in the early stages of learning to teach, students tended either not to take responsibility for children's learning at all or, if they did, they were too dominating and dictatorial in their approach. (This parallels their approach to classroom control and management.) In essence they were 'teaching for survival' rather than 'teaching for learning'.

In summary, we can say, students activities tended to be abstract, de-contextualised, fragmented, isolated and discrete. Student teachers' understandings and their practice was initially simplistic, inflexible and lacked sophistication – not only did they need to gain appropriate understandings about teaching and learning, they also needed to learn to relinquish or at least visibly 'soften' their power and control and integrate their developing knowledge and skill into a fluent performance.

Teachers' subject knowledge

When discussing 'good' activities, teachers were much more reluctant to talk about their subject knowledge than they had been to discuss their understanding of how children learn. While this reticence may, in part, reflect primary teachers' (particularly early years teachers') opposition to being seen as teachers of 'subjects' rather than 'children', in many cases it may also have reflected teachers' insecurities about their subject knowledge.

Each subject area within the curriculum (and in Wales there are ten subject areas in the National Curriculum at the primary age phase) presents teachers with its own challenges in terms of understanding and representing the substantive and syntactic knowledge and structures. Moreover, within any one curriculum area, some issues may be easier for teachers to represent and to connect to the 'real world' than others.

In conducting our research into teachers' subject knowledge, we were therefore faced with a number of problems. The breadth and complexity of subject knowledge implied by the National Curriculum meant that it was not possible to draw *generalised* understandings about teachers' subject knowledge in the way we had been able to do in relation to teachers' knowledge of how children learn. Moreover, a detailed study of teachers' knowledge of every individual subject area within the National Curriculum was simply too big a task to be undertaken in the current project. A further difficulty was that, in discussions with teachers, it was not always easy to disentangle whether their understandings arose from an appreciation of the syntactic structures of a subject area or from their understandings of how children learn best. In many cases both forms of understanding pointed in the same direction, indicating a need for enquiry or investigation.

What could be ascertained from our research, however, was that knowledge *of* the subject area – that is, substantive knowledge – appeared to be the aspect that the teachers in our study considered to be the most problematic. This may have been, in part, that their difficulties with substantive knowledge were more 'visible' to them: teachers were more likely to be aware of their difficulties with understanding a concept they were having to teach than of their lack of understanding of, for example, the 'nature' of the knowledge of a particular subject area, however profoundly this aspect might affect their teaching (Sanders 1994).

To expect primary teachers to have a 'flexible and thorough' knowledge of every curriculum area they are supposed to teach does perhaps seem unrealistic. Whether it is realistic or not, we came to recognise that lack of subject knowledge had a fundamental effect on both what and how they taught. In the sections that follow, we discuss what we discovered about their subject knowledge in a number of key areas of the curriculum.

Knowledge of mathematics

Our teachers' difficulties with substantive knowledge were particularly apparent to them in the area of mathematics and, for upper primary teachers, also in science. One teacher, for example, admitted, 'My own mathematical ability is rather dubious. I feel far less confident of really getting to grips with something like fractions because I'm not really so sure of what it is.'

Within mathematics, teachers appeared to be more reliant on using published schemes than in their teaching of many other areas of the curriculum. When schemes or workbooks were not used, although teachers were careful to contextualise their teaching, to make it as 'connected' and as meaningful as possible for the children, this seemed to us to be derived from their knowledge of children and how they learn best rather than from a deep understanding of the subject matter itself. Teachers admitted they were not always able to make connections between related concepts and ideas both within and outside the curriculum area and, with some aspects of mathematics, with real world understanding. This observation supports research by Hashweh (1987), who found that knowledgeable teachers used more representations that related a specific topic to other topics within the discipline. Student teachers' activities appeared, on occasions, to have been evaluated by teachers on how appropriate, useful and meaningful the representations were to pupils in their terms, rather than on how far they supported pupils' developing understanding of that subject area.

Of course, mathematics may present unique difficulties in this regard. As McNamara (1991) maintains, fractions, for example, are *already* a form of symbolic representation and school mathematics may entail 'learning how to *use* representations, possibly without the deeper understanding which mathematicians may argue pupils ought to acquire' (p. 122). Further, McNamara cites Desforges and Cockburn who maintain that 'pupils may gain a sudden grasp of a difficult mathematical concept after having been engaged in procedural tasks for some time' (1987: 121). The implications of this belief are problematic. Does this mean teachers do not *need* a deeper understanding of mathematics? Could it be, as McN amara suggests, that procedural knowledge actually *precedes* understanding in terms of some mathematical concepts and possibly of conceptual understanding in other sub- ject areas?

Knowledge of science

In line with their beliefs about 'experiential learning', early years teachers, in the area of science, appeared to be almost solely concerned with investigations. Their central focus was not on developing a conceptual understanding, but on the scientific process – they were essentially facilitating 'a way of thinking'. Teachers' questions therefore centred on and went no further than, 'What do you think will happen if . . .?' This was particularly apparent when the concepts being dealt with were difficult to represent in that they were complex, abstract or 'invisible' – teachers mentioned, for example, dissolving, and sinking and floating.

However, it was unclear how far this approach rested on teachers' beliefs that children would not be capable of understanding a more complex explanation or whether teachers' lack of knowledge meant that they were unable to find appropriate ways of making this knowledge accessible to pupils. One teacher maintained,

> With a lot of things you are laying foundations. With a lot of early science you are just giving them the experience of, for example, things that do sink and float. Certainly I feel with science and maths, what is important is that I don't tell them anything that is actually wrong. Even if we know, it doesn't make it accessible to six year olds because those understandings just aren't accessible.

Teachers held that where a concept was problematic to represent, giving a partial truth was acceptable – 'as long as you did not tell the children something that was actually incorrect'. Where children did ask questions that teachers found difficult to answer, one teacher said, 'I ask them a lot of questions. I get round it by throwing it back at them. If they ask me 'Why?' I ask them what they think.'

Upper primary teachers appeared to feel that they should try and find ways of answering the children's 'Why's?' – and said that they grappled with finding appropriate ways to explain and represent complex concepts. These teachers admitted that their problems often lay in their own lack of understanding. When asked 'difficult' questions by pupils, these teachers also maintained that they tended to ask the children to suggest their own hypotheses. Teachers, understandably, generally stated that 'I feel happiest with my teaching when I can answer those "whys" and most vulnerable when I am dealing with concepts that I don't understand'.

Art and technology

In subjects such as art and technology, some teachers admitted they 'lacked basic knowledge of what the subject was about'. One teacher recognised, 'If children said 'What do I need to do with this?' I don't know. I could present them with the experience, the materials and a place in which to do it. You need a thorough knowledge of the curriculum to produce good ideas.' Another teacher commented that in areas where she felt particularly confident she could take into account the children's stage of development – but, as with the previous teacher, if she felt she could not assess the children's ability, in that she didn't understand the criteria on which to assess their understanding, she would just provide 'an experience'. This teacher maintained that for these subject areas 'If you get a good response, then it's a good activity'.

As subject areas have their own body of knowledge, key ideas, 'ways of thinking' and challenges and difficulties, it would be foolish for us to attempt to draw generalisations from teachers' difficulties in any one subject area. However, from our investigations, it appeared that in many cases it was teachers' knowledge of children's learning that was most significant in their construction of 'good ideas' for teaching. Their confidence in understanding how children best learn helped to 'shore up' their insecurities in terms of subject knowledge.

STUDENT TEACHERS' SUBJECT KNOWLEDGE

I think it comes down to confidence. If you can stand at the front of the class and look as if you know what you are talking about, there aren't that many things they can ask you that you don't know something about yourself.

Initially, as the quotation above indicates, many student teachers felt that subject-matter understanding was unproblematic. This was because they appeared to lack any understanding of what was involved in having a thorough and flexible understanding of subject matter. From their point of view, knowledge in teaching did not have to be 'represented' – it was merely 'delivered'.

Interestingly, several themes, noted in our discussion of students' understanding of children's learning, were also present in their subject-matter understanding. These similarities often emerged from and reflected student teachers' simplistic beliefs about the nature of teaching and learning. For example, comments such as 'Content knowledge is the easiest because we're intelligent enough to find that out for ourselves . . . we've all got degrees',

and 'I've got to read up about ———— because that's the bit I'm
going to teach next' were again representative of the view that
teaching was primarily about 'telling' and 'conveying information'. Students also maintained, 'I am quite surprised at how
confident I feel in teaching something I know nothing about
beforehand . . . but then the level of knowledge you need isn't
that great anyway.'

Syntactic and substantive knowledge

Given their general naïvety about the nature of subject-matter
knowledge in teaching, it was perhaps unsurprising that students
often appeared to have difficulty in using the underlying processes (the syntactic structures) of a subject area in their teaching.
The fact that addressing these seriously often demanded the need
for enquiry or investigation – a strategy that students shied away
from – made them a particular problem. One teacher commented
on her student's teaching as follows: 'She's looked at the National
Curriculum "Statement of Attainment" and gone . . . "oh yes". It
was a science activity – but where are the underlying things about
science?' Where students did acknowledge these syntactic structures, there was a tendency to see these underlying processes not
as something that indicated a way of teaching but as something
separate from substantive knowledge. One student teacher commented that she was not worried about processes because, 'You
could always stick in another lesson to cover the skills'. Another
student commented, 'Some lessons I concentrate on skills, others
more on knowledge.'

Lack of substantive subject knowledge – in particular, a clear
and thorough understanding either of the concept to be taught, or
how it linked to other related concepts and to real world understanding – was also often apparent. Although, to an extent, this
was also true of the teachers in our study, with student teachers
it was far more obvious. This may have been because students
could not compensate for or conceal their lack of subject knowledge by drawing on an understanding of how children best
learn. Whatever the reason, their weaknesses were real enough.
As one student commented about her lack of substantive knowledge in Maths, 'I can't connect mathematical concepts . . . that's
because I don't know . . . I only got my O level a few years ago.'
Another said, 'I've got to understand it completely before I teach

it and how to explain it in children's terms. Some of the concepts are hard enough to understand as an adult . . . let alone as a child.'

Teaching 'tricks'

Because they lacked adequate subject-matter knowledge, and because they had simplistic notions about the nature of teaching and learning, students' teaching activities often seemed to be no more than 'empty procedural tricks' – where 'getting the right answer' rather than 'achieving understanding' appeared to be the sole aim. This was particularly the case in science and mathematics. For example, procedures in mathematics (such as length × breadth = area) and patterns (if you are multiplying by ten an easy way is to add a zero) were taught directly to the children as recipes, rather than by devising a situation where these could be 'discovered' and understood. As one student admitted:

> When I was teaching them 'tens and units' they had a series of questions and it was how many tens and how many units make the number. The top ability understood it – but lower down the only reason they got it right was because it says, for example four and four. So that's like knowing the trick of it but not understanding it.

Engaging with pupil learning

For many student teachers, an understanding of the complexity of subject knowledge was only beginning to emerge at the end of their final block of school experience. Certainly, for the student teachers in our study, it appeared that the development of an understanding of how children learn preceded or was a pre-requisite to an understanding of the need to develop a flexible and thorough subject knowledge. It was not until they had engaged with the complexities of children's learning that their lack of subject-matter understanding became apparent to them. This was perhaps because 'telling' pupils something is less demanding in terms of one's understanding of subject-matter knowledge than trying to 'elicit understanding'. It was often not until students really had to explain something to the children that they became aware of their lack of understanding. For example, one student maintained, 'I've often found when I'm doing a lesson

and I come to explain it, I think "I don't understand this" . . .
especially with maths!' Another student commented at the end of
her final teaching experience that 'You need a really thorough
subject knowledge and I don't feel I have that really.'

Having gained this understanding, the demands of 'representing' knowledge to elicit pupil learning appeared, at times, to
be almost overwhelming. One student teacher commented, 'I've
always struggled with maths and I realise I wasn't taught properly . . . and I want to teach kids properly, how to do stuff like tens
and units. But I haven't looked into how I'm going to do that yet.'
Similarly, another student said,

> Sometimes the content of what I want to teach them . . . in
> maths is especially challenging. I don't know where to start
> and they're all at different stages. I need to learn about how to
> explain it, instead of a child approaching me with a book and
> me thinking . . . 'Oh no!' . . . I don't want to say something that
> will upset their concept of tens and units for the rest of their
> lives.

Another student stated,

> With maths I don't feel I have any idea of what to do when
> they're young, and when they get older, I don't know what is
> appropriate. It's about breaking the concept down . . . where
> you start and what are the stages you go through.

On a different occasion, another student commented,

> I think representing the knowledge is the hardest thing. How
> am I to teach pollution and make it really relevant so they can
> see first hand instead of just throwing them information? . . .
> Here you just write about it . . . absorb it . . . and expect it to go
> in. Trying to think of something that really represents what I
> want them to learn is really hard . . . and I really don't like
> worksheets – 'This is it . . . I've done it all for you, you fill in the
> blanks'. It's just comprehension – it's not science, it's not geo-
> graphy. What is difficult is bringing it down to their level.
> When you're simplifying it, you're not telling them something
> that is actually wrong. I found that with photosynthesis. I said
> light helps make food – but it's not only light, it's also chloro-
> phyll and water.

Given all these difficulties, it is perhaps unsurprising that even at the end of their second teaching practice, students still relied heavily on the 'ready-made' representations they had learned as part of their college studies or remembered being taught when they were at school. Students maintained that 'in order to generate "good ideas" I need a thorough knowledge of the subject matter, of the resources available, the capabilities of the children, knowledge of what they've done before and "general knowledge" about children'.

While students recognised that their demand for ready-made 'good ideas' were just 'short cuts' – easy solutions – they maintained that on the one-year PGCE, at least, 'You just don't have the time to think'. One student commented, 'I just want to get a stock of nice little things to do. I think I could probably think of things . . . it's just not having the time.'

CONCLUSION

As a result of our investigation we developed a view of teachers' pedagogical knowledge that was somewhat different from that put forward by Shulman (1986), McDiarmid et al. (1989) and others. McDiarmid et al., in particular, describe teachers' pedagogical strategies – their 'good ideas' for teaching – as being formed through a 'bifocal' concern with how children learn and subject-matter knowledge. Our research would suggest something rather different. To follow the analogy of McDiarmid et al., we found that the teachers in our study almost always looked at the content of subject knowledge through the 'lens' of how children learn. It was in this area of their work that they felt themselves most comfortable; it was here that they would claim to be experts.

We also became aware, though we did not have the resources to investigate the issue fully, that in constructing their pedagogical strategies, teachers took into account other dimensions as well; a 'good idea' for teaching was not only forged from content knowledge and an understanding of children's learning. The teachers in our study were not only concerned with the intellectual development of their pupils; they also wanted to promote their moral, social and emotional development and to establish positive attitudes towards learning. In many cases, these dimensions of teaching were just as important to teachers in constructing pedagogical strategies as more cognitive issues. To give a concrete example, whether or not the 'best' way to teach a particular topic involved the use of, say, group work, teachers would on occasions justify the use of such a strategy because of its value in promoting social development. Similarly, teachers would struggle hard to find exciting and interesting ways to introduce new topics not merely as a strategy for teaching that topic but also as a way of stimulating among their pupils a sense of commitment to learning itself. It became clear to us that these 'non-cognitive' dimensions of teachers' pedagogical strategies were vitally important to them in constructing 'good ideas' for teaching. It may be that their neglect in contemporary research on teachers' pedagogical thinking has contributed to an overemphasis on the importance of subject knowledge in current policy debates on primary teaching. The nature and importance of these aspects of pedagogy are therefore in urgent need of further research.

Students, as we have seen, initially had inappropriate notions of how children learn and of what is involved in subject-matter knowledge. By 'inappropriate', of course, we mean inappropriate for contemporary British primary schools, for both the teachers' and the tutors' judgements of what was appropriate in this area were clearly value judgements. Views about how children best learn and therefore what sorts of understandings of subject-matter knowledge a teacher must have, are clearly not absolutes. Indeed, we came to the conclusion that although the interventions of tutors and teachers were extremely important in supporting students, it was the child-centred values of the primary school that were the greatest 'educator' of our students in relation to their pedagogical understandings. Once they had recognised and become committed to a child-centred approach to teaching and learning, they began to question for themselves their understanding of how children learn and began to recognise their own inadequacies in relation to subject-matter knowledge. Such an observation raises important questions for those close to the government (O'Hear 1988; Lawlor 1990), who have seen the development of school-based forms of teacher education as a means of suppressing 'child-centred' and 'progressive' forms of teaching in primary schools. As Cortazzi (1991) comments, 'Attempts to reform the curriculum and to effect other changes in education without considering teachers' culture (their perceptions, knowledge, attitudes, beliefs, and so on) may well founder' (p. 134).

Finally, we must comment on the fact that our study revealed that in many key areas of their work, both teachers and students felt insecure about their subject-matter knowledge. A number of points need to be made here. The teachers in our study, like all primary teachers in Britain today, faced a serious dilemma – how to teach all ten National Curriculum subjects effectively. Our teachers' solution to this dilemma was, as we have noted, to see subject-matter knowledge through the 'lens' of how children learn. And to a significant degree, this strategy, together with the use of 'ready made' teaching schemes, did allow them to 'get by' even in areas where they were insecure in their subject-matter knowledge. We became acutely sympathetic to the demands made by the National Curriculum on contemporary primary school teachers and would question whether it is realistic for *any* primary school teacher to have a thorough and flexible understanding of all aspects of all ten National Curriculum subjects. In the circumstances, therefore, it seems appropriate that primary school teachers should, first and foremost, become 'experts' in children's learning rather than in the subjects they teach. Current policy pronouncement and initiatives that serve to undermine teachers' sense of their own expertise could therefore be extremely counter-productive.

Having said that, however, our research in this area also taught us to question the frequently heard slogan, 'We teach children not subjects'. This belief (which many of our teachers explicitly supported) runs away from the reality of the importance of engaging with subject-matter knowledge. Although the teachers in our study were reluctant to talk about their subject-matter knowledge, both they and their students were clearly more confident and simply better at their job when they were teaching in an area where they had a full and flexible understanding of the substantive and syntactic structure of the subjects they were teaching. Indeed, we would suggest that if primary school teachers had better developed subject-matter knowledge in key areas of the curriculum, they would be more likely to be able to achieve their child-centred ambition of 'empowering' pupils. As Ball and McDiarmid (1990) maintain, 'A conceptual mastery of subject matter and the capacity to be critical of knowledge itself can empower [pupils] to be effective actors in their environment' (p. 438). They go on: pupils need to be able to, 'use intellectual ideas and skills as tools to gain control over everyday, real-world problems' (1990: 438). Teachers and others who deny the significance of well-founded subject-matter knowledge as a basis for good teaching are, we would suggest, being disingenuous, but the implications of this observation for initial teacher education are significant.

The conceptual level at which primary teachers need to *understand* subject matter in order to *teach* it effectively, appears to remain a debatable issue (see Kruger and Summers 1988). However, the type of questions that teachers ask, and the activities they devise for their pupils, are clearly likely to be affected by the depth of their understanding. As Kruger and Summers (1988) state: 'it is difficult to see how a teacher can give children experiences to guide them along a line of conceptual development unless the teacher knows what lies at the end' (p. 264). Similarly, effective analogies, a fundamental tool used by teachers in order to create meaning, not only rely on an understanding of children and children's learning but *also* on a thorough knowledge of the concept they are trying to represent. While primary school student teachers therefore ideally need a solid subject base in all areas of the curriculum, this is clearly unrealistic; developing appropriate forms of initial teacher education is therefore an extremely challenging task.

Is the answer, as the latest government circular on primary initial teacher education suggests (DFE 1993a), the introduction of specialist teachers in the upper primary school? On the whole we would think not. For the foreseeable future, the staffing structures of primary schools will remain built around the generalist class teacher. To produce a small number of specialist teachers does little to solve the dilemma for the majority. Moreover, we found no evidence to support the idea that a detailed and thorough subject knowledge is only necessary for teaching older pupils! Early years teachers, who have the responsibility of laying key foundations of children's understandings right across the curriculum, need just as thorough and flexible an understanding of what they are teaching as any other teachers.

Another current policy initiative designed to strengthen students' subject-matter knowledge is the introduction of the 'three-year, six-subject' B.Ed. degree. Instead of studying one or two subjects to degree level, prospective primary teachers will study six subjects to a lower level. Although there are clearly important negative implications for the teaching profession of lowering the academic status of the BEd degree, such a proposal, we would suggest, offers little prospect of solving the dilemma of how to increase student teachers' subject knowledge. Understanding the substantive and syntactic structures of subject knowledge is an advanced skill; it demands a depth of understanding that seems unlikely to be achieved by adults who have not themselves had the opportunity to study at least one subject to an advanced level. Moreover, as our study has demonstrated, much of the understanding of what is involved in developing a thorough and flexible subject knowledge comes through school-based learning. Academic learning, though clearly important, is not in itself sufficient. The idea of a six subject BEd would therefore seem to us to be a naïve response to primary school teachers' needs – a case of 'never mind the quality, feel the width!'

However, there are some aspects of current government policy that do seem to us to hold out some prospect for addressing the issue of students' subject-matter knowledge. These are the proposals that currently increase the amount of hours that must be spent in preparing students to teach the core subject of the National Curriculum – maths, science and English, and where appropriate Welsh. In the future, if course organisers are to provide the required number of hours in these subjects, then periods of school-based time will have to be specifically designated as relating to these subjects. This initiative recognises that school-based learning is an essential part of developing student teachers' subject-based understandings. Moreover, by prioritising three subjects, it recognises that, within a course of initial professional preparation, it is impossible to address all students' learning needs. Nevertheless, a sharper-focused experience in three areas will do much to lay the foundations for future professional development across the curriculum. If students leave their initial teacher education at least having recognised the importance of developing a thorough and flexible subject knowledge in the core areas of the curriculum, they will have achieved sufficient to go on developing. Induction and in-service education can then be targeted towards supporting newly qualified teachers' development in other areas of their teaching.

Chapter 8

Practical professional knowledge and student learning

The argument underlying our research has been that a fuller prescription for the role of the mentor will not be achieved until we have a more thorough understanding of the processes involved in learning to teach. Just like any form of teaching, mentoring, we have suggested, must be built on a clear understanding of the learning processes it is intended to support. Our purpose in investigating students' school-based learning has therefore been to shed more light on what the role of the mentor should be.

Any description of how students learn to teach must itself be based on an adequate conceptualisation of teachers' professional knowledge and the way that knowledge is used in the process of teaching. For example, is professional knowledge best conceived of as a series of competences and teaching as the technical following of rules (Jessup 1991)? Alternatively, is it a 'natural', common-sense process, based merely on personality and sound subject knowledge, as neo-conservative writers (Lawlor 1990 and O'Hear 1988) suggest? Yet again, is teaching a fundamentally 'moral' activity involving the exercise of complex judgements which can and should be brought to the level of consciousness (Carr and Kemmis 1986, Zeichner and Liston 1987)? In the next chapter, we argue that these different traditions of thought may indeed lead to the development of useful strategies in the training of student teachers. However, as conceptions of professional knowledge and of the process of teaching, we consider them inadequate. Hence our concern to research teachers' practical professional knowledge for ourselves.

The purpose of this chapter is to draw together what our own research indicates about the nature of teachers' practical professional knowledge – both in terms of its content (its different domains) and how that knowledge is used by teachers. We then go on to consider the processes through which students develop a body of practical professional knowledge for themselves. In this way, the chapter lays the foundations for the final chapter of the book, where we conclude our argument by presenting a model of mentoring that would support the learning processes we have identified.

THE NATURE OF TEACHERS' PRACTICAL PROFESSIONAL KNOWLEDGE

Knowledge domains

Carter (1990), in her review of research on teachers' practical professional knowledge, identifies three different approaches to work in this area: information-processing studies – generally focused on teachers' cognitive processes and decision-making; studies of teachers' practical knowledge – focused on teachers' knowledge of classroom situations and practical dilemmas; and studies of pedagogical content knowledge – focused on what teachers know about subject matter and how they 'translate' and 'represent' it to students in order to elicit pupil understanding. As we have made clear in the last three chapters, our research does not easily fall into any one of these categories, but cuts across and draws from all three.

In our work, we found it helpful to conceptualise teachers' knowledge as falling within four broad areas or domains: knowledge of pupils, knowledge of strategies, knowledge of content and knowledge of context (Maynard and Furlong 1993). For teachers, we would suggest that although each of these domains of knowledge are equally important, they are not experienced in the same way: 'pupils' and 'context' are, in a sense, given or fixed; they are what the teacher has to work with and within. By contrast, 'content' and 'strategies', while being inseparable, are experienced as being more mutable or open to choice.

But teachers' practice does not depend on knowledge drawn from a cluster of discrete domains; rather, it depends on the complex interaction and interplay between those domains. Effective practice, rather like a complex, three-dimensional jigsaw puzzle, is only achieved when all the pieces are in place, when there is a sense of 'balance'. The interdependency of these domains makes learning to teach particularly difficult.

It is also important to recognise that knowledge within each of the different domains is held at many different levels of abstraction. At the most specific level, teachers will have built up a great deal of concrete knowledge (a stock of experiences) on which they can draw in their teaching. These are experiences and knowledge of the actual children in their class, their abilities and interests, teaching strategies that are effective – what 'works' with this class, the children's achievements in different curriculum areas. They also hold a great deal of specific situational knowledge – knowledge of school policies on discipline, for example. But teachers will also hold another kind or 'level' of knowledge, for they develop concepts. Experience – that is, teaching experience – allows teachers to form concepts or schemas of the typical or likely (Berliner 1987). Teachers will, for example, know and be able to predict children's likely reactions and responses, know of strategies that are likely to work and ways of representing subject matter that are likely to elicit children's understanding. They will also know of the likely expectations of the head-teacher and of parents. Other writers have pointed to a similar process of concept development, though some describe the process in slightly different ways. Copeland (1981), for example, also describes teaching as involving the formation of 'concepts', while other writers talk of the formation of 'behavioural routines' (Leinhardt and Greeno 1986), 'schemas' (Berliner 1987) or 'scripts' (Shavelson 1986, cited in Berliner 1987). Each, we would suggest is, however, pointing in the same direction.

Knowledge *in* action

From our work with teachers, we became aware that whereas they were able to talk about some (but not all) aspects of the content of their knowledge – what they knew about pupils, contexts, lesson content and strategies – they found it much more difficult to talk about how they actually used that knowledge in their teaching.

From the various bodies of literature we reviewed, we concluded that Schön's (1983, 1987) work provided the best starting point for an understanding of how teachers use their practical professional knowledge in teaching. As we indicated in Chapter 3, for Schön, no two teaching situations are identical; they are always unique. Teaching, he believes, is a transactional process in that it involves teachers drawing on their existing stock of conrete experiences or concepts in order to 'frame' these unique teaching situations. It is through the process of 'framing' that the teacher enters into a 'dialogue' with the situation itself, achieving an understanding of it through attempting to change it. In other words, the teacher attempts to shape the situation but in conversation with it so that his or her own models and appreciations are also shaped by the situation. It is in this way that the 'phenomena that he seeks to understand are partly of his own making' (1983: 151). The teacher is actually *in* the situation that he or she is trying to understand.

As with other forms of practical expertise, experience allows teachers to put on a fluent performance – much of the normal, habitual, 'everyday' aspects of their practice and their thinking appear to become routinised and automatic. Their professional knowledge is *embedded* in skilful action. For experienced teachers, procedures like managing group work, asking appropriately pitched questions, diagnosing common learning difficulties, are undertaken with little conscious thought. Indeed, like Schön, we believe that it is only when there is some 'felt difficulty', when teachers' practice is in some way becoming noticeably out of balance, that they become consciously aware of what is happening. It is only when things go wrong that teachers find it necessary to bring the framing process to the level of consciousness in order to modify their practice or alter their intentions. However, while the routine of teaching may be carried on automatically, we would maintain that it is not, as Dewey (1910) seems to imply, thought-*less*. At some level teachers do remain constantly aware. Indeed, the teachers in our study maintained that in the classroom they could not, even for a minute, 'switch off'. As a result, they often referred to 'the sheer relentlessness' of their work.

As we reported in Chapter 5, students in our study who were new to teaching constantly complained that they could not 'see'; they found it difficult to disentangle the complexity of the classroom in ways that helped them understand the processes of teaching and learning that were going on. This, we would suggest, was because, at the beginning of their school experience, they had not built up an appropriate stock of experiences or concepts on which to draw in framing classroom situations. Without a body of practical professional knowledge it is indeed impossible to 'see'; it is impossible to engage in the process of 'framing'. Moreover, the teachers with whom they worked often found it difficult to articulate their 'taken-for-granted' practical professional knowledge. Even though, in their own professional training, teachers would have explicitly addressed the same basic issues that the students were now confronting, they often found it hard to recognise, let alone to put into words, the complex forms of professional knowledge that they used.

Perhaps because of the difficulties involved in articulating their knowledge, the teachers in our study often alluded to aspects of their knowledge-in-action in terms of gesture and metaphor (Munby 1986). One teacher, for example, tried to communicate his view of 'classroom control' through hand movements – student teachers' attempts at control he expressed by pressing one hand down flat on top of the other. However, what he maintained students needed to *learn* to do, he characterised by pressing down lightly on one hand with the fingertips of his other hand, bobbing gently up and down as they felt the 'mood' of the class. Another teacher maintained that to try and explain what she did in terms of classroom control she had told her student to *'wrap the children in her fingertips'*.

Why is teachers' knowledge-in-action so difficult to 'capture', to represent and to learn? From our own research and following Schön's work, we would suggest that there are a number of reasons. First, it is important to recognise that it is not only *teachers'* practical knowledge that is difficult accurately to represent in words. It would be equally difficult, for example, to explain *how much* pressure to put on the break pedal in order to bring the car safely to a halt, or to give a lecture on *how hard* or *when* to hit the tennis ball in order to achieve a perfect shot. Such knowledge must be 'felt', personally experienced. 'How much', 'how hard' or 'when to' would all depend on the unique circumstances of each particular situation. They also depend on the perspective, interests and ability of the 'driver' or 'player' as well as what counts as appropriate and 'acceptable' practice in each case; for example, what is understood by 'safely' or 'perfect'.

We would suggest that teachers' knowledge-in-action, is also, in part, 'felt' knowledge. The teachers in our study, for example, talked of knowing 'the *amount* to stimulate the children without getting the fidgety ones all over the place', 'giving the children *enough* room', 'knowing *when* the children need "a push" to keep them on task' and *'when* to pull the children back together again'. In each of these cases, 'how much' or 'when' would be dependent on particular and unique circumstances and on what, at that point, the teacher was trying to achieve. Because of their situational specificity, we would suggest that these understandings are very difficult to articulate; they *can* only be learned experientially.

Levels of sophistication in practical professional knowledge

Our research also made us aware of the fact that teachers' practical professional knowledge can be held at many different levels of sophistication; this observation is vitally important for understanding how students can learn. As we argued in Chapter 7, a 'bright idea', say, for teaching about life in Elizabethan Britain to year 5 pupils, may be understood at the level of a concrete recipe or routine – a strategy which students are capable of copying and implementing without fully appreciating why it takes the form that it does. Alternatively, the same lesson plan may be understood in rich and complex ways, drawing on a sophisticated appreciation of how children learn and a flexible understanding of the substantive and syntactic structures of historical knowledge incorporated within it. Recipes for teaching include and subsume within them these more complex educational, moral and other issues in ways that novice teachers seldom recognise. Our research on the stages of learning to teach, reported in Chapter 4, indicates that although it is possible to 'act like a teacher' simply by following routines and recipes established by others, becoming an effective teacher demands a deeper understanding of the processes involved in teaching and learning. Experienced teachers are able to frame teaching situations by drawing on richer and more complex understandings. When confronted by new or difficult situations they have a deeper understanding of the assumptions they are making in their framing. As a result, they are able to bring that teaching more directly under their own control.

In characterising the nature of these more complex forms of professional knowledge, it is important to recognise the role of 'theory' in their development. While it was possible, say, to recognise the influence of constructivist thought on some of our teachers' understandings of how children learn, to say that the teachers were explicitly drawing on such theories in their work would be inaccurate. As we indicated in Chapter 7, the teachers with whom we worked had a richer and more complex under-standing of pupil learning than is encapsulated in any one 'theory'. The body of professional knowledge that teachers develop through their day-to-day experience of framing classroom situ-ations is irredeemably 'practical' in its nature – first and foremost, it grows from the experience of teaching itself. However, it is also true that students as well as experienced teachers can develop more sophisticated understandings of their own practice by re-examining their practical knowledge in the light of other forms of professional knowledge, including formal educational theory. In accounting for their actions in ways that we recognised as im-plying a constructivist view of learning, it would seem that the teachers in our study had either explicitly or implicitly at some stage in their careers engaged with such ideas in relation to their own teaching.

just practical are also examined in light of other forms of prof. knowledge

VALUES AND PERSONAL LEARNING

Teachers' practical professional knowledge can therefore be understood as relating to a number of professional 'domains' – knowledge of pupils, knowledge of strategies, knowledge of con-tent and knowledge of context. We would suggest that knowledge in each of these domains takes the form of specific concrete remembered experiences as well as more abstract concepts. It is these concepts and concrete experiences, understood at a variety of different levels of sophistication, that are used in the 'framing' of specific teaching situations.

But in understanding how students develop an appropriate body of practical professional knowledge for themselves in each of these domains, it is necessary to recognise that their learning of the 'content' of professional knowledge cannot be disentangled from other forms of learning that must go on at the same time. One of the most forceful messages to come from our research was that professional development does not only depend on the acquisition of a body of knowledge; it is also dependent on stu-dents undergoing certain forms of personal learning as well as confronting fundamental issues associated with values.

According to Hartnett and Naish (1993), teaching involves the development of three different dimensions of professional knowledge, each of which must be addressed within a teacher education programme. They are 'the teacher as person', 'the teacher as worker' and 'the teacher as citizen'. We too came to recognise the significance of these three different dimensions of professional learning, though we would not necessarily interpret them in the same way as Hartnett and Naish.

The teacher as person

As we saw in Chapter 5, on the stages of development, one of our students' overriding worries during their early experiences in the classroom concerned their ability to achieve effective classroom management and control. Such an observation is hardly 'news' – worries about classroom management and control are recognised by nearly all of us who have been through the process of learning to teach. However, in understanding how students learn to teach, the issue of classroom management and control is significant in two ways. First, it is significant because its achievement is so central to other forms of learning. Second, it is significant because our research seems to indicate that its development involves rather different learning processes from those in other areas. More than any other issue in learning to teach, classroom management and control raises the issue of 'the teacher as person' for the student.

When we came to look in more detail at students' learning in this area in Chapter 6, it became apparent that during what we characterised as their 'survival' stage, students had a double agenda. Not only were they struggling to 'see' – to make sense of the processes involved in teaching and learning – they were *at the same time* learning about achieving classroom management and control. In reality, then, their learning about classroom management and control was achieved *through* their early attempts at teaching. Students selected and evaluated their early attempts at teaching almost entirely in terms of the extent to which their chosen strategies helped them achieve what they saw to be effective classroom management and control.

Our research also led us to recognise, as we have indicated in Chapter 7, that achieving effective classroom control is vitally important if students are to go on to exercise greater control over teaching and learning. If students are to 'move on' to focus on pupils' learning, they need to be able to 'de-centre' – to be less concerned about their own performance and to focus on the pupil's learning. But de-centring does not simply involve a change of focus, it also involves developing a different sort of classroom control. In the early stages of learning to teach, the students we worked with seemed to interpret control primarily in terms of achieving *power* in the classroom – they wanted to be able to dominate the classroom – to control what the children did and when and how they did it. Only slowly did they come to realise that effective teaching cannot be achieved through domination but demands the achievement of control through the fostering of *authority* in which children grant legitimate respect to the teacher. It also means that, whatever the teaching method employed, pupils must have some personal engagement in and responsibility for their own learning; such responsibility cannot be achieved through domination. In effect, we found that if they are to 'move on' in the ways we described, students have to learn to 'give away' part of the power they have so recently learned how to take on themselves.

This idea of 'giving away' power highlights the distinctive nature of learning in this aspect of teaching. At a surface level, learning about the processes involved in classroom management and control are no different from any other form of learning – students have to develop a body of professional knowledge with which to frame teaching situations. This is the sort of knowledge that has so often been described in behaviourist accounts of classroom management and control – where to stand in the classroom, how to use body language, the importance of having eyes in the back of the head and so on. Students do need to build up a body of professional knowledge of this sort – often characterised as skills – which they then use to frame teaching situations. However, while it was apparent that students in our study did indeed learn these sorts of skills, for most of them, the 'real' learning they had to do in this area of their work was of a personal kind. Whereas it seems that students can relatively easily be taught to recognise behavioural techniques in the classroom, actually using them in a way that establishes them as an authority figure with a legitimate right to manage pupils involves a very different sort of personal learning. As we indicated in Chapter 6, for many of our students, such personal learning was often painful, at times involving a fundamental reconceptualisation of themselves and their views of what teaching involved. The implications for mentoring in relation to this aspect of learning to teach may well therefore be rather different from other areas.

The teacher as citizen

Another form of learning implicit in professional development concerns what Hartnett and Naish (1993) characterise as learning about the 'teacher as citizen' – a term that indicates the importance of recognising and confronting values in teaching.

At one level, the 'agenda' of issues to be addressed in a teacher education programme seems straightforward enough – in Britain it is encapsulated in the current list of government competences grouped under three generic headings: Curriculum Content, Planning and Assessment; Teaching Strategies; and Further Professional Development (DFE 1992 and 1993a). But *what* it is that students learn about these different groups of competences, what sorts of professional knowledge they build up, will be profoundly influenced by the values they encounter within their university or college course and within their school; they will also be influenced at the most fundamental level by their own values as well.

The values enshrined within the initial teacher education courses are still extremely powerful. Despite the move to school-based forms of teacher education, tutors still retain a considerable degree of influence over the character of the learning that students do. That influence is expressed in a wide variety of different ways – within the higher education-based course, in the choice and number of schools to which students are exposed, in the character of the school-based assignments students are set, and in the questions tutors ask of the student during their school visits. Above all, it is expressed in the criteria tutors use in making assessments of students' classroom competence. Students in our study were acutely aware of the sorts of teaching their tutors wished to see on their visits to school, and both they and their class teachers recognised the importance of putting on a good 'performance' for the tutor.

However, as we also indicated in earlier chapters, the students in our study were strongly influenced by the values within their school. Much has been written on the powerful effects of the 'socialisation' of student teachers into school (Lacey 1977), and our students were no exception to this process. Sometimes the values to which they were exposed were explicit, clearly articulated in the advice teachers gave them on how to teach and manage classes. More frequently, however, these values were implicit – enshrined in the working practices and resources established by the school and the class teacher. Many of our students explicitly discussed the importance of 'fitting in' to these established ways of working, though it is unlikely that they were fully aware of the profound influence their particular school context had on their learning.

The final area of influence that we came to recognise concerned the students' own values. The importance of students' values surfaced on a number of occasions in our study. In Chapter 5 we discussed the idealised picture of teaching held by students at the beginning of their training. As we noted, when confronted with the realities of teaching, those views quickly faded. Yet underneath their more realistic views, strong values often continued to flourish. Values also emerged as important in our discussion in Chapter 7 on students' views of pupils' learning. Students' views on the nature of how children learn were often deeply held and had a profound influence on the sorts of questions they were willing and able to ask about their own teaching.

Clearly, students' own values were of considerable significance in the sorts of learning they were willing and able to take on board during their course. Sometimes those values seemed to us to be conducive to the development of more effective forms of teaching; on other occasions they seemed to inhibit students' learning. What is interesting is that in many cases it seemed that students' experiences in school and higher education did little to challenge these fundamental values. What those experiences did do, however, was to help students become clearer about the educational implications of their views and the extent to which they could be realised within schools as they currently found them.

All three areas of values – those enshrined in the school, in the higher education course as well as students' personal values – are, whether students recognise it or not, profoundly influential on the forms of professional knowledge they develop. Part of the process of gaining greater control over their own teaching involves students being helped to recognise and bring to the level of consciousness the values implicit in their own and other teacher's ways of 'framing' teaching situations.

The teacher as worker

As we have indicated above, from our own research, we recognise Hartnett and Naish's (1993) assertion that learning to teach involves a great deal of learning at the personal level and the explicit recognition of the role of values – personal, institutional, societal – in teaching. However, we would suggest that neither of these dimensions of teaching is separable from Hartnett and Naish's third dimension – 'teacher as worker'. The task of the 'teacher as worker' is to be an educationist – effectively to foster and manage pupils' learning. Following the 1988 Education Reform Act, it is to promote the pupils' 'moral, cultural, mental and physical development' and to prepare them for the 'opportunities, responsibilities and experiences of adult life'. It was the need to develop the skills, knowledge and understandings associated with this core dimension of professionalism that the students in our study were centrally concerned. This is what they rightly saw as the central focus of their professional preparation. However, as we have indicated above, it was also clear that the learning of this professional knowledge inevitably involved them in confronting issues concerned with themselves, their values and those of others. These different dimensions of professional preparation are therefore not separate entities – they are irredeemably intertwined. To use Hartnett and Naish's terms, it is through learning to be a 'teacher as worker' that one comes to confront the 'teacher as person' and the 'teacher as citizen'. All three dimensions are inevitably involved in the process of learning to teach, and all three dimensions need to be addressed by mentors and others with responsibility for supporting student teachers.

LEARNING TO TEACH

Given our views of what teaching involves, learning to teach can, we would suggest, usefully be characterised as the development of an appropriate body of practical professional knowledge with which student teachers can come to frame actual teaching situations. This body of knowledge is made up of both a stock of concrete experiences as well as more abstract concepts. As such, it needs to be broadly based – that is, derived from extensive practical teaching experience; and the concepts involved need to be understood at a variety of different 'levels' of sophistication.

The more sophisticated a student's understanding of the assumptions they are making in their framing of practical situations, the more able they are to bring their teaching under their own control.

But how and where is the body of practical professional knowledge actually acquired and what is the role of the mentor in supporting its development? One of the most common complaints made by student teachers about their professional preparation has always been that, however valuable and interesting their college-based studies, 'real' learning does not begin until they enter the classroom. No amount of college work can substitute for the experience of starting to take responsibility for the teaching and learning process itself.

The perennial nature of this complaint is a source of some irritation to teacher educators in higher education; it is a complaint that continues to be made even when they change and develop their courses to become 'professionally relevant'. However, from our point of view, such a complaint is unsurprising. Student teachers may usefully be 'prepared' in college, but such preparation will always have a degree of unreality about it. This is because teaching is an essentially practical activity. As a result, the body of professional knowledge that students need to develop through the course of their training is itself fundamentally practical in nature. Given that this is the case, the processes involved in learning are very different from learning of a more intellectual kind. Learning to teach as opposed to learning about teaching cannot really begin until one actually starts to do the job itself. In this sense, the distinction we drew earlier between the different 'domains' of professional knowledge and how that knowledge is used – knowledge-in-action – was in part an artificial one. To an important degree, a body of practical professional knowledge of pupils, of strategies, of content and of context can only be developed in dialogue with real teaching situations.

The significance of this observation is well demonstrated by looking at the processes involved in other 'practical professions'. As Schön (1987) has argued, the learning processes involved in many practical professions (architecture, music) are essentially the same. The following quotation from an Open University text on designing illustrates the point vividly. Throughout the quotation, the word 'teaching' could easily be substituted for the word 'designing':

Designing is a distinctive kind of skilled intellectual activity. It draws on some features of, say, scientific or artistic activity, but in many ways it is noticeably different. One of these principle differences is that designing is a 'solution-focused' rather than a 'problem-focused' activity. Designers tend to move fairly quickly to a solution of some kind, rather than spending a long time on trying to understand 'the problem' in abstract. The reason for this 'solution-focused' strategy is that problems encountered in designing are not fixed; they are changeable, depending on the kind of solution the designer has in mind. It is only by posing a solution, that the problem can be defined and better understood. Designing is not, therefore, a step-by-step process of analysing the problem and then optimising a solution. It is an interactive process in which both 'problem' and 'solution' are resolved and refined together.

(Open University 1983: 81–2)

We would suggest that, like designing, teaching is 'solution focused'; it demands involvement in the process and then progressive refinement of one's actions and understandings. The same, we would suggest, is true for *learning* to teach. Student teachers, at a fairly early stage in their professional preparation, need to begin the process of teaching; it is only by so doing that they can start to develop their own body of practical professional know- ledge with which to frame teaching situations.

However, the fact that the professional knowledge that students need to acquire for themselves is irredeemably practical does not mean that they do not need expert support; nor does it mean that other forms of professional knowledge that are not themselves directly practical are irrelevant. As we will indicate in the next chapter, students can usefully be prepared prior to entering the classroom. Moreover, once, through their work in schools, they have begun to develop their body of practical professional knowledge, what they, with the help of others, then have to do is progressively to refine that knowledge – extending the range of practical situations they are able to deal with and establishing a richer and more sophisticated understanding of the assumptions they are making in the concepts they have formed.

It is through this process of progressively refining their first, faltering steps as teachers that students come to gain more control over the teaching process itself. In the next and final chapter, we consider what the implications of this model of student learning are for the role of the mentor.

Chapter 9

Mentoring and the growth of professional knowledge

Existing research raises the possibility that student teachers may learn to teach in numerous ways, that different types of learning may characterise different phases in a teacher's career, and that different types of professional learning tasks may be more or less appropriate at different times.

(Calderhead 1989: 49)

In the last chapter, we indicated that within the literature there are a number of competing views of the nature of teaching – the New Right view, the competency model and so on. Each of these different conceptualisations of teaching also implies a different view of the processes involved in learning to teach and a different vision of the role of the mentor in that process. For example, in our attempt to characterise the nature of teaching, we have drawn heavily on the work of Schön; as we have indicated, we find his conception of teaching as a transactional process convincing. But in his second book (1987), Schön's concern was not so much to characterise professional action *per se*; rather, it was to consider the processes involved in professional education. For Schön, 'coaching' through reflection-on-action is central to his view of how students can and should be supported in learning by a body of professional knowledge. From this perspective, therefore, the role of the mentor is to act as a coach, helping the student teacher to reflect on their practical teaching experience.

Other writers, either explicitly or implicitly, have proposed different models of the learning process and different visions of the role of the mentor. For example, New Right thinkers such as O'Hear (1988) talk of the importance of learning through 'the emulation of an experienced practitioner' – a form of unreflective apprenticeship. Such an idea follows logically from the conception of teaching as an almost mystical process, dependent primarily on personality and 'natural' skill – not susceptible to systematic analysis. From this perspective, mentoring is not an active process nor does it involve any particular skills. To be a mentor is simply to act as a model. In sharp contrast, those supporting a competency model advocate a more systematic, skills-based approach to learning to teach. It is by separating out the different elements of teaching that students can systematically be prepared for their performance; the mentor here is a trainer. All of these models are different again from that which, in Chapter 3, we characterised as being within the tradition of Dewey (1910). Writers such as Zeichner and Liston (1987), Carr and Kemmis (1986), and many others, insist that teaching is a complex intellectual and moral activity. Drawing on Dewey's distinction between routine and reflective action, such authors insist that learning how to teach must involve students in systematic enquiry into their own and other people's practice in order to reveal the intellectual, moral and other assumptions on which it is based. It is only through such enquiry that students can establish for themselves a rational basis for their professional actions. Mentors, if they are to be given this responsibility, are therefore seen as needing special skills in order to help students in this systematic enquiry.

There is therefore no shortage of ideas when it comes to conceptualising the processes of learning to teach and defining the role of the mentor. Moreover, it is apparent that many of these different schools of thought are, in their different ways, pointing to important dimensions within that role. However, from our point of view, what is wrong with each of them is that they are partial. Once again, they are ideologically rather than empirically derived. As a consequence they take into account neither the complexities nor the developmental nature of professional learning. It has been central to our argument throughout this book that we consider learning to teach to be a complex process; it is also a developmental process as the learning needs of students change over time. It is because students typically go through different stages of learning to teach that we suggest that mentoring needs to be developmental too. However, it is important to emphasise that in arguing for a developmental approach, we are not simply suggesting that mentors should give students the sort of support that they ask for. If students are to develop fully, then there will be times when mentors will need to be assertive in their interventions, providing students with what they 'need' rather than with what they necessarily want! However, as we have stated before, in essence mentoring is no different from any other form of teaching; it needs to start from where the learners are and take their typical pattern of development into account.

Given the interpretation of what is involved in learning to teach that we have derived from our research, the central questions for mentors and others concerned with supporting students' school-based learning can be characterised as follows:

- how students can be supported in ways that help them, through experience in schools, to develop an appropriate body of practical professional knowledge (experiences and concepts) with which to frame teaching situations;
- how students can be supported in ways that will encourage them to develop deeper and more complex understandings of the assumptions they are making in that practical professional knowledge.

At one level, the range of possible strategies available for mentors to use in supporting students' school-based learning is limited. Mentors may set up opportunities for students to observe themselves and other teachers teaching; they may observe and provide feedback on the student's own teaching; and they may work alongside the student teacher, engaging in different forms of 'collaborative' teaching. But although these three strategies represent the full range available, it is clear that they can be used in many different ways. The key to effective mentoring is to utilise them in ways that will support the learning needs of students at different stages of their development.

In the remainder of this chapter we turn our attention to some of the different learning processes that go on at different 'stages' of students' development. In each stage we identify the different learning priorities the student needs to address and a different 'role' for the mentor in supporting those learning needs. We also suggest a number of key mentoring strategies. Naturally, we do not suggest that these stages are rigid. The development of any one student will be much more complex than a simple stage model implies; they will develop at their own rate and will need to revisit issues because they have forgotten them or wish to relearn them in a different context or at a deeper level. We therefore intend these stages of mentoring to be understood flexibly and with sensitivity. In fact, it is probably more appropriate to think of each stage as cumulative rather than discrete. As students develop, mentors, we would suggest, need to employ more and more strategies from the repertoire that we set out.

The different stages of mentoring considered in the remainder of this chapter are summarised below.

Stages of mentoring and student development

Beginning teaching

Focus of student learning...........	rules, rituals and routines; establishing authority
Mentoring role	model
Key mentoring strategies...........	student observation and collaborative teaching focused on rules and routines

Supervised teaching

Focus of student learning...........	teaching competences
Mentoring role	coach
Key mentoring strategies...........	observation by the student; systematic observation and feedback on student's 'performance'; mentor facilitates reflection-on-action

From teaching to learning

Focus of student learning...........	understanding pupil learning; developing effective teaching
Mentoring role	critical friend
Key mentoring strategies...........	student observation; re-examining of lesson planning

Autonomous teaching

Focus of student learning...........	investigating the grounds for practice
Mentoring role	co-enquirer
Key mentoring strategies...........	partnership teaching; partnership supervision

BEGINNING TEACHING – ROUTINES AND RITUALS

As we argued in the last chapter, because teaching is fundamentally a practical activity, student teachers are not able to begin to develop their own body of practical professional knowledge until they enter the classroom. It is through the dialogue with real teaching situations that their own professional knowledge starts to develop. However, having said this, it is also important to recognise that no student teacher enters the classroom as a complete novice – they bring with them a vast array of skills, knowledge and understandings derived from other contexts. At the very least, all student teachers have sat through many years of schooling as a pupil. In addition, in the vast majority of initial teacher education courses, students still have important preliminary college-based programmes prior to their work in school – as we noted above, these too have an important influence on students. But it is important to recognise that both of these kinds of preliminary experiences involve very different sorts of learning from that which can arise from a direct engagement with the teaching process itself. Seeing teaching from the point of view of a pupil is very different from taking responsibility for running a class. Pupils may learn a great deal about the 'surface structure' of teaching – how teachers organise the classroom, the teaching techniques they use – but much of the intention and purpose behind teachers' actions remains invisible to them.

College-based work is partial in a different way. As Furlong *et al.* (1988) noted, a great deal of what goes into courses based on higher education is highly practical in nature – it is intended to be of direct relevance to what students can 'do' in the classroom. But, as Furlong *et al.* also point out – that college-based practical work is inevitably very different in character from that which goes on in school – it is what they described as 'indirect' practical work. In learning how to prepare lessons or ask questions, students in college do not have to struggle with the complexities of working in the unpredictable context of a real classroom. Reality, in this context, is 'tidied up' – students have the opportunity to develop 'abstract' concepts, without having to use them in the framing of real teaching situations. College-based learning of this sort is therefore clearly useful; nevertheless, it is very different from the sorts of learning students need to do when they come to work in a real classroom. Once again it is important to emphasise the point that learning *to* teach involves a different developmental sequence from learning *about* teaching.

Students therefore enter the classroom with some existing concepts, though they are frequently of a different character from the forms of professional knowledge needed to frame classroom situations. If is for this reason that, despite many years of having been a pupil and despite their preliminary work in college, students still complain of not being able to 'see' when they first enter the classroom. Learning how to observe an experienced teacher and identify (let alone understand) the different skills that he or she is using is an achievement in itself; it is something that students need support in learning how to do.

The students with whom we worked frequently seemed to begin to develop their professional knowledge by copying the established routines and teaching strategies of their teachers and lecturers. By undertaking preliminary periods of classroom observation and by engaging in different forms of collaborative teaching, students were able to observe and eventually to model many of the classroom routines they witnessed. They were also able to model teaching strategies that had been used by lecturers in college-based sessions. As Furlong *et al.* (1994b) note, lecturers often deliberately choose their own pedagogy in running college-based sessions as a way of modelling different teaching strategies for students. In the very earliest stages of learning to teach, when students are searching for models of 'how to do it', it would seem that they may well find lecturers' modelling of teaching of just as much value as the content those lecturers are trying to convey!

The classroom routines and strategies that students model are, of course, no more than the 'outward expressions' of teachers' own professional knowledge. By copying them, students do not necessarily understand them; they do not 'own' them. As we emphasised in the last chapter, teachers' professional knowledge may be understood at many different levels of sophistication. Nevertheless, our students found that by modelling teachers' and lecturers' strategies, they could at least 'get by'; they could begin to 'act' like a teacher. Once they had achieved this, they could then, and only then, through a transaction with a real teaching situation begin to develop their own practical professional knowledge.

As we have indicated before, the focus for students' learning in these early days in school is likely to be their achievement of effective classroom management and control, and teaching and learning activities may well be judged almost entirely in terms of whether they contribute to that end. Mentors also need to recognise that students often find this early period of learning to teach personally highly stressful. As we have indicated, many students may well find it hard to come to terms with themselves as an authority figure. They have to get used to a new persona – 'me-as-teacher' – and for some, it is not a character they particularly like. As a consequence it is not uncommon for students to go through a period of resenting the pupils for forcing them to be more authoritarian than they really want to be.

In this initial stage of learning to teach, therefore, the role of the mentor is to support the student in this difficult transition to becoming an authority figure in the classroom. One of the best ways they can do this is by explicitly acting as a model for the student – providing examples of teaching rituals, routines and recipes that can be copied and will actually work in the classroom. Important mentoring strategies include giving the student the opportunity to observe the mentor and other teachers teach, and collaborative teaching. Collaborative teaching, where the student is party to the teacher's planning and then has some role in teaching and afterwards evaluating the lesson, is particularly powerful. By becoming an 'insider' to the planning and execution of a lesson, the student has the opportunity to model the teachers teaching at a level of great detail.

SUPERVISED TEACHING

Once students have been able to model enough simple classroom recipes and routines to allow them to begin teaching they will then start to develop their own body of practical professional knowledge. This process of transforming copied routines and rituals into professional knowledge is, it seems to us, best understood by using Schön's concept of reflection-on-action. Schön describes the process of reflection-on-action as the attempt, after the event, to put into words the complex processes involved in professional action. It is by reflecting on teaching, thinking about it and trying to express it in words that students begin to transform the behaviours they have copied into concepts which they own for themselves. It is these concepts that give them an understanding of the teaching processes they have engaged in. They are therefore essential if they are to increase their own control of their teaching.

Clearly students can and do reflect on their own teaching themselves; most students think of nothing else but teaching during their school experience. However, it is also clear that this reflective process is strengthened if it is systematically supported by an experienced practitioner. Reflection-on-action that is structured and supported in this way is what Schön characterises as 'coaching'. Coaching is, for us, an important strategy in supporting students' learning at a particular stage of development. The experienced practitioner can help the student focus on particular dimensions of teaching, 'guiding their seeing', helping them to find a language and encouraging them to discuss and articulate what they know.

The agenda for coaching in these early stages of learning to teach is, in Britain at least, now specified by the government in its list of teaching competences. Having begun to teach, students need to be encouraged to reflect on their own action in relation to, for example, 'recording pupils' progress' (competency DFE 1992, 2.4.1) or 'establishing clear expectations of pupil behaviour in the classroom' (competency DFE 9/92, 2.6.1). Supporting students at this stage of their development does therefore have something in common with competency training; the topics on which they need to be coached may indeed be expressed in this form. However, we believe that the learning processes implied by Schön's notion of coaching are fundamentally different from those described by most supporters of the competency model.

Coaching in the sense that we have described it involves important skills. Those responsible for coaching must themselves be able to recognise and articulate much of the 'sedimented' knowledge of classroom practice that is often taken for granted by experienced teachers. They also need the interpersonal skills necessary to support students in dealing with the forms of personal learning that we have indicated are so pressing in the early stages of achieving classroom control. Having these skills is, we would suggest, vital for those with responsibility for supporting students, whether they be school-based mentors or university or college lecturers. However, if teachers acting as mentors can develop such skills, they are particularly well placed to support students in this learning. As 'insiders', they have access to specific forms of practical professional knowledge – they know 'this school', 'these pupils' and 'this curriculum'. Through their dialogue with students they are therefore in a position to 'sharpen the focus' for students; coaching them in the detailed, contextspecific understandings of the teaching processes they are en- gaged in.

The strategies mentors can use at this stage of their work are familiar enough. With the government's, or their own, list of competences in mind, mentors need to encourage the student, when they are observing other teachers, to focus their attention on the specifics of teaching. They also need to observe the students teach and provide them with detailed feedback on specific competences. But the most important part of coaching is in the debriefing, for it is here that mentors can help students find a language with which to articulate and thereby establish their own conceptualisation of the teaching processes they have been engaged in. At times, mentors need to be didactic, 'giving' students this language – telling them things, pointing things out to them. At other times they need to develop a more 'discursive' style, drawing the student out, helping them find a language for themselves with which to characterise their teaching experiences. However it is achieved, it is by finding an appropriate language to talk about specific competences that students can refine their own understandings of the processes involved in teaching. Following such a discussion, they are then in a stronger position to re-enter the classroom and begin again their practical 'dialogue' with teaching situations.

FROM TEACHING TO LEARNING

In Chapter 4, on the stages of learning to teach, we indicated that many of the students with whom we worked seemed to 'hit a plateau' after several weeks in the classroom. They had found one particular way of teaching that seemed to 'work', and they were going to stick to it. Some of them even appeared to go backwards. After what seemed like early satisfactory progress, mentors would accuse them of 'trying to cut corners' and 'not paying enough attention to detail'. What seemed to us to be happening was that the students had still only partially developed the professional knowledge of the teachers they were trying to emulate; they had become proficient at copying the surface structure of other teachers' strategies but their understandings of the underlying professional knowledge on which teachers drew remained rudimentary.

This lack of understanding was particularly evident in their attempts to cut corners and act like 'real' teachers. For example, they were aware that the teachers with whom they worked did not plan their lessons in the same detail that they were required to do. However, their own attempts to reduce their degree of planning sometimes resulted in disaster. Experienced teachers know how to reduce their overt planning without compromising their teaching; this is because they have a deeper understanding of the educational purposes underlying their professional action. For the experienced teacher, what on the surface looks like a simple plan can encapsulate a complex and flexible understanding of the teaching and learning processes they intend to set up.

Our research evidence would suggest that after the first few weeks in the classroom a key area of practical professional knowledge students still lack concerns the way pupils learn. Their first period in the classroom is, for most students, primarily focused on developing their own *performance* as teachers; they concentrate on 'acting like a teacher' – copying and refining those overt aspects of teaching behaviour that they can see teachers engaging in. There is, however, an important difference between 'acting like a teacher' and 'thinking like a teacher'. We would suggest that a key difference between these two states is that experienced teachers devote most of their attention to thinking about their pupils' learning rather than focusing on their own 'performance'; in other words, they are able to 'de-centre' from themselves to the pupils. If, after the first few weeks in the classroom, students are to improve the quality of their teaching, we would argue that it is essential that they too learn to de-centre. However, evidence from our work and from elsewhere (Calderhead 1987) suggests that without external support, students often find this transition difficult.

In supporting students in this transition, mentors need to adopt different strategies from those they have employed earlier. Given that teachers' understandings of how pupils learn are largely implicit rather than explicit, then Schön's notion of coaching – getting students to reflect by articulating their *own* understandings – may well not be sufficient. Students need to be encouraged to consider more deeply the educational purposes underlying their teaching. As a result, a rather different form of intervention is, we would suggest, essential. It is here that we turn to a different tradition of thought on reflection – that derived from the work of John Dewey (1910) – to characterise the role of the mentor.

In our discussion of models of reflection in Chapter 3, we indicated that authors writing in the tradition of Dewey define reflective action as involving systematic enquiry into one's own action. Dewey and his followers argue that it is only by such systematic enquiry that the rational basis for professional action can be established. Although we recognise that, in certain contexts, systematic enquiry of the type advocated by Dewey is valuable, we would agree with McIntyre (1993) that such an approach can have only a limited role in an initial teacher education programme. Systematic enquiry into one's own practice can be a highly potent form of professional development for the experienced practitioner; but students, in the earliest stages of their professional development, have neither the time nor the breadth of experience to do more than experiment with such an approach. As a model for understanding how student learning should be supported, Dewey's definition of reflective action is of limited value.

Yet even if the opportunities for systematic enquiry into students' own practice are limited, the thrust of Dewey's approach does seem to us to have value. The aim of reflective action as far as Dewey was concerned was to help teachers establish more secure grounds for their own professional practice. As we saw in Chapter 3, more contemporary writers (van Manen 1977; Zeichner and Liston 1987; Carr and Kemmis 1986) in the same tradition have frequently distinguished a number of different dimensions of teaching that need to be addressed in this manner. Van Manen (1977), for example, distinguishes three levels of reflection. After focusing on 'the practical', he suggests that teachers need to consider the educational justifications of their teaching, posing questions about the nature and quality of pupils' learning. At a deeper level yet again, he suggests that they need to consider moral and political questions, focusing on the 'worth of knowledge and the nature of the social conditions necessary for raising the questions of worthwhileness in the first place' (1977: 227).

Even if students have neither the time nor the experience to explore such questions through *systematic enquiry* into their own teaching, we would still argue that they remain important issues to be confronted. Students, we would suggest, do need to be encouraged to consider the nature and quality of the educational experiences they are making available to their pupils, for it is only by so doing that they will come to appreciate the educational purposes behind the teaching strategies they have developed. As we will suggest below, in the final stages of their initial teacher education, they also need to confront broader questions concerning the social context in which teaching takes place and the 'worthwhileness' of their teaching.

Difficulties students face

Students who find difficulty in moving on to consider pupils' learning often have difficulties in common. First, they may hold views that are not supportive of this switch in focus. For example, they may believe: that teaching is simply about the transmission of knowledge and the accumulation of factual information; that children are blank slates; that school learning is 'discrete' and separate from learning going on elsewhere in pupils' lives; that giving correct answers denotes understanding.

Until these sorts of beliefs have been challenged and student teachers have begun to recognise the complexities involved in teaching and learning, they will not be open to developing a more 'educational' dimension to their practical professional knowledge.

A second difficulty may be that the student has insufficient confidence in classroom management and control. An appreciation of how pupils learn demands a willingness to experiment with different strategies of classroom organisation. In particular, it demands that pupils take an active role in their learning and, when appropriate, participate in investigation and enquiry. For some student teachers, especially those who have only a tentative hold on classroom control, this may appear very threatening. How much easier it is to keep pupils sitting in their places and have their attention focused on you!

Student teachers have to come to realise that effective classroom control is attained primarily through 'well-matched' activities – activities that take account of pupils' needs and interests, that take account of how pupils best learn, and are supportive of pupils' developing understanding of the subject area.

The development of a fuller understanding of effective teaching is often a slow and difficult process for students. Their understanding of how pupils learn, and what their role as a teacher should be, may initially be naïve and simplistic. If students are to move on to develop a more realistic understanding of the processes involved in effective teaching, they need to be encouraged to look critically at the teaching procedures they have established and evaluate their effectiveness. However, as they are often still extremely insecure about their teaching abilities, they also need considerable support if they are going to achieve this.

The task of the mentor is thus doubly challenging at this stage of the student's development. We would characterise the role as being a 'critical friend'. The mentor needs to be able to challenge the student to re-examine their teaching, while at the same time providing encouragement and support.

Two specific mentoring strategies are particularly pertinent at this stage of a student's development. First, students need to return to classroom observation but now focusing their attention very specifically on how pupils learn. Mentors might encourage this by, for example, asking them to observe pupils when they are engaged in classroom work, and make notes on how the pupils tackle their work and talk to their peers; or to engage a small group of pupils in discussion in order to explore their understanding of a particular task or concept.

A second strategy is to focus again on lesson planning. This might be achieved by asking the student to plan a lesson or sequence of lessons. The mentor can then focus discussion of the lesson plans on the content of the planned lesson rather than on the 'performance' of the student. In discussing lesson content, it might be useful to focus questions under headings such as the following:

Pupils' learning	• What do you want the pupils to learn?
	• Why?
	• How does this relate to their previous or future learning or their lives outside school?
Subject matter	• What is the nature of the intended learning – factual, conceptual, procedural?
	• How does it relate to other aspects of this subject area?
	• Does it take account of the underlying processes associated with this subject area?

Broader questions   • What do you understand to be the nature
                       of the teacher's role in fostering learning
                       – a transmitter, a facilitator, etc.?
                     • How do children learn best – by being
                       told, by constructing their own
                       understanding, by doing?

The practical professional knowledge of experienced teachers
involves more than how to 'perform' in the classroom; it also
includes an appreciation of complex issues such as how children
learn and how best to represent subject knowledge to pupils.
These forms of knowledge are largely implicit, subsumed within
teachers' teaching plans. As we have argued, the aim of mentoring after students have achieved some basic competence and
confidence in their classroom performance must therefore be to
help them develop these additional 'educational' dimensions to
their practical professional knowledge.

AUTONOMOUS TEACHING

There is one further stage of learning to teach that we would
identify from our research and that concerns the development of
the student as an 'autonomous teacher'. Defining with any precision what is involved in being an autonomous teacher is clearly
difficult, and, however it is defined, a course of initial professional preparation can do no more than lay the foundations for its
development. Nevertheless, our research demonstrated that as
the students we studied gained in confidence, they were capable
of taking more responsibility for their own professional development; of broadening their repertoire of teaching strategies; of
deepening their understanding of the complexities of teaching
and learning; and of considering the social, moral and political
dimensions of educational practice.

Many of those in higher education argue that the aim of developing students' abilities to address the social, political and
moral dimensions of teaching is of particular importance. As
Hartnett and Naish (1993) put it, 'in a developed democratic
society, teachers should be a critically reflective group who are
given difficult and complex tasks to do. Their status, prestige,
development and education has to reflect the complexity and
social importance of these tasks' (p. 337).

Moreover, teacher educators frequently insist that these are issues that should be addressed throughout a course of initial teacher education; right from their first days on their course, students should be encouraged to read, to assess and to question all aspects of the educational process. We too recognise the importance of this 'critical' dimension to professional education though we would insist that there are other dimensions of 'autonomous teaching' that are equally important. However, we would suggest that once again there is an important difference between learning *about* teaching and learning *to* teach. Much of what goes on in a university or college concerns learning *about* teaching, and it is right and proper that issues addressed in that context are done so in a manner appropriate to higher education. The aspects of professional preparation based on higher education should involve reflection, analysis and open-minded critique.

Our primary concern in this book has been rather different; it has been with the practical process of learning *to* teach that takes place in school. As we have argued throughout, in learning a practical activity like teaching, the processes involved are very different from learning in an intellectual sense. Learning how to recognise the moral, social and political assumptions implicit in one's practical professional knowledge is a vitally important aspect of professional development. As teacher educators should have learned from many years of bitter experience, if students are not supported in developing these abilities in relation to their own teaching in school, then no amount of university- or college-based work will develop them. But we have found that students are unlikely to be able to address such issues in relation to their *own* teaching until they have achieved at least basic confidence and competence in the classroom. It is for this reason that we believe that it is only at a later stage in their school experience that developing students' abilities in this direction should become a major priority for mentors.

How can mentors support the development of students as autonomous teachers? We would suggest that the focus for student learning in this final stage of development should include: broadening the student's repertoire of teaching strategies; encouraging the student to take more responsibility for their own professional development; deepening their understanding of the complexities involved in teaching and learning including the social, moral and political dimensions.

As the student begins to acquire greater skill and knowledge and develop a more appropriate and realistic understanding of the nature of teaching, so the mentor should begin to modify his or her role yet again. While there will still be times when they need to act as 'model', 'trainer' or 'critical friend', they should also develop the role of 'co-enquirer' (Rudduck and Sigsworth 1985). As a co-enquirer, they will have a more open and equal relationship with their student, spending more time working as equal professionals. Such a relationship has the advantage of encouraging the student to take greater responsibility for their own learning and allows both student and mentor to address some of the complexities of teaching in a spirit of open enquiry.

Mentors should also use the key mentoring strategies of partnership supervision and partnership teaching. These strategies are in many ways similar to the strategies of systematic observation and feedback and collaborative teaching referred to earlier. However, we suggest that at this point in a student's training, they should be developed in ways appropriate to a more equal professional relationship between student and mentor. For example, in partnership supervision, it is the student, rather than the mentor, who should select the focus for the mentor's observation. The topics students choose may vary widely. They may, for example, wish to sharpen particular classroom 'skills' such as the use of praise or handling group work; they may wish to experiment with a new teaching strategy or piece of work. Whatever the focus, the student should be encouraged to take responsibility for selecting it. It should then be the task of the mentor merely to observe the student, record evidence and provide feedback afterwards.

The strategic use of partnership supervision in the later stages of school experience can do much to encourage students to take responsibility for their own professional development, and careful analysis of the observational evidence provided by the mentor can help the student learn how to evaluate themselves.

Once students have gained considerable confidence in their own teaching, we would suggest that there are also advantages in their returning occasionally to teaching alongside their mentor or another experienced teacher; at this stage of development we would characterise this strategy as partnership teaching. In partership teaching, like collaborative teaching, the student and the mentor should engage in a cycle of joint planning, joint teaching and debriefing, though in each case, the roles they adopt are likely to be more equal than in the early stages of professional preparation.

Partnership teaching can have many uses. For example, it might be used for encouraging the student to broaden their repertoire of teaching strategies or allowing both student and mentor to experiment with new teaching techniques. However, its most valuable role is in providing a context for mentor and student to discuss planning and teaching at a more fundamental level than before. No longer should the mentor present themselves as an authority, knowing the 'right' answers. Rather, through discussion of their planning and teaching, mentors should attempt to 'open up' their practical professional knowledge. This can be achieved by, for example: focusing on the *complexity* of thinking underlying professional decisions; exposing the moral, practical and other *dilemmas* underlying professional decisions; evaluating the *consequences* of particular professional decisions; discussing the social, institutional and political *context* in which professional decisions have to be made.

It is by participating in such open, professional discussions in relation to their own practice that students can be encouraged to confront the complexities of teaching more deeply. If such discussions are linked to a programme of reading and writing based in higher education, then students will indeed start to confront and develop a deeper and more secure understanding of the grounds on which their practical professional knowledge is based.

CONCLUSION

In the two years since we began our research project on the role of the mentor, secondary initial teacher education in England and Wales has changed dramatically; over the next two years, primary initial teacher education is now set to change just as much. As we indicated in Chapter 1, the British government first started to insist that schools and practising teachers should have a larger role in initial teacher education as early as 1984. However, recent government interventions (particularly the insistence on the transfer of resources out of higher education and into schools) have quickened the pace of change. As a result, schools, rather than universities and colleges, are rapidly becoming the dominant partner in the professional preparation of the next generation of teachers. The implications of these changes are profound.

As a result of our research, we have become even more convinced of the importance and complexity of the role of the mentor. As financial constraints start to bite, universities and colleges are finding it necessary to withdraw the degree of support they are able to give to students while they are in school. As this shift in responsibility takes hold, developing the role of the mentor takes on even greater urgency; the quality of the next generation of teachers will, in large part, depend on the quality of the mentoring support they are given.

What we have tried to do in our work is to highlight the complexity of students' school-based learning and to highlight the importance of carefully constructed mentoring strategies. Schools need to come to recognise that mentoring is an active process; it demands more than simply *supporting* students up to the level of minimum competence, challenging though that is. As we indicated in Chapter 4, the more we came to recognise how much students' development was dependent on systematic and carefully timed intervention, the more we ourselves began to work in this way.

However, mentoring strategies cannot be developed in a vacuum. What we have tried to show through our research is that they must be built on an informed understanding of how students develop and on a clear vision of the forms of professionalism they are trying to engender. If mentors are to take the responsibility for ensuring the continued high levels of professionalism that teaching demands, then it is essential that they too develop an understanding of how students learn to teach and enter the debate about the forms of professionalism that effective teaching demands. What we hope is that our text will make some small contribution to understanding and discussion in this crucial area of educational policy.

References

Adams, R.D. (1982) 'Teacher Development: A Look at the Changes in Teacher Perception Across Time', Paper presented at the meeting of the Educational Research Association, New York (March).

Aldrich, A. (1990) 'The Evolution of Teacher Education', in N. Graves, *Initial Teacher Education: Policy and Progress*, London: Kogan Page.

Alexander, R. (1984) *Primary Teaching*, Eastbourne: Holt, Rinehart & Winston.

Alexander, R., Craft, M. and Lynch, J. (1984) *Change in Teacher Education*, Eastbourne: Holt, Rinehart & Winston.

Alexander, R., Rose, J. and Woodhead, C. (1992) *Curriculum Organization and Classroom Practice in Primary Schools*, London: HMSO.

Allen, D. and Ryan, K. (1967) *Micro-Teaching*, Boston, Mass.: Addison-Wesley.

Bailey, C. (1984) *Beyond the Present and Particular: A Theory of Liberal Education*, London: Routledge.

Ball, D. and McDiarmid, G.W. (1990) 'The Subject-matter Preparation of Teachers', in W.R. Houston (ed.) *Handbook of Research on Teacher Education*, Basingstoke: Macmillan.

Ball, S.J. (1990) *Politics and Policy-making in Education: Explorations in Policy Sociology*, London: Routledge.

Baron, S., Finn, D., Grant, N., Green, M. and Johnson, R. (eds) (1981) *Unpopular Education: Schooling and Social Democracy in England since 1944*, London: Hutchinson Centre for Contemporary Cultural Studies.

Barrett, E. and Galvin, C. (1993) *The Licensed Teacher Scheme: A MOTE Report*, London: University of London, Institute of Education.

Barrett, E., Barton, L., Furlong, J., Galvin, C., Miles, S. and Whitty, G. (1992a) 'New Routes to Qualified Teacher Status', *Cambridge Journal of Education*, 22(3): 323–6.

Barrett, E., Whitty, G., Furlong, J., Galvin, C. and Barton, L. (1992b) *Initial Teacher Education in England and Wales: A Topography*, Modes of Teacher Education Project, London: Goldsmiths' College.

Beardon, T., Booth, M., Hargreaves, D. and Reiss, M. (1992) 'School-led Teacher Training: The Way Forward', *Cambridge Education Papers No. 2*, Cambridge: University of Cambridge Department of Education.

Bell, A. (1981) 'Structure, Knowledge and Relationships in Teacher Education', *British Journal of Sociology of Education*, 2(1): 3–23.

Bennett, N. and Carré, C. (eds) (1993) *Learning to Teach*, London: Routledge.

Benton, P. (1990) *The Oxford Internship Scheme: Integration and Partnership in Initial Teacher Education*, London: Calouste Gulbenkian Foundation.

Berliner, D.C. (1987) 'Ways of Thinking about Students and Classrooms by More and Less Experienced Teachers', in J. Calderhead (ed.) *Exploring Teachers' Thinking*, London: Cassell.

Berrill, M. (1994) Review of *Cambridge Journal of Education* special edition 22(3), 'Initial Teacher Education at the Crossroads', *Cambridge Journal of Education*, 24(1).

Booth, M., Furlong, J., Hargreaves, D., Reiss, M. and Ruthven, K. (1989) *Teacher Supply and Teacher Quality: Solving the Coming Crisis*, Cambridge Education Papers No. 1, Cambridge: University of Cambridge Department of Education.

Booth, M., Furlong, J. and Wilkin, M. (1991) *Partnership in Initial Teacher Training*, London: Cassell.

Brown, S. and McIntyre, D. (1993) *Making Sense of Teaching*, Buckingham: Open University Press.

Buchmann, M. (1987) 'Teaching Knowledge: The Lights that Teachers Live By', *Oxford Review of Education*, 13: 151–64.

Burden, P. (1990) 'Teacher Development', in W.R. Houston (ed.) *Handbook of Research on Teacher Education*, Basingstoke: Macmillan.

Butterworth, G. (1992) 'Context and Cognition in Models of Cognitive Growth', in P. Light and G. Butterworth (eds) *Context and Cognition: Ways of Learning and Knowing*, Hemel Hempstead: Harvester Wheatsheaf.

Calderhead, J. (1987) 'The Quality of Reflection in Student Teachers' Professional Learning', *European Journal of Teacher Education*, 10(3): 269–78.

—— (1988) 'Learning from Introductory School Experience', *Journal of Education for Teaching*, 14(1): 75–83.

—— (1989) 'Reflective Teaching and Teacher Education', *Teaching and Teacher Education* 5(1): 43–51.

Calderhead, J. and Gates, P. (eds) (1993) *Conceptualizing Reflection in Teacher Development*, Lewes: Falmer Press.

Calderhead, J. and Robson, M. (1991) 'Images of Teaching: Student Teachers' Early Conceptions of Classroom Practice', *Teaching and Teacher Education*, 7: 1–8.

Carr, W. and Kemmis, S. (1986) *Becoming Critical: Education, Knowledge and Action Research*, Lewes: Falmer/Deakin University Press.

Carter, K. (1990) 'Teachers' Knowledge and Learning to Teach', in W.R. Houston (ed.) *Handbook of Research on Teacher Education*, Basingstoke: Macmillan.

Carter, K. and Doyle, W. (1987) 'Teachers' Knowledge Structures and Comprehension Processes', in J. Calderhead (ed.) *Exploring Teachers' Thinking*, London: Cassell.

Chomsky, N. (1968) *Language and Mind*, New York: Harcourt Brace Jovanovich.

Clandinin, D.J. (1986) *Classroom Practice: Teacher Images in Action*, Lewes: Falmer Press.

Clark, C.M. and Peterson, P.L. (1986) 'Teachers' Thought Processes', in M.C. Whittrock (ed.) *Handbook of Research on Teaching*, 3rd edn, London: Macmillan.

CNAA (1992) *Competency Based Approaches to Teacher Education: Viewpoints and Issues*, London: Council for National Academic Awards.

Copeland, W.D. (1981) 'Clinical Experiences in the Education of Teachers', *Journal of Education for Teaching*, 7(1): 3–16.

Cortazzi, M. (1991) *Primary Teaching, How It Is: A Narrative Account*, London: David Fulton Publishers.

Cox, C. and Boyson, R. (1975) *The Black Papers*, London: Dent.

Dale, R. (1989) *The State and Educational Policy*, Lewes: Falmer Press.

DENI (1993) *Review of Initial Teacher Training in Northern Ireland. Working Group 1: Competences*, Belfast: Department of Education, Northern Ireland.

Dent, H. (1977) *The Training of Teachers in England and Wales 1800–1975*, Sevenoaks: Hodder & Stoughton.

DES (1983) *Teaching Quality*, London: DES.

—— (1984) *Initial Teacher Training: Approval of Courses (Circular 3/84)*, London: DES.

—— (1988) *Qualified Teacher Status, Consultation Document*, London: DES.

—— (1989) *Initial Teacher Training: Approval of Courses (Circular 24/89)*, London: DES.

Desforges, C. and Cockburn, A. (1987) *Understanding the Mathematics Teachers: A Study of Practice in First Schools*, Lewes: Falmer Press.

Dewey, J. (1910) *How We Think*, London: D.C. Heath.

—— (1933) *How We Think: A Restatement of the Relation of Reflective Thinking in the Educative Process*, Chicago: Henry Regnery.

DFE (1992) *Initial Teacher Training (Secondary Phase) (Circular 9/92)*, London: DFE.

—— (1993a) *The Initial Training of Primary School Teachers: New Criteria for Course Approval (Circular 14/93)*, London: DFE.

—— (1993b) *School Centred Initial Teacher Training (SCITT). Letter of Invitation, 5.3.93*, London: DFE.

Elbaz, F. (1983) *Teacher Thinking: A Study of Practical Knowledge*, London: Croom Helm.

Elliott, J. (1990) 'Competency-based Training and the Education of the Professions: Is a Happy Marriage Possible?' Unpublished paper, Norwich: University of East Anglia, Centre for Applied Research in Education.

Elliott, J. (1992) 'The Role of a Small Scale Research Project in Developing a Competency Based Police Training Curriculum', Unpublished paper, Norwich: University of East Anglia, Centre for Applied Research in Education.

Feiman-Nemser, S. and Buchmann, M. (1987) 'When is Student Teaching Teacher Education?', *Teaching and Teacher Education*, 3: 255–73.

Flanders, N. (1970) *Analysing Teaching Behaviour*, Boston, Mass.: Addison-Wesley.

French, J.P. and Peskett, R. (1986) 'Control Instructions in the Infant Classroom', *Educational Research*, 28(3): 210–19.

Fuller, F. (1969) 'Concerns of Teachers: A Developmental Conceptualization', *American Educational Research Journal*, 6(2): 207–26.

Fuller, F.F. and Bown, O.H. (1975) 'Becoming a Teacher', in K. Ryan (ed.) *Teacher Education: The Seventy-fourth Yearbook of the National Society for the Study of Education*, Chicago: University of Chicago Press.

Furlong, V.J. (1992) 'Reconstructing Professionalism: Ideological Struggle in Initial Teacher Education', in M. Arnot and L. Barton (eds) *Voicing Concerns: Sociological Perspectives on Contemporary Educational Reforms*, Wallingford: Trinagle.

Furlong, V.J., Hirst, P.H., Pocklington, K. and Miles, S. (1988) *Initial Teacher Training and the Role of the School*, Milton Keynes: Open University Press.

Furlong, J., Maynard, T., Miles, S. and Wilkin, M. (1994a) *The Secondary Active Mentoring Programme*, vol. 1, Cambridge: George Pearson.

Furlong, J., Whitty, G., Barrett, E., Barton, L. and Miles, S. (1994b) 'Integration and Partnership in Initial Teacher Education – Dilemmas and Possibilities', *Research Papers in Education*, 9(3).

Galloway, D. and Edwards, A. (1991) *Primary School Teaching and Educational Psychology*, Harlow: Longman.

Gamble, A. (1983) 'Thatcherism and Conservative Politics', in S. Hall and M. Jaques (eds) *The Politics of Thatcherism*, London: Lawrence & Wishart.

Gardner, P. (1993) 'The Early History of School Based Teacher Training', in D. McIntyre, H. Hagger and M. Wilkin (eds) *Mentoring: Perspectives on School-based Teacher Education*, London: Kogan Page.

Goodman, J. (1985) 'Field-based Experience: A Study of Social Control and Student Teachers' Response to Institutional Constraints', *Journal of Education for Teaching*, 11(1): 26–49.

Grace, G. (1978) *Teachers' Ideology and Control*, London: Routledge & Kegan Paul.

—— (1987) 'Teachers and the State in Britain: A Changing Relation', in M. Lawn and G. Grace (eds) *Teachers: The Culture and Politics of Work*, Lewes: Falmer Press.

Guillaume, A. and Rudney, G. (1993) 'Student Teachers' Growth Towards Independence: An Analysis of their Changing Concerns', *Teaching and Teacher Education*, 9(1): 65–80.

Habermas, J. (1970) 'Towards Theory of Communicative Competence', *Inquiry*, 13.

—— (1974) *Theory and Practice*, London: Heinemann.

Hagger, H., Burn, K. and McIntyre, D. (1993) *The School Mentoring Handbook*, London: Kogan Page.

Handal, G. and Lauvas, P. (1987) *Promoting Reflective Teaching: Supervision in Practice*, Milton Keynes: Society for Research into Higher Education and Open University Press.

Hargreaves, D. (1990) 'Another Radical Approach to the Reform of Initial Teacher Training', *Westminster Studies in Education*, 13: 5–11.

Hartnett, A. and Naish, M. (1993) 'Democracy, Teaching and the Struggle for Education: An Essay in the Political Economy of Teacher Education', *Curriculum Studies*, 7(3): 335–45.

Hashweh, M.Z. (1987) 'An Exploratory Study of Teacher Knowledge and Teaching: The Effects of Science Teachers' Knowledge of Subject Matter and their Conceptions of Learning on their Teaching', Unpublished doctoral dissertation, Stanford University, Stanford, CA.

Hencke, D. (1977) Colleges in Crisis, Harmondsworth: Penguin.

HMI (1982) *The New Teacher in School*, London: HMSO.

—— (1983) *Teaching in Schools: The Content of Initial Teacher Training*, London: DES.

—— (1987) *Quality in Schools: The Initial Training of Teachers*, London: DES.

—— (1988a) *The New Teacher in School*, London: HMSO.

—— (1988b) *Initial Teacher Training in Universities in England, Northern Ireland and Wales*, London: HMSO.

—— (1991) *School Based Initial Teacher Training in England and Wales*, London: DES.

Hillcole Group (1989) *The Charge of the Right Brigade*, Brighton: Hillcole.

Hillgate Group (1989) *Learning to Teach*, London: Claridge Press.

Hirst, P. (1990) 'Internship: A View from Outside', in P. Benton (ed.) *The Oxford Internship Scheme*, London: Calouste Gulbenkian Foundation.

Hollingsworth, S. (1989) 'Prior Beliefs and Cognitive Change in Learning to Teach', *American Educational Research Journal*, 26(2): 160–89.

Houston, W.R. and Howsam, R.B. (1972) *Competency Based Teacher Education*, Science Research Associates.

Jacques, K. (1992) 'Mentoring in Initial Teacher Education', *Cambridge Journal of Education*, 22(3): 337–50.

James, Lord (1972) *Teacher Education and Training (The James Report)*, London: HMSO.

Jessup, G. (1991) *Outcomes: NVQs and the Emerging Model of Training*, Lewes: Falmer Press.

Johnston, S. (1992) 'Images: A Way of Understanding the Practical Knowledge of Student Teachers', *Teaching and Teacher Education*, 8(2): 123–36.

Katz, L.G. (1972) 'Developmental Stages of Pre-school Teachers', *The Elementary School Journal*, 73(1): 50–4.

King, R. (1978) *All Things Bright and Beautiful? A Sociological Study of Infants' Classrooms*, Chichester: John Wiley & Sons.

Klemp, C.O. (1980) *Three Factors of Success in the World of Work: Implications for Curriculum in Higher Education*, Boston: McBer & Co.

Korthagen, F.A.J. (1988) 'The Influence of Learning Orientations on the Development of Reflective Teaching', in J. Calderhead (ed.) *Teachers' Professional Learning*, Lewes: Falmer Press.

Kounin, J.S. (1970) *Discipline and Group Management in Classrooms*, New York: Holt, Rinehart & Winston.

Kruger, C. and Summers, M. (1988) 'Primary School Teachers' Understanding of Science Concepts', *Journal of Education for Teaching*, 14(3).

Kyriacou, C. (1991) *Essential Teaching Skills*, Hemel Hempstead: Simon & Schuster.

LaBoskey, V. (1993) 'A Conceptual Framework for Reflection in Pre-service Teacher Education', in J. Calderhead and P. Gates (eds) *Conceptualizing Reflection in Teacher Development*, Lewes: Falmer Press.

Lacey, C. (1977) *The Socialization of Teachers*, London: Methuen.

Lawlor, S. (1990) *Teachers Mistaught*, London: Centre for Policy Studies.

Leinhardt, G. and Greeno, J. (1986) 'The Cognitive Skill of Teaching', *Journal of Educational Psychology*, 78(2): 75–95.

Lortie, D.C. (1975) *School Teacher: A Sociological Study*, Chicago: University of Chicago Press.

McDiarmid, G.W., Ball, D.L. and Anderson, C. (1989) 'Why Staying One Chapter Ahead Doesn't Really Work: Subject-specific Pedagogy', in M. Reynolds (ed.) *Knowledge Base for the Beginning Teacher*, The American Association of Colleges for Teacher Education, New York: Pergamon.

McElvogue, M. and Salters, M. (1992) 'Models of Competence and Teacher Training', Unpublished paper, Belfast: Queen's University, Belfast.

McIntyre, D. (1990) 'Ideas and Principles Guiding the Internship Scheme', in P. Benton (ed.) *The Oxford Internship Scheme: Integration and Partnership in Initial Teacher Education*, London: Calouste Gulbenkian Foundation.

—— (1991) 'The Oxford Internship Scheme and the Cambridge Analytical Framework: Models of Partnership in Initial Teacher Education', in M. Booth, J. Furlong and M. Wilkin, *Partnership in Initial Teacher Training*, London: Cassell.

—— (1993) 'Theory, Theorising and Reflection in Initial Teacher Education', in J. Calderhead and P. Gates (eds) *Conceptualising Reflection in Teacher Development*, Lewes: Falmer Press.

McIntyre, D. and Hagger, H. (1994) *Mentoring in Initial Teacher Education: Findings from a Research Initiative Funded by the Paul Hamlyn Foundation*, Oxford: Oxford University Department of Educational Studies.

McIntyre, D., Hagger, H. and Wilkin, M. (1993) *Mentoring: Perspectives on School-based Teacher Education*, London: Kogan Page.

McNair, A. (1944) *Teachers and Youth Leaders (The McNair Report)*, London: HMSO.

McNamara, D. (1990) 'Research on Teachers' Thinking: Its Contribution to Educating Student Teachers to Think Critically', *Journal of Education for Teachers*, 16(2): 147–60.

—— (1991) 'Subject Knowledge and its Application: Problems and Possibilities for Teacher Educators', *Journal of Education for Teaching*, 17(2): 113–28.

McNamara, D. and Desforges, C. (1978) 'The Social Sciences and Teacher Education and the Objectification of Knowledge', *British Journal of Teacher Education*, 4(1): 17–36.

Marshall, K. (1991) 'NVQs: An Assessment of the "Outcomes" Approach to Education and Training', *Journal of Further and Higher Education*, 15 (3): 50–64.

Marx, K. (1941) 'Theses on Feuerbach', in A. Engels (ed.) *Ludwig Feuerbach*, New York: International Publishers.

Maynard, T. and Furlong, J. (1993) 'Learning to Teach and Models of

Mentoring', in D. McIntyre, H. Hagger and M. Wilkin (eds) *Mentoring: Perspectives on School-based Teacher Education*, London: Kogan Page.

Meadows, S. (1993) *The Child as Thinker*, London: Routledge.

Medley, D.N. (1977) *Teacher Competence and Teacher Effectiveness*, American Association of Competency Based Teacher Education.

Miles, S., Barrett, E., Barton, L., Furlong, J., Galvin, C. and Whitty, G. (1993) 'Initial Teacher Education in England and Wales: A Topography', *Research Papers in Education*, 8(3).

Munby, H. (1986) 'Metaphor in the Thinking of Teachers: An Exploratory Study', *Journal of Curriculum Studies*, 8(2).

Munn, P., Johnstone, M. and Chalmers, V. (1992) *Effective Discipline in Primary Schools and Classrooms*, London: Paul Chapman Publishing.

NCVQ (1989) *National Vocational Qualifications: Criteria and Procedures*, London: National Council for Vocational Qualifications.

Nias, J. (1989) *Primary Teachers Talking: A Study of Teaching as Work*, London: Routledge.

O'Hear, A. (1988) *Who Teaches the Teachers?*, London: Social Affairs Unit.

O'Keefe, D. (1990) *The Wayward Elite: A Critique of British Teacher Education*, London: Adam Smith Institute.

Patrick, H., Bernbaum, G. and Reid, K. (1982) *The Structure and Process of Initial Teacher Education within Universities in England and Wales*, Leicester: University of Leicester, School of Education.

Pigge, F. and Marso, R. (1987) 'Relationship between Student Characteristics and Changes in Attitudes, Concerns, Anxieties, and Confidence About Teaching During Teacher Preparation', *Journal of Education Research*, 81(2): 109–15.

Pollard, A. (1985) *The Social World of the Primary School*, London: Cassell.

Pollard, A. and Tann, S. (1987) *Reflective Teaching in the Primary School*, London: Cassell.

Popkewitz, T. (1987) *Critical Studies in Teacher Education: Its Folklore, Theory and Practice*, Lewes: Falmer Press.

Ransom, S. (1990) 'From 1944 to 1988: Education Citizenship and Democracy', in M. Flude and M. Hammer (eds) *The Education Reform Act 1988: Its Origins and Implications*, Lewes: Falmer Press.

Robbins, Lord (1963) *Higher Education (The Robbins Report)*, London: HMSO.

Robertson, J. (1989) *Effective Classroom Control – Understanding Teacher–Pupil Relationships*, London: Hodder & Stoughton.

Roderick, R. (1986) *Habermas and the Foundations of Critical Theory*, London: Macmillan.

Rosenshine, B. and Furst, N. (1971) 'Research on Teacher Performance Criteria', in B.O. Smith (ed.) *Research in Teacher Education*, Englewood Cliffs, NJ: Prentice-Hall.

Rudduck, J. and Sigsworth, A. (1985) 'Partnership Supervision (or Goldhamer Revisited)' in D. Hopkins and K. Reid (eds) *Rethinking Teacher Education*, London: Croom Helm.

Ryle, G. (1949) *The Concept of Mind*, London: Hutchinson.

Sanders, D. and McCutcheon, G. (1986) 'The Development of Practical Theories of Teaching', *Journal of Curriculum and Supervision*, 2(1): 50–67.

Sanders, S. (1994) 'Mathematics and Mentoring', in B. Jaworski and A. Watson (eds) *Mentoring in Mathematics Teaching*, Lewes: The Mathematical Association and Falmer Press.

Schön, D. (1983) *The Reflective Practitioner*, New York: Basic Books.

—— (1987) *Educating the Reflective Practitioner*, San Francisco: Jossey Bass.

Schwab, J. (1969) 'The Practical: A Language for Curriculum', *School Review* 78(1): 1–24.

—— (1971) 'The Practical: Arts of Eclectic', *School Review*, 79(4): 493–542.

—— (1973) 'The Practical 3: Translation into Curriculum', *School Review*, 81(4): 501–22.

—— (1978) 'Education and the Structure of the Disciplines', in I. Westbury and N.J. Wilkof (eds) *Science, Curriculum and Liberal Education*, Chicago: University of Chicago Press.

Shavelson, R. (1983) 'Review of Research on Teachers' Pedagogical Judgements, Plans and Decisions', *Elementary School Journal*, 83: 392–413.

—— (1986) 'Interactive Decision-making: Some Thoughts on Teacher Cognition', Paper presented at the First International Congress on Teacher Thinking and Decision-making, La Rabida, Huelva, Seville, Spain (June).

Shaw, R. (1992) *Teacher Training in the Secondary School*, London: Kogan Page.

Shulman, L. (1986) 'Those who Understand: Knowledge Growth in Teaching', *Educational Researcher*, 15(2): 4–14.

—— (1987) 'Knowledge and Teaching: Foundations of the New Reform', *Harvard Education Review*, 57(1): 1–22.

Sitter, J.P. and Lanier, P.E. (1982) 'Student Teaching: A Stage in the Development of a Teacher or a Period of Consolidation!', Paper presented at the meeting of the American Educational Research Association, New York (March).

Squirrell, G., Gilroy, P., Jones, D. and Rudduck, J. (1990) 'Acquiring Knowledge in Initial Teacher Education', *Library and Information Research Report 79*, London: British Library Board.

Sternberg, R. and Caruso, D. (1985) 'Practical Modes of Knowing in Learning and Teaching the Ways of Knowing', in Eisner, E. (ed.) *84th Yearbook of the National Society for the Study of Education*, Chicago: University of Chicago Press.

Stones, E. (1976) 'Teaching Teaching Skills', *British Journal of Teacher Education* 2(1): 59–78.

Tabachnick, B. and Zeichner, K. (1984) 'The Impact of the Student Teaching Experience on the Development of Teacher Perspectives', *Journal of Teacher Education*, Nov.–Dec.: 28–36.

Tann, S. (1993) 'Eliciting Student Teachers' Personal Theories', in J. Calderhead and P. Gates (eds) *Conceptualising Reflection in Teacher Development*, Lewes: Falmer Press.

Taylor, W. (1965) 'The University Teacher of Education in England', *Comparative Education*, 1(3): 193–201.

—— (1969) *Society and the Education of Teachers*, London: Faber & Faber.

Tom, A.R. (1984) *Teaching as a Moral Craft*, New York: Longman.

van Manen, M. (1977) 'Linking Ways of Knowing with Ways of Being Practical', *Curriculum Inquiry*, 6: 205–28.

Walker, J.C. (1992) 'A General Rationale and Conceptual Approach to the Application of Competence Based Standards to Teaching', Unpublished paper, Canberra: National Project on the Quality of Teaching and Learning.

Watkins, C. and Whalley, C. (1993) *Mentoring: Resources for School-based Development*, Harlow: Longman.

Weber, M. (1948) *From Max Weber: Essays in Sociology*, H.H. Gerth and C. Wright Mills (trans. and ed.), London: Routledge & Kegan Paul.

Whitty, G. (1990) 'New Right and the National Curriculum: State Control or Market Forces', in M. Flude and M. Hammer (eds) *The Education Reform Act 1988: Its Origins and Implications*, Lewes: Falmer Press.

Whitty, G. and Willmott, E. (1991) 'Competence Based Teacher Education: Approaches and Issues', *Cambridge Journal of Education* 21(3): 309–18.

Whitty, G., Barrett, E., Barton, L., Furlong, J., Galvin, C. and Miles, S. (1992) 'Initial Teacher Training in England and Wales: A Survey of Current Practices and Concerns', *Cambridge Journal of Education* 22(3): 293–306.

Wilkin, M. (1991) 'The Development of Partnership in the United Kingdom', in M. Booth, J. Furlong and M. Wilkin (eds) *Partnership in Initial Teacher Training*, London: Cassell.

—— (1992a) 'The Challenge of Diversity', *Cambridge Journal of Education*, 22(3): 307–22.

—— (1992b) *Mentoring in Schools*, London: Kogan Page.

—— (1993) 'Initial Training as a Case of Post Modern Development: Some Implications for Mentoring', in D. McIntyre, H. Hagger and M. Wilkin (eds) *Mentoring: Perspectives on School-Based Teacher Education*, London: Kogan Page.

Wilkin, M. and Sankey, D. (1994) *Collaboration and Transition in Initial Teacher Training*, London: Kogan Page.

Wilson, S., Shulman, L. and Richert, A. (1987) '150 Different Ways of Knowing: Representations of Knowledge in Teaching', in J. Calderhead (ed.) *Exploring Teachers' Thinking*, London: Cassell.

Winter, R. (1990) 'Beginning to Identify Post-qualifying Professional Competences in Social Work', *ASSET Working Paper No. 1*, Chelmsford: Anglia Polytechnic.

Wragg, E. (1984) *Teaching Skills*, Beckenham: Croom Helm.

—— (1991) 'Two Routes to Teaching', in M. Booth, J. Furlong and M. Wilkin (eds) *Partnership in Initial Teacher Training*, London: Cassell.

Wragg, E.C. and Wood, E.K. (1984) 'Teachers' First Encounters with their Classes', in E.C. Wragg, *Class Management and Control: A Teaching Skills Workbook*, London: Macmillan.

Yeomans, R. and Sampson, J. (1994) *Mentoring in the Primary School*, Lewes: Falmer Press.

Zeichner, K. and Liston, D. (1987) 'Teaching Student Teachers to Reflect', *Harvard Educational Review*, 57(1): 23–49.

Zeichner, K. and Tabachnick, B.R. (1985) 'The Development of Teacher Perspectives: Social Strategies and Institutional Control in the Socialization of Beginning Teachers', *Journal of Education for Teaching*, 11(1): 1–25.

Index